Lecture Notes in Computer Science 8454

Commenced Publication in 1973
Founding and Former Series Editors:
Gerhard Goos, Juris Hartmanis, and Jan van Leeuwen

Laurent George   Tullio Vardanega (Eds.)

Reliable Software Technologies – Ada-Europe 2014

19th Ada-Europe International Conference
on Reliable Software Technologies
Paris, France, June 23-27, 2014
Proceedings

 Springer

Volume Editors

Laurent George
University of Paris-Est
Champs sur Marne, France
E-mail: Laurent.George@univ-mlv.fr

Tullio Vardanega
University of Padua, Italy
E-mail: tullio.vardanega@math.unipd.it

ISSN 0302-9743   e-ISSN 1611-3349
ISBN 978-3-319-08310-0   e-ISBN 978-3-319-08311-7
DOI 10.1007/978-3-319-08311-7
Springer Cham Heidelberg New York Dordrecht London

Library of Congress Control Number: 2014941454

LNCS Sublibrary: SL 2 – Programming and Software Engineering

Typesetting: Camera-ready by author, data conversion by Scientific Publishing Services, Chennai, India

Printed on acid-free paper

Springer is part of Springer Science+Business Media (www.springer.com)

Preface

The 19th edition of the International Conference on Reliable Software Technologies (Ada-Europe 2014) took place in the fascinating venue of Paris, graciously hosted by the École d'Ingénieurs, ECE, on their spectacular campus very close to the Eiffel Tower. With this edition, the conference returned to France for the third time after Toulouse in 2003 and Brest in 2009. Two other countries have hosted the conference three times since its inception: Spain (Santander, 1999, Palma de Mallorca, 2004, and Valencia, 2010), and the UK (London, 1997, York, 2005, and Edinburgh, 2011). Three countries hosted it twice: Switzerland (Montreux, for the inauguration in 1996, and Geneva, 2007), Sweden (Uppsala, 1998, and Stockholm, 2012), and Germany (Potsdam, 2000, and Berlin, 2013). Four countries have their hosting counter still at one: Belgium (Leuven, 2001), Austria (Vienna, 2002), Portugal (Porto, 2006) and Italy (Venice, 2008).

The conference series is run and sponsored by Ada-Europe, in collaboration with local organizers, whenever possible (and luckily, often enough) representing the local Ada communities. This was the case this year, with Ada-France leading the organizing team, with precious reinforcement from members of the host institution, ECE. There were two main reasons for the conference to come to Paris. One was to facilitate an encounter between the vast industrial pole based around Paris and the 2012 revision of the Ada language standard, which makes it especially attractive where reliability is a factor. The other was to start the celebrations of the 20th anniversary of the first validation of GNAT, which actually happened in 1995, before building a home in Paris after its birth in New York. These celebrations will peak in 2015, in nice sync with the 20th anniversary of the conference series.

The conference took place during June 23-27, 2014, featuring a rich and attractive program on both technical and social grounds. In building the program, the organizers had to choose from 68 submissions, 37 of which were for peer-reviewed papers, 12 for industrial papers, 16 for tutorials, and three for workshops. Out of this healthy batch of material, ten tutorials for the equivalent of 12 half-day sessions were scheduled on Monday and Friday, together with two full-day workshops on themes of high relevance to industrial research, one on the engineering of "Dependable Cyber-Physical Systems" (Monday), and the other on "Mixed-Criticality Systems." The core program, run from Tuesday to Thursday, included three keynote talks, 12 presentations from peer-reviewed papers, six industrial presentations, three experience reports positioned between industry and research, one vendor session with an accompanying industrial exhibition, and a retrospective session on the first 20 years of GNAT and its ecosystem. On the Wednesday of the conference week, Ada-France also organized a special event dedicated to presenting Ada 2012 to high-ranking members of French industry.

The proceedings contained in this volume cover two of the three keynote talks that opened each day of the core conference program, and the full set of peer-reviewed papers. The remainder of the conference proceedings were published, in successive instalments, in the *Ada User Journal*, the quarterly magazine of Ada-Europe.

- *Lessons Learned and Easily Forgotten*, Robert Lainé, SPACINOV, France, delivered insights drawn from over 40 years of experience in leading large space projects.
- *From ARTEMIS to ECSEL: Growing a Large Eco-System for High-Dependability Systems*, Alun Foster, ARTEMIS, Belgium, gave testimony of the power of larger-scale collaborative research, and the importance of the public–private partnership model for R&D investments.
- *Future Challenges in Design Tools and Frameworks for Embedded Systems; Application to Intelligent Transportation Systems*, Mohamed Shawky, Université de Technologie Compiègne, France, presented a synopsis of the new challenges that future designers and tool developers for intelligent transportation systems will face in the near future.

Submissions to the peer-reviewed track of the conference program came from 18 countries and 87 distinct authors, from Europe, Asia, Australia, North America, and Africa. The selection was very competitive and resulted in the making of four technical sessions, all covered in this volume, on topics ranging from formal verification to real-time scheduling via Ada technology and critical applications.

The tutorial program covered a rich spectrum of topics in close match with the central themes of the conference, as follows:

- *Proving Safety of Parallel/Multi-Threaded Programs*, Tucker Taft, AdaCore, USA
- *Multicore Programming Using Divide-and-Conquer and Work Stealing*, Tucker Taft, AdaCore, USA
- *Debugging Real-Time Systems*, Ian Broster and Andrew Coombes, Rapita Systems, UK
- *Developing Mixed-Criticality Systems with GNAT/ORK and Xtratum*, Alfons Crespo, Alejandro Alonso, and Jon Perez, Universidad Politècnica de València, Universidad Politécnica de Madrid, IKERLAN, Spain
- *High-Integrity Object-Oriented Programming with Ada 2012*, Ben Brosgol, AdaCore, USA
- *Ada 2012 (Sub)type and Subprogram Contracts in Practice*, Jacob Sparre-Andersen, JSA R&I, Denmark
- *Technical Basis of Model-Driven Engineering*, William Bail, MITRE, USA
- *An Overview of Software Testing with an Emphasis on Statistical Testing*, William Bail, MITRE, USA
- *Robotic Programming*, Lars Asplund, Asplund Data AB, Sweden
- *Introduction to Verification with SPARK 2014*, Rod Chapman and Yannick Moy, Altran, UK, and AdaCore, France.

The industrial session featured six presentations centered on various aspects of reliable software development:

- *From Ada 83 to Ada 2012*, Philippe Gast and David Lesens, Astrium EADS, France
- *Test Means at Airbus Defence and Space, Military Aircraft Business Line: Making Ada the Heart of an All •Encompassing Aircraft Test Life •Cycle*, Javier Arroyo and Bartolome Lozano, Airbus Defence and Space, Spain
- *PolarSys: Open Source Tools for Embedded Systems, and Use Cases*, Gael Blondelle, Pierre Gaufillet and Silvia Mazzini, Eclipse Foundation, France, Airbus, France, Intecs, Italy
- *Agile Software Development Compliant to Safety Standards?*, Christian Scholz, Thales Transportation Systems GmbH, Germany
- *Critical Software for the First European Rail Traffic Management System*, Ana Rodriguez, Silver Atena, Spain
- *AdDoc (Beyond a Document Generator)*, Robert Cholay, Systerel, France.

The program also included an experience report session, which contained the following presentations:

- *Modified Condition/Decision Coverage (MC/DC) of Ada Case Statements*, Antoine Colin, Roger Braff and Andrew Coombes, Rapita Systems, UK
- *Privacy Leaks in Java Classes*, Jacob Sparre Andersen, JSA R&I, Denmark
- *Experience in Spacecraft On •Board Software Development*, Juan Antonio de La Puente, Alejandro Alonso, Juan Zamorano, Jorge Garrido, Emilio Salazar and Miguel A. De Miguel, Universidad Politécnica de Madrid, Spain.

Before closing this preface, we must acknowledge those who, serving in various roles – some in the foreground, others in the background – were central to the making of the conference program. The first to deserve gratitude are the authors of all presentations: They had a large take in the success of the event. Next come the members of the Program Committee – their reviewing and advising were essential to achieving a high standard of quality in the conference proceedings, in its various guises – Springer's LNCS for the peer-reviewed papers, and the *Ada User Journal* for the industrial presentations and the workshops. A smaller group of people ran, for a full year, the preparation, construction and execution of the conference program: Local Chair Magali Munoz; Conference Chair Jean-Pierre Rosen; Industrial Chair Jørgen Bundgaard; Publicity Chair Dirk Craeynest; Exhibition Co-chairs Jamie Ayre and Guillaume Foliard; Tutorial Co-chairs Liliana Cucu and Albert Llemosì; Finance Chair Paul Duquennoy. They all deserve a big thank you.

We hope that the attendees enjoyed the conference, in both its technical and social program, as much as we did in organizing it.

June 2014   Laurent George
                                                                   Tullio Vardanega

Organization

Conference Chair

Jean-Pierre Rosen, Ada-France

Finance Chair

Paul Duquennoy, Ada-France

Program Co-chairs

Laurent George	University of Paris-Est, Marne La Vallée, France
Tullio Vardanega	University of Padua, Italy

Industrial Chair

Jørgen Bundgaard	Ramboll, Denmark

Tutorial Co-chairs

Liliana Cucu	Inria, France
Albert Llemosì	Universitat des Illes Balears, Spain

Exhibition Co-chairs

Jamie Ayre	AdaCore, France
Guillaume Foliard	Thales, France

Publicity Chair

Dirk Craeynest	Aubay Belgium & K.U. Leuven, Belgium

Local Chair

Magali Munoz	ECE, France

Sponsoring Institutions

AdaCore
Altran
Rapita Systems Ltd
Squoring
TNI – Ellidiss Software

Program Committee

Mario Aldea	Universidad de Cantabria, Spain
Ted Baker	US National Science Foundation, USA
Johann Blieberger	Technische Universität Wien, Austria
Bernd Burgstaller	Yonsei University, Korea
Maryline Chetto	University of Nantes, France
Liliana Cucu	Inria, France
Christian Fraboul	ENSEEIHT, France
Laurent George	LIGM/UPEMLV – ECE Paris, France
Xavier Grave	Centre National de la Recherche, France
Emmanuel Grolleau	ENSMA, France
Jérôme Hugues	ISAE Toulouse, France
Albert Llemosí	Universitat de les Illes Balears, Spain
Kristina Lundqvist	Mälardalen University, Sweden
Franco Mazzanti	ISTI-CNR Pisa, Italy
John McCormick	University of Northern Iowa, USA
Stephen Michell	Maurya Software, Canada
Laurent Pautet	Telecom ParisTech, France
Luís Miguel Pinho	CISTER Research Centre/ISEP, Portugal
Erhard Plödereder	Universität Stuttgart, Germany
Juan A. de la Puente	Universidad Politécnica de Madrid, Spain
Jorge Real	Universitat Politécnica de València, Spain
José Ruiz	AdaCore, France
Sergio Sáez	Universidad Politécnica de Valencia, Spain
Amund Skavhaug	NTNU, Norway
Yves Sorel	Inria, France
Tucker Taft	AdaCore, USA
Theodor Tempelmeier	University of Applied Sciences Rosenheim, Germany
Elena Troubitsyna	Âbo Akademi University, Finland
Tullio Vardanega	University of Padova, Italy
Juan Zamorano	Universidad Politécnica de Madrid, Spain

Industrial Committee

Jacob Sparre Andersen	JSA Consulting, Denmark
Roger Brandt	Roger Brandt IT Konsult AB, Sweden
Ian Broster	Rapita Systems, UK
Jørgen Bundgaard	Rambøll Denmark A/S, Denmark
Dirk Craeynest	Ada-Belgium & KU Leuven, Belgium
Peter Dencker	ETAS GmbH, Germany
Ismael Lafoz	Airbus Military, Spain
Maria del Carmen Lomba Sorrondegui	GMV, Spain
Ahlan Marriott	White Elephant, Switzerland
Robin Messer	Altran-Praxis, UK
Quentin Ochem	AdaCore, France
Steen Palm	Terma, Denmark
Paolo Panaroni	Intecs, Italy
Paul Parkinson	Wind River, UK
Ana Rodriguez	Silver-Atena, Spain
Jean-Pierre Rosen	Adalog, France
Alok Srivastava	TASC, USA Claus Stellwag, Elektrobit AG, Germany
Jean-Loup Terraillon	European Space Agency, The Netherlands
Rod White	MBDA, UK

Table of Contents

Applications

Lessons Learned and Easily Forgotten

Robert Lainé

SPACINOV
www.spacinov.com

Abstract. The author has had the privilege of leading a number of important and challenging spacecraft development projects in his long professional career. At the request of the organizers of the 19th International Conference on Reliable Software Technologies, this short paper summarizes some lessons learned on the exercise of leadership. This paper is more like a retrospective reflection on a vast personal experience than a scientific essay on the art of project and team management. In the hope that this contribution can benefit others, these personal reflections are offered first to the community that keeps this conference series alive and kicking, and then to those who consult the conference proceedings, who – I have learned – are not a small number.

1 Introduction

It is my pleasure to address the Ada community, to whom I am grateful for its contribution to some of the space projects I had to lead.

A common element in those projects was the significant part of innovation they involved. Having retired after 41 years of technical leadership in space projects, and in "debugging" a number of others, I have now had time to think about what contributes to making projects successful. This paper shares my findings with the readers of these proceedings.

Perhaps a surprise to some, my discussion will not address technical issues; rather it will dwell on what I regard as the root cause of projects major problems: the human factor. Please sit back and take this opportunity to look at project leadership from a different perspective.

2 Some Definitions about Projects and Project Team

Projects are the visible part of development activities. It is there that all the expertise is glued together (in system work) to achieve something useful. It underlines our ability to lead and develop people expertise in various fields.

A project is a task with a clearly identified objective to be reached, with finite resources and within a finite time. Once the objective is reached, the project cease to exist. A project that goes on forever is no longer a project; it has become a sort of administration or worse, a bureaucracy working for the single purpose of maintaining its existence!

L. George and T. Vardanega (Eds.): Ada-Europe 2014, LNCS 8454, pp. 1–6, 2014.

A project team is a group of people who individually take the project objective as a personal objective and voluntarily agree to work together to make the project a success. One cannot force people to work successful on a project if they do not agree on its objective.

These notions are easily forgotten.

3   Key Factors in Project Success

In a spacecraft development budget, the cost of raw material is irrelevant: 99% of the time and money goes to human activities. In software, that human activity ratio gets very close to 100 %. In other Hi-Tech fields, that ratio may be only 80%, but, still, the quality of the result is essentially that of the human contribution in innovation and work.

In space projects, there is no second chance for a launch: it must work the first time round! Once a spacecraft is in orbit, it is too late to remove an error or fix a fault.

The success of any large project, aerospace or software or Hi-Tech, bases on teamwork, with several subcontractors and players. Managing, or rather Leading (with capital L) projects successfully is first of all leading people, which means:

- interacting continuously with people,
- identifying what hampers their progress,
- helping them to perform and solve problems,
- making sure that no mistake gets through the verification net.

Let us look at each such task in isolation.

3.1   Interacting with People

All European space projects are international undertakings. Europe's space community is small, highly qualified, but with wide differences of culture and language, which cause a lot of room for misunderstanding and lasting aggravations. For a project leader, there is no point trying to reduce these differences, which are deeply embedded in the human nature; recognizing them, accepting them and working with them is the only solution to remain sane.

In a project, everyone depend on others doing their share of work on time. As we cannot afford the luxury of duplicating all work packages and pick the first to deliver, all individuals contributing to the project are to be treated as partners and definitely not as upper/lower/junior citizens of an improbable hierarchy.

Consequently, it is essential to split the work according to the capability of each partner. Recognizing and respecting the work done by each partner is as essential as being prepared to help anyone who runs into problems.

Sometime, things do not go as planned. Accepting and facing that reality is vital. The «Wait and See» attitude or worse its «Don't bring me problems, I pay you to solve them» variant, never pays, since problems do not go away by themselves.

People never drive themselves intentionally into problems, if problems arise, they have to be dealt with promptly and honestly while respecting people rather than judging them. In these situations where a solution has to be found, we must remember that there is always a solution to a problem and finding it is what counts. Asking the right questions and listening to what individuals have to propose often brings that solution to solve the problem. Asking the same questions to an «Organization», which is supposed to have avoided or solved the problem, will mostly add confusion.

3.2   Identifying What Hampers Progress

The number One source of trouble in a project is a «customer» who does not know what he actually needs in the way of a product, but is very good at defining strict rules he wants followed! In this context, it is important to remember that, in all complex projects, many partners are both the supplier but also the customer of someone else. For example, a system engineer is the customer of a number of sub-systems suppliers who are themselves the customers of components suppliers, and so forth.

The absence of clear understandable objective for each task cannot be replaced by Rules that, by definition, are only formalizing what has already been done. Rules are the prerogative of administration ("management" in English): the leader of an innovative project would be well advised to know them, but be prepared to at least bend them or ignore them if they do not help meeting the objective of the project. The only fixed rule a leader should respect is that his project must succeed. Project failure is not an option, even with a good excuse.

Another source of trouble is a set of self-imposed constraints, negative thinking and talking, easily recognized by such expressions as: «this is the way we always do it»; «customer will not accept our way of doing it»; «these guys are unable to do anything right»; and variants of this tune. If people talk negatively, they think negatively, and quickly they will focus on the possibility of failure and consider covering their track under the false protection of hypothetical rules and practices. When it comes to innovative solution, it is impossible to identify a priori who is the innovator (supplier) and who is the customer. In this situation, everyone can be a source of innovation provided the other members of the team are prepared to accept and build on innovative ideas of others. It is there that the «Not Invented Here» (NIH) syndrome can do a lot of damage. When combined with negative talking, it will discourage anyone from venturing new ideas and solutions.

The negative thinking and NIH have to be stopped at once, and people have to be refocused on going forward.

Very often, the above negative thinking is associated with poor or even absence of human-to-human communication. One should be aware of what I call the «email and memo broadcasting escalation trap». These e-mails with copy to the world just add noise and encourage people to spend their time hitting their keyboards to show that they too exist, instead of thinking of how to move the project forward. Very quickly, such emails turn sour with underlying or explicit judgment of value being passed to one another. These judgments of value will send everyone down in their bunker to think hard on how to retaliate, and the project will halt! The only solution there is to block the email flow and call the team for a serious discussion on how to meet the project objective.

Emotional relations in the decision process, where someone will surely think that he lost out in a decision; personal ambition driving decisions; hiding errors to make sure that one cannot be seen to be wrong; playing « games » to obtain a favor, etc. These are all common practices that degrade very quickly the positive spirit needed for a project to succeed.

3.3   Helping People to Perform

Individuals have different personalities, with competences, strength and weaknesses. Teamwork is the summation of these strengths and competences. It is therefore important not to dwell on weaknesses – we all have some and we don't like to have them exposed – but rather make sure that these weaknesses are not in a critical path.

Reformulating the task objective until it is positively understood is essential, in particular when the culture and language of the partner is different from yours. The answer «Yes» to the question «Do you understand?», is no proof of understanding, particularly in some culture where saying «No» is considered impolite. The only way to make sure that people really understand is to ask them to reformulate the objective in their own language, and even that may leave room to some doubt.

Give people the freedom to do their job. Innovation often comes from failure, as such failure will reveal which underlying assumptions were wrong. It is therefore important to assure the people that trying new routes may indeed lead to failures, and this is OK as long as we know about it and understand why it failed.

When something does not work, it is often necessary to provide alternatives routes to explore, which may even include known solutions. In those circumstances, it is important to leave it to the partner to implement the alternative, so that he regains confidence and succeeds in delivering their part of the project.

Regular, transparent reporting on real progress at all levels is important such that everyone sees where the others are toward the project objective. It greatly helps reduce the attitude of hiding behind the delays of others, an attitude that slows down the project and degrades to a competition at not being the last rather than at being in front. To that extent, public acknowledgement of success is a form of reward to be used without limitation. It does create a positive feedback motivating the people.

3.4   System Engineering and Human Factor

The job of system engineering is to design and specify for others to do. System engineers will set and explicit the common objective for the technical groups and will keep track of progress toward it. The following list of common pitfalls has been drawn from experience:

- Fuzzy requirements mean that various interpretation can allowed leaving a lot of room for creativity and mistakes. «KIS»: Keep It Simple, is the golden rule to follow when writing requirements. One requirement per sentence, one explicit verification criteria per requirement. If in doubt about the usefulness of a requirement, move it to the wish list for later decision.

- Design must be achievable and verifiable. There is no point in asking for the impossible or something that cannot be verified.
- At system level, be aware of the «almighty software» solution. In particular in safety critical missions, it can become virtual reality replacing reality until reality catches up! Sometime a little piece of hardware can be more practical, more predictable and safer than complicated software.
- Be as strict in defining software as you are with hardware. It is surprising that very often the system engineering group is unable to describe in simple words what they expect the software to do. They leave it to the software team to define their own requirements and hope it will work. This often leads to a number of «undocumented features», which are just booby traps waiting for someone to trigger them.
- Mistakes are made all the time by humans. Everyone has his bad day, sooner or later. It is important to accept that reality and not rate it as «unacceptable»! The issue is not the mistake being made, that is reality, the issue is to organize the work and set the right state of mind in the team to find them. Once a mistake is found, it can always be tracked, corrected and the earlier it is found, the cheaper it will be.
- Organizing the work to help remove mistakes is a matter of being clear about what each function shall do and shall not do in which environment, and having methods for proving it. Many tools exists to achieve that but managers (not leaders) will often skip them as they cost and in the mind of managers people are supposed to be perfect. Be extremely careful with things that seemingly work but have not been formally verified.
- The norm to be set across the team is that a day without finding a mistake is a day lost! That norm is true for everyone in the team from the leader to all partners and contributors. To help this, transparency and absence of judgment of value about the people having made mistakes is vital. Transparency means that other team members can then check that they have not made similar error. Be very sensitive to the body language of individuals, it often gives the best warning about up-coming problems and remember that in engineering, a majority of people saying it is OK cannot overrule a minority saying it is NOT OK. Either side must be able to prove rationally that it is OK/NOK. In doubt, assuming the worse is safer than going with a majority of hand wavers.
- No judgment of value passed on individuals means that people will feel comfortable with reporting doubts and mistakes instead of hiding them. If a judgment of value is passed in the heat of events, it is important to quickly and publicly acknowledge that this was inappropriate to avoid a negative thinking spiral development.

4   Summary: Preferred Project Leadership Style

Over the years, I have observed that successful project leaders share a common set of values, which is worth itemizing:

- Acceptance and respect for the competences and responsibilities of all partners, despite cultural differences.
- Transparent, open and direct communication of the project objective to reach.
- Encourage lateral and upward communication as opposed to strictly hierarchical reporting, encourage peer review of critical points within the team.
- Provide regular feedback to all participants.
- Open minded to different approaches to achieve the result. This is particularly important when a large part of the project depend on innovation.
- Keep the team focused strictly on the project end objective and finding mistakes.
- Do not shoot at people just solve problems.
- Be honest and stay honest with people; do not play games on them.

Finally, always keep in mind that a random success is just a missed random failure.

References

1. National Transportation Safety Board. Their reports provide analysis of the incidence of the human factor in various accidents, http://www.ntsb.gov/
2. Morel, C.: Les décisions absurdes, Sociologie des erreurs radicales et persistantes. Bibliothèque des Sciences Humaines, Gallimard (2002)

Future Challenges in Design Frameworks for Embedded Systems: Application to Intelligent Transportation Systems

Mohamed Shawky

Université de Technologie de Compiègne, Heudiasyc Laboratory,
Joint Research Unit with CNRS, Compiègne, France
shawky@utc.fr

Abstract. Environment perception technologies and sophisticated signal processing algorithms yield today mature understanding of dynamics of transportation vectors. Uncertainty management became inherent to decision making following such environment understanding processes. However, designers of critical embedded systems remain skeptical about considering uncertainty, probably as design tools and frameworks have not yet integrated advances in state-of-the-art of confidence management approaches. Furthermore, hesitant multicore programming tools do not provide yet enough native redundancy for applications offered by such technologies, which would have been a precious contribution to increase their reliability. In this paper, which outlines the conference keynote, we present a synopsis of these new challenges that will face in the near future designers and tool developers for Intelligent Transportation Systems.

Keywords: Intelligent Transportation Systems, design tools for critical embedded systems, multicore for native redundancy.

1 Introduction

Intelligent Transportation Systems (ITS) are excellent representatives of critical systems, either for their relation to time determinism and constraints, or for their requirements from safety point of view. Recent advances in ITS domain are greatly visible for example in automatic driving in automotive sector, where millisecond comprehensive reactivity of the vehicle became a mandatory reference. Along with these developments, information technology has raised the expectations of ordinary users from a computerized system to unprecedented level of interaction intelligence. We will present in this keynote how the need to "cognitive behavior" from Intelligent Transportation Systems has driven researches in the last decade, mainly to set up novel perception algorithms, but oddly neglecting implementation of tools and frameworks to let them become definite references in the domain.

L. George and T. Vardanega (Eds.): Ada-Europe 2014, LNCS 8454, pp. 7–10, 2014.

2   Cognitive Behavior in ITS

Environment understanding, which includes detecting neighboring vehicles, pedestrians, infrastructure signs or other obstacles, is relying today on various sensing technologies. Whatever are the accuracy and the precision of a single sensor, inherent uncertainties remain in the returned values, representing the measured physical magnitudes. Multisensor data fusion is meant to increase the reliability of environment detection process (Fig. 1). Hence, a clearly defined need emerged for methods that correctly combine data issued from different sensors.

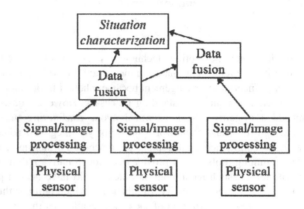

Fig. 1. Multisensor Data Fusion for driving situation recognition

Evidence theory has brought up satisfying paradigm to deal with such problematic [1, 2]. A belief mass is assigned to each subset of the repertory of hypothesis.

By cognitive behavior, or automatic reasoning, we do not consider here "intellectual" reasoning, like text understanding, but we are dealing with intermediate reasoning, as recognizing of "driving situations", for example: "I am following a light vehicle and being followed by a truck and we are all on the rightmost lane" [3].

To activate automatically a breaking system in case a dangerous situation is recognized, a degree of autonomy in decision making has to be granted to the centralized decision module. Managing uncertainty may be used as a basic building block to increase the reasoning ability of such decision component, in order to improve their autonomy.

Programming tools should enable designers and programmers to add or subtract belief masses. Compilers should be able to overload usual arithmetic operators by corresponding belief masses arithmetic functions.

Unfortunately, thorough analysis of current programming frameworks shows that very few tools are positioned on that niche today.

3   Critical Embedded Systems and ITS

Critical embedded systems are best portrayed by a collection of common characteristics. In most of the corresponding applications, a distributed architecture of processing elements is used. Tasks are statistically assigned to processing elements, with no adaptive behavior, or very few, especially in avionics and spatial domains. Hence, hard partitioning of memory is a usual approach. Considering communications between processing elements, even if originally asynchronous network protocols are used, their implementation would be so distorted to come up finally with almost completely synchronous protocols [4].

3.1   Uncertainty in Critical Systems

Although Intelligent Transportation Systems sphere is often comprehended as ground transportations, latest researches in avionic domain had positive fallouts on all other transportation fields, especially through several recent European Integrated Projects. Nevertheless, critical system designers continue to regard uncertainty management with considerable precaution, possibly for the lack of tools for managing uncertainty, adequately positioned in the engineering lifecycle.

3.2   Impact on Component Based Design

In order to implement such type of tools, new design paradigm is needed that would probably accentuate the trend for Model Driven Engineering and Component Based Design, by distributing the intelligence of the tool over the components themselves, so that each component includes part of the tool verification code.

This verification code would be activated only during the design phase to fulfill the model checking stage, yielding "inference" ability to individual components. However, few research works have extrapolated these approaches for complex components that could not be any more considered as simple ones, but as a sub-system or even a whole system by itself.

4   Multicore Implementation and Redundancy

Despite recent progress in multi-core technology, few research works have considered sacrificing number of cores to the advantage of redundant resources, at the expense of performance [5].

Several existing frameworks and runtime environments for parallel and distributed programming like OpenMP have been cross-dressed to support redundancy design and its real time operation.

Other works have addressed other challenges to automatically generate redundant architecture and software code, including the necessary runtime middleware over a given operating system [6].

However, the contest is still open until we reach satisfying industrial tools where a simple sliding cursor should enable to choose the number of cores dedicated to architecture and code redundancy and others assigned to application code execution.

References

1. Cattaneo, M.E.G.V.: Combining belief functions issued from dependent sources. In: Bernard, J.M., Seidenfeld, T., Zaffalon, M. (eds.) Proceedings of the Third International Symposium on Imprecise Probabilities and Their Applications (ISIPTA 2003), Carleton Scientific, Lugano, Switzerland, pp. 133–147 (2003)
2. Denœux, T.: A k-nearest neighbor classification rule based on Dempster–Shafer theory. IEEE Transactions on Systems Man and Cybernetics 25(05), 804–813 (1995)
3. Nigro, J.-M., Rombaut, M.: IDRES: A rule-based system for driving situation recognition with uncertainty management. Information Fusion 4(4), 309–317 (2003)
4. Persson, M., Bonnet, S., Shawky, M.: In: Rajan, A., Wahl, T. (eds.) CESAR - Cost-efficient Methods and Processes for Safety-relevant Embedded Systems. Springer (2013)
5. Smolens, J.C., Gold, B.T., Falsafi, B., Hoe, J.C.: Reunion: Complexity-Effective Multicore Redundancy. In: 39th Annual IEEE/ACM International Symposium on Microarchitecture, pp. 223–234. IEEE Computer Society, Washington, DC (2006)
6. Tahan, O., Shawky, M.: Using Dynamic Task Level Redundancy for OpenMP Fault Tolerance. In: Herkersdorf, A., Römer, K., Brinkschulte, U. (eds.) ARCS 2012. LNCS, vol. 7179, pp. 25–36. Springer, Heidelberg (2012)

Rigorous Development of Fault-Tolerant Systems through Co-refinement

Ilya Lopatkin and Alexander Romanovsky

CSR, School of Computing Science, Newcastle University,
Newcastle upon Tyne, NE1 7RU, UK
{ilya.lopatkin,alexander.romanovsky}@ncl.ac.uk

Abstract. With our increasing dependency on computer-based systems, ensuring their dependability becomes one the most important concerns during system development. This is especially true for safety-critical systems. Critical systems typically use fault tolerance mechanisms to mitigate runtime errors. However, fault tolerance modelling and, in particular, rigorous definitions of fault tolerance requirements, fault assumptions and system recovery have not been given enough attention during formal system development. This paper proposes a development method for stepwise modelling of high-level system fault tolerant behaviour. The method provides an environment for explicit modelling of fault tolerance and modal aspects of system behaviour and is supported by tools that are smoothly integrated into an industry-strength development environment. A case study is used to demonstrate the proposed method.

1 Introduction

Our society is becoming increasingly dependent on computer-based systems due to the falling costs and improving capabilities of computers. There is a class of systems called *critical* that operate with resources of the highest value and defects of which can have a significant impact on the environment, assets, and human life. Critical systems have to be *dependable* [2], so that they can be justifiably trusted to provide the required services.

It is well-known that one cannot produce a faultless system functioning in a perfect fault-free environment [8]. A number of safety and reliability analysis techniques are being successfully used nowadays in industry such as Failure Modes and Effects Analysis (FMEA), Fault Tree Analysis, and HiP-HOPS. Deterioration of physical components makes it necessary for systems to employ *fault tolerance* mechanisms [8] in both hardware and software.

Furthermore, the design complexity of modern systems requires additional means for reducing the number and criticality of design faults. One of the prominent solutions to ensuring systems dependability by fault prevention and/or fault removal is the inclusion of formal modelling in various stages of the software development process. Usage of formal methods in development of dependable systems is increasing and is proven to be cost-effective [13]. Among the main current obstacles to adopting formal methods by industry are the lack of tools

L. George and T. Vardanega (Eds.): Ada-Europe 2014, LNCS 8454, pp. 11–26, 2014.

and engineers' experience in formal development. We believe this situation can be significantly improved by teaching best practices of modelling and providing modelling guidelines and reusable solutions.

The development method proposed in this work builds on our study of the requirements descriptions and formal models produced by deployment partners of the FP7 DEPLOY project [4]. The study showed that up to 35-40% of requirements to critical systems can be devoted to fault tolerance. However, typically, formal models do not adequately represent the fault tolerant behaviour due to the fact that the fault tolerance component of requirements is intertwined with the functional one and is difficult to address during the modelling phase.

There are a number of studies on formal modelling of fault tolerance. Some research is done on extending original semantics of formal methods with additional fault tolerance modelling constructs [5]. Other techniques provide patterns and modelling styles for modelling fault tolerance within the formal semantics of a particular formalism. For example, [7] provides a guidance to modelling fault tolerant control system in the B formalism. The authors focus on modelling low-level component failures that may be masked at a system level. Another example of a style-based approach is introduced in [6]. The paper describes a general formal specification pattern to be applied in development of dependable systems with a layered architecture. The pattern adds exception handling mechanism to each system layer and organizes communication between components within a hierarchical structure by means of exceptions. The layered exception hierarchy pattern is based on top-down refinement. The pattern follows the idea of *idealised fault tolerant component* (IFTC) introduced in [8]. The IFTC is a generic component which explicitly differentiates between its normal and abnormal operation, and specifies the conditions under which it switches between the two. The system is thus constructed as hierarchical layers of IFTCs. Each component can handle certain exceptions, and it propagates the unhandled exceptions to the abnormal part of its higher-level component. The idea of IFTC implies sequential composition of component executions, and its application may undermine the ability to express system-level safety properties for some proof-based methods.

We follow a pattern-based approach and propose a method for modelling high-level fault tolerant system behaviour. In contrast to the above-mentioned studies, we focus on reactive style of system-level fault tolerant behaviour, and provide support for explicit reasoning about safety properties. Although the present work focuses on refinement-based development of reactive systems, we follow the IFTC-based ideas of top-down system structuring and explicitness of system abnormal operation.

The paper is organised as follows. We give an overview of the proposed method in Section 2. Then we describe the basic modelling principles behind the method and the proposed refinement strategy in Sections 3 and 4 accordingly. We describe the method by applying it to a case study in Section 5, and draw conclusions in Section 6.

2   Overview

In this paper we demonstrate a method for top-down development of fault toler-ant systems with a focus on abstract levels of modelling. The method focuses on verification of safety properties of fault tolerant systems and ensures traceability of the relevant safety and fault tolerance requirements.

The method accommodates two formalisms: a traditional state-based formal-ism and a diagrammatic formalism from our previous work [10]. Any state-based formalism with interleaving semantics can be used with the proposed method such as Action Systems, B, Event-B, Z, and VDM with refinement-based for-malisms benefiting the most. In this paper we exemplify our approach on the Event-B formalism [1]. The second formalism used in the method constitutes an additional viewpoint called Fault Tolerance (FT) Views for modelling modal and fault tolerant behaviour [10]. The FT viewpoint is also refinement-based. The refinement chains for the two formalisms coexist in a single development and formally relate to each other. At each refinement level, the two formal mod-els essentially represent the same system at the appropriate level of abstraction (Figure 1).

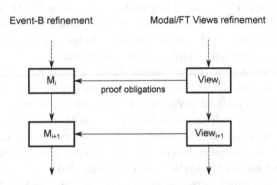

Fig. 1. Refinement chain of a bi-model development

The development method includes the following three constituents:
- the *modelling principles* stating the key rules and reasoning behind the mod-elling process of the method,
- the *refinement strategy* defining a sequence of refinement steps that need to be performed to arrive at a meaningful model of a fault tolerant system, and
- a set of *modelling patterns* and *FT view templates* that provide a reuse mechanism during modelling.

The three constituents together represent modelling guidelines for building fault tolerant systems in refinement-based formal methods in a systematic way.

3   Modelling Principles

The development method is based on a number of modelling principles. These postulate a set of terms and rules that are used in definitions of modelling patterns and the refinement strategy described later.

The first principle of the method defines the style for modelling fault tolerant systems. The method facilitates the expression of safety properties by providing patterns that follow a *reactive style* of modelling. By the reactive modelling style we mean such a way of behaviour definition that uses atomic reactions and allows developers to express high-level properties in the following form:

$$cause \Rightarrow reaction$$

One of the most important principles used in the method is the principle of *behaviour restriction*. We treat the system model as a transition system that is "composed" of two parts: an *unconstrained behaviour* and a set of functional and fault tolerance *constraints*. An unconstrained behaviour contains all system states and all transitions, it is merely a declaration of the system structure using variables. A model without constraints has a non-deterministic behaviour. During its evolution, it can go from any state to any other state. In the proposed method, the development departs from an unconstrained declaration of the state space and step-wise arrives at a model which "behaves" in a safe and sensible manner within the given constraints, i.e. requirements.

In our method, we assume that a system observes some part of its environment and reacts to its changes. To represent the environment adequately in the models, we require all state transitions occurring during system execution to satisfy the *implementable causality rule*: a cause (environmental change) must not depend on a reaction (system change). In other words, a system being in a certain state may not "forbid" environment to change. Otherwise, the model would contain unrealistic assumptions about system environment that cannot be implemented.

To structure the formal development in such a way that follows the implementable causality and the behaviour restriction principles, we offer a term *fault tolerant component*. A fault tolerant component is a structural system unit that is described by its *functional* and *error* state variables which are explicitly separate in the model. In this regard, the term is similar to the Idealised Fault Tolerant Component [8]. Note that an FT component is a modelling concept and does not necessarily represent a physical object or a design-level module.

4   Refinement Strategy

The development method prescribes a number of modelling steps that need to be performed to arrive at a correct and meaningful model of a fault tolerant system. The schematic procedure of the development method is shown on Figure 2. The development method is divided into two parts: the first part contains steps for a generic development of reactive fault tolerant systems and is applicable in any problem domain, the second part focuses on control systems and facilitates modelling of low-level components with an intention to support the implementation step.

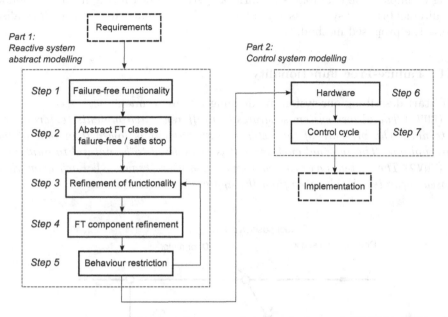

Fig. 2. The steps of the method

Abstract modelling of a reactive fault tolerant system starts with defining a *failure-free* functionality of the system (Step 1). By failure-free functionality we mean the abstract behaviour that is only restricted by functional requirements.

At the first abstract level where fault tolerance requirements impact the system model, a designer has to choose an *abstract fault tolerance class* of the system (Step 2). We give more details on system FT classes in Section 5.2.

Steps 3, 4 and 5 form the core of the method. They are repeated iteratively until all the required properties of the reactive system behaviour are expressed and verified. Step 3 is a refinement of functionality which is project-specific. Step 4 is called the *fault tolerant component refinement*: it refines the abstract component errors and FT behaviour into sub-component errors. This step is described in Section 5.3. Step 5 is the *behaviour restriction* step that is used to restrict the functional behaviour with operational conditions dictated by the environment. The details of this step are given in Section 5.4.

The second part of the method refines the reactive model into a model of a control system. Here we reuse our previous work on modelling control cycles and incorporating FMEA into Event-B specifications [11] and omit description of this step due to space restriction. It is important to note that the first part focuses on verification of safety properties whereas the second part of the method facilitates further implementation of the system.

5   Method Application

In this section we describe the steps of the proposed method applied to a running example. The example is an airlock system shown in Figure 3. We define requirements to the system as a set of informal statements that we then formalise using the proposed method.

5.1   Failure-Free Functionality

We start describing our system by defining its environment:

(ENV1) *The airlock system separates two different environments (external and internal). The pressure of the external environment is lower than that of the internal one. The internal environment is considered to be natural to humans.*

(ENV2) *The system has two doors and a chamber (Figure 3). Each door when closed separates the chamber from the appropriate environment.*

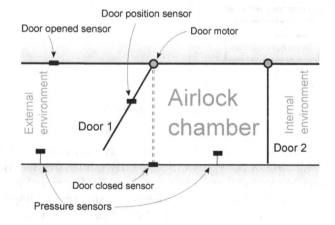

Fig. 3. The airlock system

The primary function of the system can be expressed in the following form:

(FUN1) *When in operation, the airlock system must be able to let users pass safely between the two environments via the airlock.*

In order to allow a user to pass from the internal area through the airlock into the external area, the system needs to perform the following steps:

1. equalise the chamber pressure to that of the internal environment,
2. open the second door to allow the user in the chamber,
3. close the second door,
4. equalize the pressure in the airlock to that of the external environment,
5. open the first door to allow the user out,

and vice versa for the opposite direction.

To provide such operations, the system is equipped with a number of sensors and actuators as shown on Figure 3. We assume that the details of such a low level are given in requirements on which we base our abstractions. In this paper, we omit the low-level modelling steps due to lack of space and focus on modelling and proving safety properties at a high level of abstraction. We define the following safety requirements for the airlock system:

(SAF1) *The pressure in the chamber must always be between the lower external pressure and the higher internal one*

(SAF2) *A door can only be opened if the pressure values in the chamber and the conjoined environment are equal*

(SAF3) *At most one door is allowed to be opened at any moment of time*

(SAF4) *The pressure in the chamber shall not be changed unless both doors are closed*

---

axioms

    axm1: $partition(DOOR\_STATE, \{OPENED\}, \{CLOSED\}, \{OPENING\},$
        $\{CLOSING\}, \{STOPPED\})$
    axm2: $LOW\_PRESSURE = 0$
    axm3: $HIGH\_PRESSURE = 2$

invariants

    inv1: $door1 \in DOOR\_STATE$
    inv2: $door2 \in DOOR\_STATE$
    inv3: $pressure \in \mathbb{N}$
    inv4: $door1 \neq CLOSED \Rightarrow pressure = LOW\_PRESSURE$
    inv5: $door2 \neq CLOSED \Rightarrow pressure = HIGH\_PRESSURE$
    inv6: $door1 = CLOSED \vee door2 = CLOSED$
    inv7: $pressure > LOW\_PRESSURE \Rightarrow door1 = CLOSED$
    inv8: $pressure < HIGH\_PRESSURE \Rightarrow door2 = CLOSED$
    inv9: $pressure \geq LOW\_PRESSURE \wedge pressure \leq HIGH\_PRESSURE$

events

event open1 $\widehat{=}$

  when

    grd1: $door1 = CLOSED \vee door1 = STOPPED$
    grd2: $pressure = LOW\_PRESSURE$
    grd3: $door2 = CLOSED$

  then

    act1: $door1 := OPENING$

  end

Snippet 1. Definitions, invariants, and behaviour of M0

At this stage, we only define the *failure-free functionality* of the system. That is, no failures are considered and the system is assumed to work in a flawless manner forever. We formalise the given requirements in an Event-B model M0 (see Snippet 1). In the model, section **axioms** contains axiomatic definitions such as a given set of door states (*opened, closed*, etc). We represent the two environments described in (ENV1) by their pressure values $LOW\_PRESSURE$ and $HIGH\_PRESSURE$ that we assume to be constant. Section **invariants** contains variable type definitions and safety properties that must always hold during system evolution. For example, we represent the physical components from (ENV2) by variables *door*1 and *door*2 for the two doors correspondingly, and the current value of pressure in the chamber by variable *pressure*. The rest of the invariants correspond to the safety requirements. Namely, *inv*9 ensures the pressure limits required by (SAF1). Invariants *inv*4 and *inv*5 correspond to requirement (SAF2). Requirement (SAF3) is ensured by *inv*6. Invariants *inv*7 and *inv*8 together represent (SAF4).

The **events** section formalises the behaviour of the system. It consists of a set of events each of which represents a guarded labelled transition. The guard of each event is given as a set of predicates in section **when**. When the guard becomes true, the event fires thus atomically making a transition described in section **then** by a set of assignments. The system evolves by making transitions in an interleaving fashion. During evolution, invariants must always hold, and the modeller is obliged to prove that the action of each event preserves all of the invariants. In model M0, there are five events for each door that ensure the safe traversal of the corresponding door through its set of possible states, and two events for changing the level of pressure in the chamber. For brevity, we only show an event of a door behaviour (*open*1) in Snippet 1. Event *open*1 starts opening the first door if it is either closed or stopped at some intermediate position.

5.2   Abstract Class of System Fault Tolerance

The next step is to identify the class of the system from the fault tolerance perspective. In the proposed method, we identify two abstract classes of systems from the fault tolerance modelling perspective: a class of *failure-free* systems, and a class of *safe stop* systems. Any system belongs to one of these classes depending on whether stop conditions are defined in requirements.

At this stage, we include an additional type of formal models into the development process, Modal Views, and define a formal relationship with Event-B models. A modal view consists of *modes* and *mode transitions*. A mode describes the functionality of a system by its *guarantee* predicate, and the operating conditions under which the system provides this functionality by its *assumption* predicate. A mode is mapped into a set of Event-B events and represents a superstate of a system. A mode transition represents an instantaneous switch of the system between two modes. More details on formal definitions of Modal Views and relationship with Event-B can be found in [10,3,12,9]. Here it is important to understand that such a relationship between two different types of models produces formal consistency conditions in a form of additional proof obligations. These require developers to focus more on the modelling activity and, thus, add rigour to the development process.

We associate the two classes of system fault tolerance with two possible initial modal views accordingly (Figure 4). Systems of the first class can mask all internal errors and operate indefinitely long. This is represented by a single mode *Normal*. Systems of the second class cannot tolerate certain errors and can eventually stop. The errors that can cause a system stop are called *unrecoverable* and are collectively represented by the abstract transition to mode *Stop*.

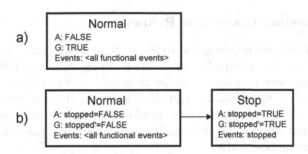

Fig. 4. Two abstract classes of fault tolerant systems: a) Failure-free, b) Safe-stop

The airlock system so far contained only failure-free functionality reflecting the absence of failures in requirements. Now we assume that some components of the system can fail, and the whole system may eventually stop due to such errors. We accommodate this behaviour in model M1 (Snippet 2). We define variable *stopped* representing the operational availability of the system, and separate the functional behaviour from the stopped state by using this variable. We refine all functional events by strengthening their guards and add two new events as shown in Snippet 2. The changes we made to the model are generic in that they are applicable to any safe stop system. These constitute the *safe stop pattern* that should be applied as the first refinement step for modelling fault tolerant behaviour in case of a safe stop system.

---

event open1 $\widehat{=}$ **extends open1**
    when grd_stopped: *stopped* $= FALSE$

event stop $\widehat{=}$
    when grd_stopped: *stopped* $= FALSE$
    then act_stopped: *stopped* $:= TRUE$

event stopped $\widehat{=}$
    when grd: *stopped* $= TRUE$
    then *skip*

Snippet 2. Part of M1 after applying the safe stop pattern

We also associate the modal view *b* on Figure 4 with Event-B model M1. This produces additional formal obligations to prove for M1 and ensures that the model indeed contains the safe stop behaviour.

The purpose of this refinement step is to "reserve" an abstract representation of the overall system fault tolerant behaviour for further refinements. Event *stop* represents an abstraction of all unrecoverable errors that will be introduced later.

5.3   Fault Tolerant Component Refinement

On top of the functional requirements to the system, we also introduce a "fragile" environment where the physical components of the system may fail:

(**ENV3**) *Sensors and actuators may fail to provide a correct function.*

From this fault assumption, description of sensors (which we omit due to lack of space), and description of available redundancy in the system we can construct an adequate abstraction for modelling. We define the three possible error states of the two doors in model M2:

$$door1\_cond, door2\_cond : \{BROKEN, DEGRADED, OK\}$$

Such a definition of error states constitutes the *error state variable pattern*.

Fault assumption (**ENV3**) raises a number of requirements that concern system fault tolerance:

(**FT1**) *The system shall disallow opening a degraded door.*

(**FT2**) *The system shall stop if at least one of the doors is broken.*

(**FT3**) *If both doors are degraded, the system shall stop unless there is a user in the chamber. If the user is present in the chamber, the system shall allow opening the inner door.*

In order to represent these requirements formally, we refine the modal view shown in Figure 4b by splitting the normal behaviour of the system into four modes: the normal operation mode and three degraded modes (Figure 5). The system stays in mode *Door1* when the first door is degraded and the second door is fully operational, and vice versa for mode *Door2*. When both doors are degraded and there is a user present in the chamber, the system stays in mode *Trapped* until the user leaves the chamber. The new mode *Normal* together with the three degraded modes formally refine abstract mode *Normal* as shown by a dashed area. Such a refinement of a mode by a chain of degraded modes constitutes the *mode split template*. The degraded modes in Figure 5 represent different sets of available components and the associated subsets of system behaviour. The assumption predicates of the modes split the possible combinations of the components' error states into disjoint sets. The mode assumptions cover all the system states which must be demonstrated through the well-definedness proof obligation COVER [12].

We refine the abstract system failure transition by four concrete transitions depicting the sources of failure. Transitions *Stop on degrade* and *User leaves* initiate at the new modes. Transition *Break* can initiate at any of the four modes within the dashed area. All three formally refine the abstract error transition,

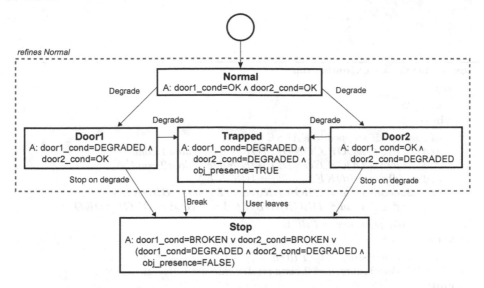

Fig. 5. Modal view of the airlock M2 model

and this is an example of an application of the *transition split template*. The two templates shown here (mode split and transition split templates) provide a means for step-wise construction of complex modal behaviour and ensure traceability of modal views into fault tolerance requirements.

Modal view M2 represents fault tolerant behaviour of the system in terms of its *fault tolerant components*, two doors and the chamber. In order to ensure formal refinement between M1 and M2, we define a relationship between the abstract error state variable *stopped* and the newly defined door error state variables as a gluing invariant *inv4*:

$$door1\_cond = BROKEN \lor door2\_cond = BROKEN\lor$$
$$(door1\_cond = DEGRADED \land door2\_cond = DEGRADED\land$$
$$obj\_presence = FALSE) \Leftrightarrow stopped = TRUE$$

Definition of gluing invariants over error state variables constitutes the *error state invariant pattern*. This pattern is necessary for establishing the refinement relation between each two subsequent modelling steps. Note that the gluing invariant also refers to functional variable *obj_presence* that we introduced to meet requirement (FT3). This variable shows whether a user is present in the chamber. Such reference to a functional variable highlights the point that the fault tolerance properties of the system are inevitably tied to the functional state and both need to be taken into account during refinement.

The defined error states are used in definition of fault tolerant behaviour using the *fault tolerant behaviour pattern*: we refine the events that represent the reactions of the system to errors by error detection events. In this way we associate the causes of failures with system reactions. Snippet 3 shows three

---

event break $\widehat{=}$ **extends stop**

  any

    $d1c$ $d2c$

  where

    grd_stopped: $stopped = FALSE$
    grd2_0: $d1c \in DOOR\_CONDITION \land d1c \leq door1\_cond$
    grd2_1: $d2c \in DOOR\_CONDITION \land d2c \leq door2\_cond$
    grd2_2: $d1c = BROKEN \lor d2c = BROKEN$
    grd2_3: $door1\_cond \neq BROKEN \land door2\_cond \neq BROKEN$
    grd2_4: $door1\_cond = DEGRADED \land door2\_cond = DEGRADED \Rightarrow$
        $obj\_presence = TRUE$

  then

    act_stopped: $stopped := TRUE$
    act2_0: $door1\_cond, door2\_cond := d1c, d2c$

  end

event degrade $\widehat{=}$

  any

    $d1c$ $d2c$

  where

    grd0: $stopped = FALSE$
    grd1: $d1c \in \{OK, DEGRADED\} \land d1c \leq door1\_cond$
    grd2: $d2c \in \{OK, DEGRADED\} \land d2c \leq door2\_cond$
    grd3: $(door1\_cond = OK \land d1c = DEGRADED \land door2\_cond = d2c) \lor$
        $(door2\_cond = OK \land d2c = DEGRADED \land door1\_cond = d1c)$
    grd4: $d1c \neq DEGRADED \lor d2c \neq DEGRADED \lor obj\_presence = TRUE$

  then

    act1: $door1\_cond, door2\_cond := d1c, d2c$

  end

event stop_on_degrade $\widehat{=}$ **extends stop**

  when

    grd0: $stopped = FALSE$
    grd1: $door1\_cond = DEGRADED \lor door2\_cond = DEGRADED$
    grd2: $obj\_presence = FALSE$
    grd4: $door1\_cond = OK \lor door2\_cond = OK$

  then

    act_stopped: $stopped := TRUE$
    act1: $door1\_cond := DEGRADED$
    act2: $door2\_cond := DEGRADED$

Snippet 3. The airlock M2 model after refining fault tolerant components events *break*, *degrade* and *stop_on_degrade* changing the door error states in three different situations. Events *break* and *stop_on_degrade* extend abstract event *stop* with actions putting the doors into degraded and broken states to satisfy gluing invariant *inv*4. This shows how an abstract fault tolerant reaction is refined into more specific component failures. Event *degrade* is new at M2, it changes the doors' error states and continues the system operation. It represents the tolerance of the system to certain errors. The three events represent a part of requirements (FT1), (FT2), (FT3). Two events *degrade* and *stop_on_degrade* depict the same abstract detection of a door failure but they lead to different reactions, and the choice depends on the current system state. We have to have both events in the model to cover all relevant system states at the moment of component failure to satisfy the implementable causality rule.

Thus, error detection transitions are also system reactions: they change FT components' error states as well as functional states. Such behaviour conforms to the reactive style of modelling and allows us to express safety properties which include both functional and error states.

5.4   Behaviour Restriction

During the previous steps, we refined the error states of the airlock system into error states of its components and defined events that provide transitions between those states. However, the functional behaviour of the system does not take the current error states into account. For example, a broken door can still "operate" in our model M2 as if it was in a normal condition. In this step, we remedy such an omission and restrict the functional behaviour to satisfy the fault tolerance requirements.

Firstly, we refine the M2 modal view by applying the behavioural split template to modes *Door1*, *Door2* and *Trapped* (Figure 6). For example, mode *Door2_closing* now restricts the system to only operate with the second door, and only contains events that close or stop the door but do not open it. Upon the door closure, the system switches to mode *Door2* that guarantees that the pressure is set to low and the door is closed, and thus only allows operating the first door.

Secondly, in order to satisfy the consistency conditions enforced by the modal view, we restrict the system behaviour expressed in the Event-B model. Specifically, to satisfy proof obligation *EVT_A* [12], we strengthen the guard of event *open*1 by the following condition:

$$door1\_cond = OK$$

We strengthen every event in model M3 in a similar manner thus ensuring that (FT1) is satisfied. Such a restriction constitutes the *behaviour restriction pattern*: we restrict the functional transitions that are not allowed with respect to the error states of components. In this regard, we treat modal views as diagrammatic specifications of the system fault tolerant behaviour, and their assumption/guarantee pairs as one of the two formalisations of fault tolerance requirements.

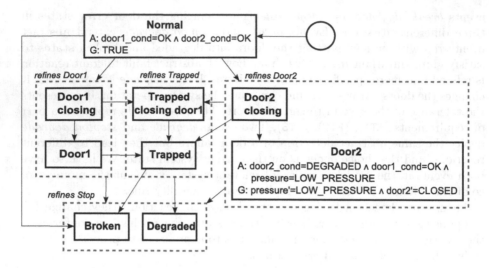

Fig. 6. Modal view of airlock M3 model

The component refinement and the behaviour restriction steps are performed in a top-down manner until the reactive model of the system contains the required safety and fault tolerance properties.

6   Conclusions

Development of correct fault tolerance is a major challenge in designing complex dependable systems as evidenced by major failures such as the crash of the Ariane 5 launcher and the August 2003 Blackout in the US and Canada. Analysis of these and more recent failures shows that a (typically substantial) support for tolerating faults in many modern systems often fails or has a lower quality than the rest of the systems.

In this paper, we described a top-down development method for formal modelling of fault tolerant systems starting from the early stages of abstract modelling and following to modelling control systems. The early consideration of fault tolerance in refinement-based methods can reduce the modelling efforts, and helps to ensure the overall dependability of the resulting systems.

The method proposed incorporates a separate viewpoint for modelling modal and fault tolerance features of systems. This viewpoint adds rigour to the formal development process, contributes to readability of formal models by engineers, and bridges the gap between requirements and formal models. The method ensures the reuse of formal modelling by supporting patterns typical for modelling fault tolerance. The use of refinement as a formal basis for step-wise development, separation of FT concern in a formal viewpoint, and a pattern-based approach to modelling contribute to tackling complexity of critical system models.

We demonstrated the application of the method by modelling an airlock system. The refinement chain of the airlock case study consists of 5 Event-B machines and 3 associated modal views; overall the development produced 417 proof obligations, 356 of which were proven automatically. Most of the rest 61 proof obligations that required interactive proof were generated by the Rodin tools. The full Rodin project containing the models and views can be downloaded from the Modal Views wiki page [12].

The method is tool supported. The modal viewpoint is implemented as a plug-in for the Rodin environment which includes a diagram editor and a smooth integration with prover facilities [12].

Acknowledgements. This work is supported by the ICT DEPLOY IP and the EPSRC/UK TrAmS-2 platform grant. We are grateful to Alexei Iliasov for fruitful discussions and support.

References

1. Abrial, J.-R.: Modeling in Event-B - System and Software Engineering. Cambridge University Press (2010)
2. Avizienis, A., Laprie, J.-C., Randell, B., Landwehr, C.: Basic Concepts and Taxonomy of Dependable and Secure Computing. IEEE Transactions on Dependable and Secure Computing 1(1), 11–33 (2004)
3. Dotti, F.L., Iliasov, A., Ribeiro, L., Romanovsky, A.: Modal systems: Specification, refinement and realisation. In: Breitman, K., Cavalcanti, A. (eds.) ICFEM 2009. LNCS, vol. 5885, pp. 601–619. Springer, Heidelberg (2009)
4. FP7 DEPLOY Project: Industrial deployment of system engineering methods providing high dependability and productivity (2008 - 2012), http://www.deploy-project.eu/
5. Jeffords, R., Heitmeyer, C., Archer, M., Leonard, E.: A Formal Method for Developing Provably Correct Fault-Tolerant Systems Using Partial Refinement and Composition. In: Cavalcanti, A., Dams, D.R. (eds.) FM 2009. LNCS, vol. 5850, pp. 173–189. Springer, Heidelberg (2009)
6. Laibinis, L., Troubitsyna, E.: Fault Tolerance in a Layered Architecture: A General Specification Pattern in B. In: Proceedings of the 2nd International Conference on Software Engineering and Formal Methods, SEFM 2004, pp. 346–355. IEEE Computer Society (September 2004)
7. Laibinis, L., Troubitsyna, E.: Refinement of Fault Tolerant Control Systems in B. In: Heisel, M., Liggesmeyer, P., Wittmann, S. (eds.) SAFECOMP 2004. LNCS, vol. 3219, pp. 254–268. Springer, Heidelberg (2004)
8. Lee, P.A., Anderson, T.: Fault Tolerance: Principles and Practice. Springer-Verlag New York, Inc. (1990)
9. Lopatkin, I.: A Method for Rigorous Development of Fault-Tolerant Systems. PhD thesis, School of Computing Science, Newcastle University (2013)
10. Lopatkin, I., Iliasov, A., Romanovsky, A.: Rigorous Development of Dependable Systems using Fault Tolerance Views. In: Proceedings of the 22nd International Symposium on Software Reliability Engineering, ISSRE 2011, Hiroshima, Japan, pp. 180–189 (December 2011)

11. Lopatkin, I., Iliasov, A., Romanovsky, A., Prokhorova, Y., Troubitsyna, E.: Patterns for Representing FMEA in Formal Specification of Control Systems. In: The 13th IEEE International High Assurance Systems Engineering Symposium (HASE 2011), Boca Raton, FL, USA, pp. 146–151 (November 2011)
12. Wiki page for Modal and Fault Tolerance Views language and tool support, http://wiki.event-b.org/index.php/Mode/FT_Views
13. Woodcock, J., Larsen, P.G., Bicarregui, J., Fitzgerald, J.S.: Formal methods: Practice and experience. ACM Computing Surveys 41(4), 19:1–19:36 (2009)

Kronecker Algebra for Static Analysis of Ada Programs with Protected Objects*

Bernd Burgstaller[1] and Johann Blieberger[2]

[1] Yonsei University, Korea
[2] Vienna University of Technology, Austria

Abstract. Kronecker algebra has proven useful in analyzing multi-threaded programs when semaphores are the only synchronization primitives. In contrast, Ada uses higher level synchronization primitives, namely protected objects. In this paper we show how Kronecker algebra can be generalized to statically analyze Ada multi-tasking programs that employ protected objects for synchronization issues.

1 Introduction

With the advent of multi-core processors, scientific and industrial interest focuses on analysis and verification of multi-threaded applications. The scientific challenge comes from the fact that the number of thread interleavings grows exponentially in a program's number of threads. All state-of-the-art methods suffer from this so-called *state explosion problem.*

Kronecker algebra is a useful vehicle to model multi-threaded shared memory programs and stochastic automata [5,14,15,16]. Kronecker sum and Kronecker product are applied to the adjacency matrices of the underlying concurrent programs' control flow graphs and the synchronization primitives' graph representations. Until now Kronecker algebra analysis has only been applied to multi-threaded concurrent programs being synchronized via *semaphores*. Applying Kronecker algebra to higher level synchronization primitives like Ada's *protected objects* (POs) is novel in this area. The contributions of this paper are as follows.

1. We show how to model Ada's protected objects such that Kronecker algebra can be employed for static analysis. This covers several more or less semaphore-like synchronization primitives.
2. We provide graph templates that can be plugged into the graph model used by Kronecker algebra when a guarded entry call, a procedure, or function call is contained in a task body.
3. We apply symbolic analysis (SA) to the graph resulting from Kronecker algebra. SA provides predicates associated with graph edges which can be used to eliminate dead program paths.

* This project has been supported by the National Research Foundation of Korea (NRF) funded by the Korean government (MEST) under grant number 2012-K2A1A9054713, and by the Austrian Science Fund (FWF) project I 1035N23.

L. George and T. Vardanega (Eds.): Ada-Europe 2014, LNCS 8454, pp. 27–42, 2014.

2   Preliminaries

Tasks and synchronization primitives are represented by slightly adapted control flow graphs (CFGs). Each CFG is represented by an adjacency matrix. We assume that the edges of CFGs are labeled by elements of a semiring. Definitions and properties of the semiring can be found in [10,14]. A prominent example of such semirings are regular expressions describing the behavior of finite state automata. Our semiring consists of a set of labels $\mathcal{L}$ which is defined by $\mathcal{L} = \mathcal{L}_V \cup \mathcal{L}_S$, where $\mathcal{L}_V$ is the set of non-synchronization labels and $\mathcal{L}_S$ is the set of labels representing calls to synchronization primitives ($\mathcal{L}_V$ and $\mathcal{L}_S$ are disjoint).

Semiring $\langle \mathcal{L}, +, \cdot, 0, 1 \rangle$ consists of a set of labels $\mathcal{L}$, two binary operations $+$ and $\cdot$, and two constants 0 and 1 such that $\langle \mathcal{L}, +, 0 \rangle$ is a commutative monoid, $\langle \mathcal{L}, \cdot, 1 \rangle$ is a monoid, $\forall l_1, l_2, l_3 \in \mathcal{L} : l_1 \cdot (l_2 + l_3) = l_1 \cdot l_2 + l_1 \cdot l_3$ and $(l_1 + l_2) \cdot l_3 = l_1 \cdot l_3 + l_2 \cdot l_3$ hold, and $\forall l \in \mathcal{L} : 0 \cdot l = l \cdot 0 = 0$. Examples for semirings include regular expressions (cf. [19]).

Intuitively, our semiring is a unital ring without subtraction. For each $l \in \mathcal{L}$ the usual rules are valid, e.g., $l + 0 = 0 + l = l$ and $1 \cdot l = l \cdot 1 = l$. In addition we equip our semiring with the unary operation $*$. For each $l \in \mathcal{L}$, l^* is defined by $l^* = \sum_{j \geq 0} l^j$, where $l^0 = 1$ and $l^{j+1} = l^j \cdot l = l \cdot l^j$ for $j \geq 0$.

Since our matrix calculus manipulates the edges of CFGs, we need to have basic blocks on the (incoming) edges. To keep things simple we refer to edges, their labels and the corresponding entries of the adjacency matrices synonymously. A basic block consists of multiple consecutive statements without jumps. For our purpose we need a finer granularity which we achieve by splitting edges. We employ edge splitting for calls to synchronization primitives (e.g. p- and v-calls to semaphores) and require that such a call referred to as s_i has to be the only statement on the corresponding (split) edge. Edge splitting maps a CFG edge e whose corresponding basic block contains k semaphore calls to a subgraph $\circ \xrightarrow{e_1} \circ \xrightarrow{s_1} \circ \xrightarrow{e_2} \circ \xrightarrow{s_2} \circ \cdots \circ \xrightarrow{e_k} \circ \xrightarrow{s_k} \circ \xrightarrow{e_{k+1}} \circ$, such that each s_i represents a single semaphore call, and e_i and e_{i+1} represent the consecutive parts before and after s_i, respectively ($1 \leq i \leq k$). Applying edge splitting results in a refined CFG (RCFG).

Kronecker product and Kronecker sum form Kronecker algebra. In the following we define both operations. Proofs, additional properties, and examples can be found in [3,7,9,14]. In addition, we find it convenient to sometimes refer to CFGs as automata, both of which are represented by matrices. From now on we use matrices out of $\mathcal{M} = \{M = (m_{i,j}) \mid m_{i,j} \in \mathcal{L}\}$ only.

Definition 1 (Kronecker product). *Given an m-by-n matrix A and a p-by-q matrix B, their* Kronecker product *$A \otimes B$ is an mp-by-nq block matrix defined by*

$$A \otimes B = \begin{pmatrix} a_{1,1} \cdot B & \cdots & a_{1,n} \cdot B \\ \vdots & \ddots & \vdots \\ a_{m,1} \cdot B & \cdots & a_{m,n} \cdot B \end{pmatrix}.$$

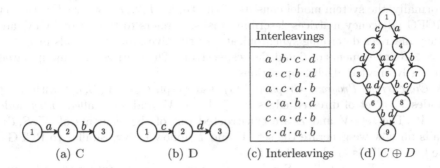

Fig. 1. A simple example

Given two automata, the Kronecker product synchronously executes them. This means that both automata perform a single step at the same time. Thus the Kronecker product is too restrictive for modeling tasks that synchronize via a synchronization primitive. However, we will show below how we can achieve our goal to model concurrent systems (see also [5,14,16]).

Definition 2 (Kronecker sum). *Given a matrix A of order m and a matrix B of order n, their Kronecker sum $A \oplus B$ is a matrix of order mn defined by $A \oplus B = A \otimes I_n + I_m \otimes B$, where I_m and I_n denote identity matrices of order m and n, respectively.*

The Kronecker sum calculates all possible interleavings of two concurrently executing automata (see, e.g., [11] for a proof) even if the automata contain conditionals and loops. The following example illustrates the interleaving of two simple tasks and how the Kronecker sum handles it.

Example 1. Consider matrices $C = \begin{pmatrix} 0 & a & 0 \\ 0 & 0 & b \\ 0 & 0 & 0 \end{pmatrix}$ and $D = \begin{pmatrix} 0 & c & 0 \\ 0 & 0 & d \\ 0 & 0 & 0 \end{pmatrix}$. The CFGs of matrices C and D are shown in Fig. 1a and Fig. 1b, respectively. The regular expressions associated with the CFGs are $a \cdot b$ and $c \cdot d$. All possible interleavings by executing C and D in an interleavings semantics are shown in Fig. 1c. In Fig. 1d the graph represented by the adjacency matrix $C \oplus D$ is depicted. It is easy to see that all possible interleavings are generated correctly. Note, however, that $\oplus$ provides correct results even if the operands contain branches and loops.

The system model presented so far (see, e.g., [14]) consists of a finite number of tasks and synchronization primitives which are represented by RCFGs. The RCFGs are stored in form of adjacency matrices. The matrices have entries which are referred to as labels $l \in \mathcal{L}$ as defined in Sect. 2. The only synchronization primitives used until now are semaphores. In the following we first give the general system model used by the Kronecker approach leading to (1). Then we describe how Ada's protected objects can be modeled such that Kronecker algebra can be employed for analyzing concurrent Ada programs.

Formally, the system model consists of the tuple $\langle \mathcal{T}, \mathcal{S}, \mathcal{L} \rangle$, where $\mathcal{T}$ is the set of RCFG adjacency matrices describing tasks, $\mathcal{S}$ refers to the set of RCFG adjacency matrices describing synchronization primitives, and the labels in $T \in \mathcal{T}$ and $S \in \mathcal{S}$ are elements of $\mathcal{L}$ and $\mathcal{L}_S$, respectively. The matrices are manipulated by using Kronecker algebra operations.

A *Concurrent Program Graph* (CPG) is a graph $C = \langle V, E, n_e \rangle$ with a set of nodes V, a set of directed edges $E \subseteq V \times V$, and a so-called *entry* node $n_e \in V$. The sets V and E are constructed out of the elements of $\langle \mathcal{T}, \mathcal{S}, \mathcal{L} \rangle$. Details on how we generate the sets V and E follow below. Similar to RCFGs, the edges of CPGs are labeled by $l \in \mathcal{L}$.

Let $T^{(i)} \in \mathcal{T}$ and $S^{(j)} \in \mathcal{S}$ refer to the matrices representing thread i and synchronization primitive j, respectively. We obtain matrix T representing k interleaved tasks and matrix S representing r interleaved synchronization primitives by

$$T = \bigoplus_{i=1}^{k} T^{(i)}, \text{ where } T^{(i)} \in \mathcal{T} \text{ and } S = \bigoplus_{j=1}^{r} S^{(j)}, \text{ where } S^{(j)} \in \mathcal{S}.$$

Because the operations $\otimes$ and $\oplus$ are associative (cf. [14]), the corresponding n-fold versions are well defined. In the following we define the selective Kronecker product which we denote by $\oslash_L$. This operator limits synchronization of the operands to labels $l \in L \subseteq \mathcal{L}$.

Definition 3 (Selective Kronecker product). *Given an m-by-n matrix A and a p-by-q matrix B, we call $A \oslash_L B$ their selective Kronecker product. For all $l \in L \subseteq \mathcal{L}$ let $A \oslash_L B = (a_{i,j}) \oslash_L (b_{r,s}) = (c_{t,u})$, where*

$$c_{(i-1)\cdot p + r, (j-1)\cdot q + s} = \begin{cases} l & \text{if } a_{i,j} = b_{r,s} = l, \ l \in L, \\ 0 & \text{otherwise.} \end{cases}$$

The selective Kronecker product ensures that, e.g., a semaphore p-call in the left operand is paired with the p-operation in the right operand and not with any other operation in the right operand.

Definition 4 (Filtered Matrix). *We call M_L a filtered matrix and define it as a matrix of order $o(M)$ containing entries $l \in L \subseteq \mathcal{L}$ of $M = (m_{i,j})$ and zeros elsewhere:*

$$M_L = (m_{L;i,j}), \text{ where } m_{L;i,j} = \begin{cases} l & \text{if } m_{i,j} = l, \ l \in L, \\ 0 & \text{otherwise.} \end{cases}$$

The adjacency matrix representing program $\mathcal{P}$ is referred to as P. In [14] it has been shown that P can be computed efficiently by

$$P = T \oslash_{\mathcal{L}_S} S + T_{\mathcal{L}_V} \otimes I_{o(S)}. \tag{1}$$

Intuitively, the selective Kronecker product term on the left allows for synchronization between the tasks represented by T and the synchronization primitives S.

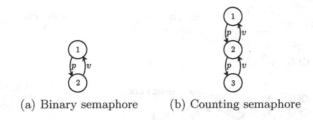

(a) Binary semaphore   (b) Counting semaphore

Fig. 2. Semaphores (synchronization primitives)

Both T and S are Kronecker sums of the involved tasks and synchronization primitives, respectively, in order to represent all possible interleavings of the concurrently executing tasks. The right term allows the tasks to perform steps that are not involved in synchronization. Summarizing, the tasks (represented by T) may perform their steps concurrently where all interleavings are allowed, except when they call synchronization primitives. In the latter case the synchronization primitives (represented by S) together with Kronecker product ensure that these calls are executed in the order prescribed by the deterministic finite automata (DFA) of the synchronization primitives.

So, for example, a task cannot do semaphore calls in the order v followed by p when the semaphore DFA only allows a p-call before a v-call. The CPG of such an erroneous program will contain a node from which the final node of the CPG cannot be reached. This node is the one preceding the v-call. Such nodes can easily be found by traversing CPGs. Thus deadlocks of concurrent systems can be detected with little effort.

In Fig. 2a and 2b a binary and a counting semaphore are depicted. The latter allows two threads to enter at the same time. In a similar way it is possible to construct semaphores allowing n non-blocking p-calls ($n \in \mathbb{N}, n \geq 1$).

Figure 3 shows a small example. The program in Fig. 3a has two branches. The left one employs calls p and v to an initially unlocked semaphore (Fig. 2a) in the correct order, the second one contains two p-calls. Applying Kronecker algebra (cf. (1) and Fig. 3b) we obtain the CPG in Fig. 3c. Node 6 shows that there is a self-deadlock in the underlying program.

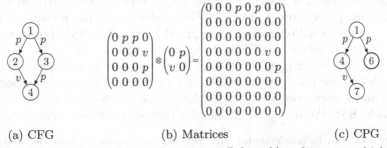

(a) CFG   (b) Matrices   (c) CPG

Fig. 3. (a) An example program with a correct (left path) and incorrect (right path) use of a binary semaphore that is initially unlocked; (b) Kronecker matrix operation; (c) CPG after Kronecker analysis with the self-deadlock in CPG-node 6

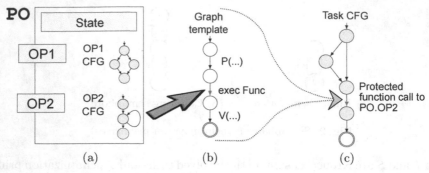

Fig. 4. Protected object PO (a), CFG template for protected functions (b) and task CFG containing a call to the protected function PO.OP2 (c). CFGs generated from user source code are shaded in grey O. Instantiation proceeds from left to right: the CFG of the protected function OP2 is inserted into the protected function graph template in place of the highlighted edge labelled "exec Func". The instantiated graph template is inserted into the task CFG to replace the highlighted edge marking the call to PO.OP2.

3   Modelling Ada's Protected Objects

Kronecker algebra until now has only been applied to concurrent programs that use semaphores for synchronization. Ada's protected objects (POs) are a higher level synchronization primitive. For reasons explained in the latter part of this section, simple Kronecker algebra-based semaphores are insufficient to model POs.[1] However, the Kronecker algebra approach is not limited to simple semaphores. Its general idea is that DFAs are employed to model synchronization primitives. The Kronecker product ensures that concurrent programs use the operations of the modeled synchronization primitives (e.g., p and v with semaphores) in the correct order, i.e., the order prescribed by the DFA. For this reason we are free in setting up DFAs that describe the semantics of Ada POs.

Our approach is outlined in Fig. 4. We build on our prior work from [8] to create CFGs from user-provided source code. CFGs are created for (1) the main program, (2) all tasks in the concurrent Ada program, and (3) for all protected operations. We provide graph templates for all types of protected operations, i.e., functions, procedures, and entries. Templates model the mutual exclusion semantics of protected operations as required by the Ada RM. Templates provide placeholders where the CFG of the user-supplied code of the protected operation is inserted. E.g., with the template for protected functions in Fig. 4b, the placeholder for the protected function call ("exec Func") is wrapped by a pair of P and V operations that enforce the mutual exclusion semantics required by the Ada RM. We note that standard binary or counting semaphores, e.g.,

---

[1] Clearly POs can be *implemented* with help of semaphores. Semaphores employed within Kronecker algebra, however, differ from semaphores used in practical implementations in several ways. For example, tasks in the Kronecker algebra model are not blocked and queued when a semaphore is not available.

from Fig. 2, are insufficient for this purpose: a counting semaphore would allow concurrent execution of multiple protected function calls, but it cannot model the exclusive access for protected procedure and entry calls at the same time. We will develop the full semantics of graph templates in the latter part of this section. For this introductory example we assume the simplified semantics provided by the binary semaphore from Fig. 2a to exclusively lock the protected object PO.

At a protected operation call-site, a graph template is instantiated. E.g., with the task CFG in Fig. 4c, the highlighted edge represents a call to the protected function PO.OP2. Template instantiation inserts the CFG of the protected operation (Fig. 4a) into the graph template (Fig. 4b). The instantiated graph template is inserted at the call site of the protected operation (Fig. 4c). The effect of this protected operation "inlining" is that the protected operation call-site is expanded into a CFG of the respective, user-provided protected operation-functionality wrapped by the mutual-exclusion semantics of the graph template. Insertions of CFGs are done in a manner similar to derivations in graph grammars [17]. In the remainder of this section we describe our model in more detail, accompanying it by a running example.

Our static analysis for concurrent programs with Ada POs extracts the program semantics from the CFG of the user-supplied input program. As we have already observed in the overview in Fig. 4, the user-supplied source code must be complemented by functionality that ensures the mutual-exclusion semantics of POs. The PO mutual-exclusion semantics is complex, because it involves guarded entries, protected procedures, and functions. Implementation permissions of the Ada RM add complexity, because they allow multiple run-time system implementations which are correct with respect to Ada semantics, but which differ considerably in the run-time behavior of the concurrent program. E.g., Ada allows a task to execute an entry on behalf of another task [4, 9.5.3(22)]. So-called proxy-model implementations [13] make use of this permission, which limits the parallelism inherent in an application: because a proxy-task that executes an entry on behalf of another, queued, task delays execution of its own code, parallelism is temporarily reduced. Entry queuing policies determine the order in which queued tasks are served and thus influence the run-time behavior of the program.

It is *essential* for a static analysis method for concurrency bugs to anticipate all possible parallel executions of tasks in the program under consideration. If the analysis misses out on a particular, incorrect parallel execution (e.g., one that leads to a deadlock), analysis will yield a false negative result. To cover the complexity of Ada's PO synchronization constructs, and to cope with concurrency-related variations from permissible implementations, we chose a template-based approach. Our graph templates constitute semantic models of the underlying execution semantics of Ada's POs. Graph templates contain all synchronization primitives necessary to ensure the correct mutual-exclusion semantics imposed by the Ada RM. Synchronization primitives comprise standard semaphores, three-phase (counting) semaphores with operations Pe, V and

```
 1   procedure Running_Example is
 2
 3      protected type Buffer (Max: Integer) is
 4         entry Load (S: in String);
 5         entry Get (C: out Character);
 6      private
 7         Data: String(1..Max);
 8         Start: Integer := 1;
 9         Finish: Integer := 0;
10      end Buffer;
11
12      protected body Buffer is
13         entry Load(S: in String)
14            when Start > Finish is
15         begin
16            Start := 1;
17            Finish := S'Length;
18            Data(Start..Finish) := S;
19         end Load;
20
21         entry Get(C: out Character)
22            when Start <= Finish is
23         begin
24            C := Data(Start);
25            Start := Start + 1;
26         end Get;
27      end Buffer;
28
29      B: Buffer(16);
30
31      task Getter;
32      task body Getter is
33         C: Character;
34      begin
35         loop
36            B.Get(C);
37         end loop;
38      end Getter;
39
40   begin
41      B.Load("Hello Ada!");
42   end Running_Example;
```

Fig. 5. Running example

Px, and counting semaphore-like DFAs. Graph templates capture the semantics of guards and their queuing policies. Our template-based approach offers the following advantages.

1. Graph templates separate concerns: they isolate the semantics of the language run-time system from user-level code. Graph templates provide few and well-defined insertion points where user-level code of protected operations is automatically inserted during template instantiation.
2. Graph templates can be plugged into the Kronecker algebra-based PO analysis: multiple graph templates covering different PO implementations can co-exist to be selected according to the run-time system at hand.
3. The graph template mechanism is extensible and generic and not restricted to POs.

In the following we describe the graph templates necessary to model Ada PO semantics. We chose the proxy-model where a task that opens the guard of an entry with a queued task will execute the entry on behalf of the queued task [13]. In particular, if a guard of an entry evaluates to *false*, the calling task T_1 has to wait until the guard's value changes. If, later on, a different task T_2, after executing a PO operation, detects that a guard now evaluates to *true* and that task T_1 is waiting for this guard to become *true*, T_2 executes the PO entry on behalf of task T_1 and after that releases T_1. T_2 continues with the proxy execution of entries until all tasks waiting on *true* (open) guards have been released. In the meantime no other task can use the affected PO. Thus our model corresponds to the semantics of Ada's POs ([18]) and to the eggshell model implemented in GNAT ([2,13]). Other PO implementations such as self-service where tasks do not delegate entry call executions have been omitted due to space considerations; their implementation will follow along the same lines.

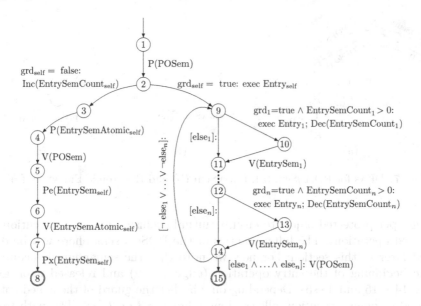

Fig. 6. Graph template for protected entries

We use the running example depicted in Fig. 5. The example is originally from [2] and contains a string buffer implemented as a PO. The **Load** entry (lines 13–19) allows filling the buffer, subject to the guard condition that the buffer is empty. The **Get** entry allows character-by-character retrieval of the buffer string, subject to the guard condition that the buffer is not empty. The program's main task, in the following called the Loader, fills the buffer once by invoking the PO's **Load** entry (line 41). The Getter task uses an infinite loop (lines 35–37) to read characters from the buffer through repeated invocations of the **Get** entry. After depleting all characters from the Loader's initially loaded string, the guard of the **Get** entry (line 22) becomes *false*.

Our graph template for protected entry operations is depicted in Fig. 6. This template is to be instantiated at each protected entry call site in the program. The purpose of the graph template is to encapsulate the semantics of a protected entry operation in the form of a CFG which is inserted in place of the entry call (see also the overview in Fig. 4). For the CFG of the running example from Fig. 5, the template will be instantiated for the **Get** entry call in line 36 and the **Load** entry call in line 41.

Template execution starts at Node 1 and proceeds along the edges of the graph until a final node (depicted as a double-circle) is reached. Each edge contains a label of the form ⟨cond⟩ : ⟨side-effect⟩, where cond is a condition that must be true for execution to follow along this edge, and side-effect is the activity performed as a result of edge execution. Trivial true conditions are omitted, and null-statements are left empty, denoted by ⟨cond⟩ :.

For this exposition, the entries of a PO are numbered from 1 to n. We use variable *self* to contain the number of the called entry. We employ one semaphore,

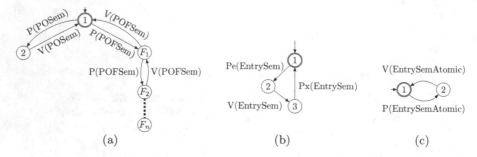

Fig. 7. DFAs for PO(F)Sem (a), EntrySem (b) and the atomic EntrySem (c)

POSem, per protected object to ensure mutual exclusion with the execution of protected operations. The full semantics of the POSem semaphore will be discussed later in this section; For now we note that the semaphore is acquired at the beginning of the entry operation (edge $1 \to 2$) and released upon exit (edges $14 \to 15$ and $4 \to 5$). Depending on whether the guard of the called entry is closed or open, execution follows along edge $2 \to 3$ or $2 \to 9$. The path from node 2 to node 8 is used to queue a task that called an entry with a closed guard, expressed by the edge-condition grd_{self} =false. For each entry we maintain a counter for the number of queued tasks. This counter ($EntrySemCount_{self}$) is incremented along edge $2 \to 3$. (The counter will be used later when the guard becomes open to decide whether a task is queued on this entry.) The task is then queued (blocked) as follows: it relinquishes the POSem on edge $4 \to 5$ to allow other tasks into the PO. The task then attempts to acquire the entry's $EntrySem_{self}$ semaphore on edge $5 \to 6$. Because the $EntrySem_{self}$ semaphore is initially closed, the attempted acquisition will block the task. To cover the three phases of (1) attempting to acquire the semaphore, (2) signaling the semaphore by another task, and (3) releasing the blocked task, EntrySem semaphores have three phases, as depicted in Fig. 7b. After the to-be-blocked task has executed the Pe(EntrySem) operation, it cannot proceed until another task signals the semaphore by executing V(EntrySem). Only then can the blocked task proceed to its Px(EntrySem) operation (edge $3 \to 1$ in Fig. 7b corresponding to edge $7 \to 8$ in Fig. 6) and resume execution. We note that the three phases applied in our model for EntrySem semaphores correspond to the behavior of "real", e.g., POSIX semaphores, where the P-operation of a closed semaphore is interleaved with the V-operation of the signaling process.

With our entry-call graph template, a blocked task delegates entry call execution to another task, the so-called proxy-task. This behavior is explicitly allowed in the Ada RM [4, 9.5.3(22)]. Proxy execution is captured by nodes 9–14 of Fig. 6: a task that is past the execution of its own entry call (edge $2 \to 9$) will look for open guards. For an open guard, a blocked task is detected by an EntrySemCount value greater than zero. The entry is executed and the EntrySemCount decremented (edges $9 \to 10$ and $12 \to 13$), followed by the release of the blocked task (edges $10 \to 11$ and $13 \to 14$). Guards are evaluated in a loop

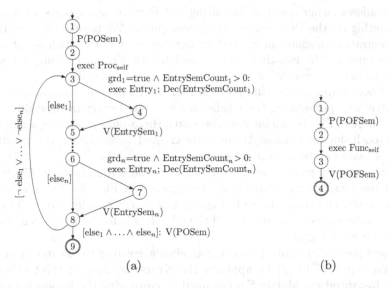

(a)   (b)

Fig. 8. Templates for protected procedures (a) and functions (b)

until proxy-execution and task-release has been achieved for all tasks blocked on open guards. Only then will the proxy-task exit the PO by relinquishing the POSem semaphore (edge $14 \to 15$). This behavior of favoring already queued tasks over newly-arriving tasks is informally called the eggshell model.

A note is due on the EntrySemAtomic semaphore employed with the blocking of tasks on closed entries (edges $3 \to 4$ and $6 \to 7$ in Fig. 6, and Fig. 7c): the purpose of this semaphore is to enforce that relinquishing of the POSem and queuing on the EntrySem happens atomically in our PO model. Note that the nesting of the $V(EntrySemAtomic_{self})$ operation within the P-operation (Pe and Px) is not possible with real, e.g., POSIX, semaphores. However, the graph template is concerned with the *model* of the mutual exclusion semantics, and the stated nesting of calls in conjunction with the semantics of the Kronecker algebra ensure that the model correctly represents the queuing of tasks.

The graph template for protected procedures depicted in Fig. 8a is simpler than protected entries, because protected procedures are not guarded and hence there is no need to block a calling task conditionally on a protected procedure. Once the POSem has been acquired, the protected procedure is executed. As with the entry call template, guards and EntrySemCounts are then repeatedly evaluated for possible proxy-execution of entry-calls of blocked tasks.

Figure 8b contains the graph template for protected function calls. Because functions are not allowed to change the state of a PO, multiple protected functions are allowed inside the PO as long as mutual exclusion with protected entries and procedures is ensured. We model this semantics as a counting semaphore extension of the POSem used with protected entries and procedures. As depicted in Fig. 7a, POSem and POFSem operations are combined in one DFA:

the DFA allows either one task acquiring the POSem semaphore, or multiple tasks counting up the POFSem counting semaphore. We note again that this is a synchronization mechanism created for our model of POs, which is not necessarily the same as the run-time system implementation mechanism, but which correctly models the execution semantics of the run-time system.

A final note is due on the EntrySem in Fig. 7c: if a program contains multiple tasks potentially performing entry calls on a protected entry or procedure, then the semaphore in Fig. 7c can be extended into a three-phase counting semaphore. Our approach does not allow dynamically created tasks, hence the maximum number of tasks can be statically bound.

The instantiation process for the running example is illustrated in Fig. 9. The CFGs of the Loader and Getter task are depicted in Fig. 9b. The CFGs after template instantiation are shown in Fig. 9c. For space considerations CFG edge labels are abbreviated. The relation of the edge labels to the graph template in Fig. 6 is stated in Fig. 9a.

The next step is to apply Kronecker algebra according to (1) to our graphs. We obtain matrix T in (1) by applying the Kronecker sum to the CFGs after template instantiation. Matrix S is obtained by employing the Kronecker sum to the CFGs of Fig. 7a, of two instances of Fig. 7b (for the Load and Get EntrySem semaphores), and two instances of Fig. 7c (again for the Load and Get entries of the Buffer object). The result is a CPG that contains all possible interleavings of the Loader and Getter task subject to the synchronization imposed by the Buffer PO. The resulting matrix has size 7560x7560, it defines a CPG consisting of 171 nodes, 298 edges, and 13 deadlock nodes. Incorporating conditions and side-effects of the CPG edge labels into our analysis, we find that several deadlock nodes are unreachable, i.e., all paths from the root of the CPG to such a deadlock node are infeasible and the deadlock thus constitutes a false positive. To illustrate unreachable paths through the CPG, we consider the CPG subgraph of our running example depicted in Fig. 10. The subgraph is rooted at the CPG root node. The path along the edges G.gcz→G.p1→G.7→G.lcm→L.lcz is infeasible, because the guard of the Get entry will be initially closed (the loader has not filled the buffer yet). Thus the condition along edge G.7 will evaluate to false and execution cannot proceed along this edge. Further consideration reveals that all paths from the root of the CPG to the depicted deadlock node are across edge G.7. Along all such paths, the condition on edge G7 is false and the deadlock node is thus unreachable and constitutes a false positive.

CPGs contain infeasible paths because the Kronecker algebra does not consider the conditions and side-effects on the edge-labels of CPGs. In the following section we will apply symbolic analysis of the computations along edges to avoid infeasible CPG paths and thereby increase the precision of the analysis.

4   Symbolic Analysis

Static program analysis is concerned with the design of algorithms that determine the dynamic behavior of programs without executing them. Symbolic analysis is an advanced static program analysis technique. It has been successfully

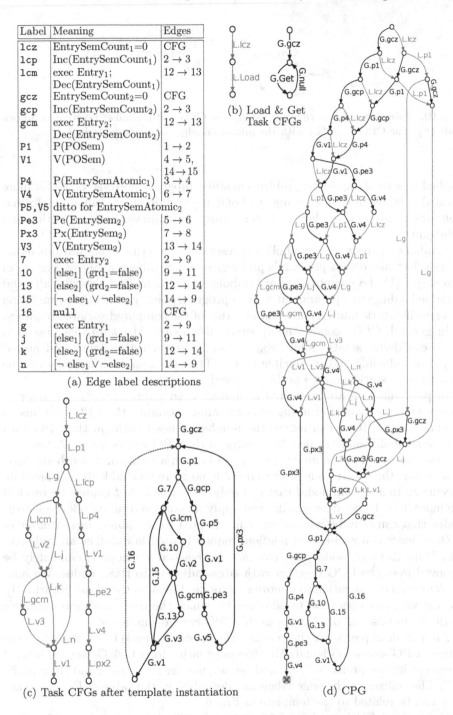

Label	Meaning	Edges
lcz	$EntrySemCount_1=0$	CFG
lcp	$Inc(EntrySemCount_1)$	$2 \to 3$
lcm	exec $Entry_1$; $Dec(EntrySemCount_1)$	$12 \to 13$
gcz	$EntrySemCount_2=0$	CFG
gcp	$Inc(EntrySemCount_2)$	$2 \to 3$
gcm	exec $Entry_2$; $Dec(EntrySemCount_2)$	$12 \to 13$
P1	$P(POSem)$	$1 \to 2$
V1	$V(POSem)$	$4 \to 5,$ $14 \to 15$
P4	$P(EntrySemAtomic_1)$	$3 \to 4$
V4	$V(EntrySemAtomic_1)$	$6 \to 7$
P5,V5	ditto for $EntrySemAtomic_2$	
Pe3	$Pe(EntrySem_2)$	$5 \to 6$
Px3	$Px(EntrySem_2)$	$7 \to 8$
V3	$V(EntrySem_2)$	$13 \to 14$
7	exec $Entry_2$	$2 \to 9$
10	$[else_1]$ $(grd_1=false)$	$9 \to 11$
13	$[else_2]$ $(grd_2=false)$	$12 \to 14$
15	$[\neg\ else_1 \vee \neg else_2]$	$14 \to 9$
16	null	CFG
g	exec $Entry_1$	$2 \to 9$
j	$[else_1]$ $(grd_1=false)$	$9 \to 11$
k	$[else_2]$ $(grd_2=false)$	$12 \to 14$
n	$[\neg\ else_1 \vee \neg else_2]$	$14 \to 9$

(a) Edge label descriptions

(b) Load & Get Task CFGs

(c) Task CFGs after template instantiation

(d) CPG

Fig. 9. (a) Relation of edge labels to the template in Fig. 6 and the task CFGs, (b) task CFGs, (c) task CFGs with protected operations expanded (dashed edges remain from the task CFGs), and (d) pruned CPG with deadlock node (✖)

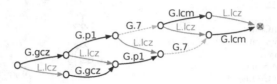

Fig. 10. Subgraph of the running example's CPG with a false positive deadlock node (✖). The CPG edge G.7 with the infeasible edge condition is dashed.

applied to several important problems in static program analysis (cf. [6] for more details). The results gained using symbolic analysis provide invaluable information for optimizing compilers, code generators, program verification, testing and debugging.

Symbolic analysis uses symbolic expressions to describe computations as algebraic formulæ over a program's problem space. Symbolic analysis consists of two steps: (1) the computation of symbolic expressions that describe all valid variable bindings of a program at a given program point, and (2) the formulation of a specific static analysis problem in terms of the computed variable bindings.

In general, CPGs contain many irreducible loops. The approach presented in [6] can derive solutions for arbitrary nodes (even within loops and nested loops) of reducible and irreducible CFGs. Thus the approach from [6] can be used to solve static analysis problems based on CPGs.

In particular, we are interested in finding dead paths in CPGs in order to reduce false positives. Returning to our running example, the CPG contains 13 deadlock nodes. If we can reduce the number of dead paths in the CPG with help of symbolic analysis, deadlock nodes in the CPG will be reduced, too.

After we have located an edge $e = (s \to t)$ with a path condition being false in all cases, the target node of this edge t is no more reachable during program execution. In addition, nodes that can only be reached via t cannot be reached anymore, too. To be more specific and applying notions from dataflow analysis, nodes that can only be reached via t are related to the *dominance frontier* of t. *Dominance* is a well-known relation frequently used in dataflow analysis (cf., e.g., [12]). Anyway, nodes that can only be reached via node t, can safely be removed from the CPG together with edges adjacent to these nodes. We have implemented an operation to remove such nodes based on the boost libraries [1]. By applying this operation to all edges for which the path condition evaluates statically to false, all dead paths in the CPG can be eliminated.

After all dead paths have been removed from our example CPG, we obtain the pruned CPG shown in Fig. 9d. All edges originating from task Getter are labeled starting with the prefix "G", while those originating from task Load show prefix "L". The suffixes of the edge labels are described in the table of Fig. 9a. Thus they can be related to the template in Fig. 6.

Our pruned CPG consists of 56 nodes and 87 edges. Out of the 13 potential deadlock nodes in the original CPG, only one deadlock node remains after pruning. The pruned CPG is depicted in Fig. 9d, with the deadlock node (✖) at the bottom left. Because we have eliminated all dead paths, we can be sure that our example program eventually deadlocks. Studying the graph more closely, we distinguish two parts:

1. One part reflects the Getter task calling entry `Buffer.Get` before the main task calls entry `Buffer.Load`. In this case, the Getter task is blocked because the corresponding guard is closed. Eventually `Buffer.Load` is called by the main task. During its execution the first call to `Buffer.Get` is executed and the Getter task is released. Later the Getter task issues the remaining calls to `Buffer.Get` until all characters have been read from the `Buffer` object.
2. The other part reflects the main task executing the call to `Buffer.Load` before the Getter task issues its first call to `Buffer.Get`. After the execution of `Buffer.Load` is finished, the Getter task does its calls to `Buffer.Get` until all characters have been read.

In both cases, after the last character has been read from the `Buffer`, the Getter task again calls `Buffer.Get`. Since, however, the `Buffer` is empty now, the Getter task is blocked because the guard of `Buffer.Get` is closed. As no task issues a further call to `Buffer.Load`, the program deadlocks.

Instead of doing an accurate analysis, an alternative approach is to study only one single path from the start node to the deadlock node of the pruned CPG. On such a path, conditions can be identified that yield a deadlock. These conditions provide enough facts to correct the erroneous program.

5 Conclusions

We have shown how Kronecker algebra can be employed for static analysis of concurrent Ada programs that use protected objects for synchronization. In more detail, we have provided graph templates that can be plugged into the graph model used by Kronecker algebra when a guarded entry call, a procedure, or function call is contained in a task body. Our graph model corresponds to the well-known eggshell model for implementing PO semantics. In addition, we have elaborated on how the graph resulting from Kronecker algebra can be pruned by eliminating dead program paths.

Since Kronecker algebra is based on the theory of finite automata, dynamically allocated tasks and dynamically allocated protected objects cannot be modeled by our approach. As our analysis targets safety related systems, we do not consider this a severe limitation.

The usefulness of our approach has been proved by a lazy implementation of Kronecker algebra done in Ada. The implementation is very memory efficient and has been parallelized to exploit modern many-core hardware architectures [14]. In addition, our implementation for pruning the resulting CPG is based on the boost C++ libraries [1]. Generating CFGs for Ada programs is based on [8].

References

1. The Boost Graph Library: User Guide and Reference Manual. Addison-Wesley Longman Publishing Co., Inc., Boston (2002)
2. Barnes, J.: Programming in Ada 2005. Addison Wesley (2006)
3. Bellman, R.: Introduction to Matrix Analysis. Classics in Applied Mathematics, 2nd edn. Society for Industrial and Applied Mathematics (1997)
4. Brukardt, R.L. (ed.): Ada 2012 Annotated Reference Manual (2012)
5. Buchholz, P., Kemper, P.: Efficient Computation and Representation of Large Reachability Sets for Composed Automata. Discrete Event Dyn. Systems 12(3), 265–286 (2002)
6. Burgstaller, B., Scholz, B., Blieberger, J.: A symbolic analysis framework for static analysis of imperative programming languages. Journal of Systems and Software 85(6), 1418–1439 (2012)
7. Davio, M.: Kronecker Products and Shuffle Algebra. IEEE Trans. Computers 30(2), 116–125 (1981)
8. Fechete, R., Kienesberger, G., Blieberger, J.: A framework for CFG-based static program analysis of Ada programs. In: Kordon, F., Vardanega, T. (eds.) Ada-Europe 2008. LNCS, vol. 5026, pp. 130–143. Springer, Heidelberg (2008)
9. Graham, A.: Kronecker Products and Matrix Calculus with Applications. Ellis Horwood Ltd., New York (1981)
10. Kuich, W., Salomaa, A.: Semirings, Automata, Languages. Springer (1986)
11. Küster, G.: On the Hurwitz Product of Formal Power Series and Automata. Theor. Comput. Sci. 83(2), 261–273 (1991)
12. Lengauer, T., Tarjan, R.E.: A fast algorithm for finding dominators in a flow graph. ACM Transactions on Programming Languages and Systems 1(1), 121–141 (1979)
13. Miranda, J.: A Detailed Description of the GNU Ada Run Time (2002), http://www.iuma.ulpgc.es/users/jmiranda/gnat-rts/
14. Mittermayr, R., Blieberger, J.: Shared Memory Concurrent System Verification using Kronecker Algebra. Technical Report 183/1-155, Automation Systems Group, TU Vienna (September 2011), http://arxiv.org/abs/1109.5522
15. Mittermayr, R., Blieberger, J.: Timing Analysis of Concurrent Programs. In: Vardanega, T. (ed.) 12th International Workshop on Worst-Case Execution Time Analysis, Dagstuhl, Germany. OpenAccess Series in Informatics (OASIcs), vol. 23, pp. 59–68. Schloss Dagstuhl–Leibniz-Zentrum fuer Informatik (2012)
16. Plateau, B.: On the Stochastic Structure of Parallelism and Synchronization Models for Distributed Algorithms. ACM SIGMETRICS 13, 147–154 (1985)
17. Rozenberg, G.: Handbook of Graph Grammars and Computing by Graph Transformation: Volume I. Foundations. World Scientific Publishing Co., Inc. (1997)
18. Taft, S.T., Duff, R.A., Brukardt, R.L., Plödereder, E., Leroy, P.: Ada 2005 Reference Manual. LNCS, vol. 4348. Springer, Heidelberg (2006)
19. Tarjan, R.E.: A Unified Approach to Path Problems. J. ACM 28(3), 577–593 (1981)

A TASM-Based Requirements Validation Approach for Safety-Critical Embedded Systems

Jiale Zhou, Yue Lu, and Kristina Lundqvist

School of Innovation, Design and Engineering
Mälardalen University, Västerås, Sweden
{zhou.jiale,yue.lu,kristina.lundqvist}@mdh.se

Abstract. Requirements validation is an essential activity to carry out in the system development life cycle, and it confirms the completeness and consistency of requirements through various levels. Model-based *formal methods* can provide a cost-effective solution to requirements validation in a wide range of domains such as safety-critical applications. In this paper, we extend a formal language Timed Abstract State Machine (TASM) with two newly defined constructs *Event* and *Observer*, and propose a novel requirements validation approach based on the extended TASM. Specifically, our approach can: 1) model both functional and non-functional (e.g. timing and resource consumption) requirements of the system at different levels and, 2) perform requirements validation by utilizing our developed toolset and a model checker. Finally, we demonstrate the applicability of our approach in real world usage through an industrial case study of a Brake-by-Wire system.

1 Introduction

With the growing complexity of safety-critical systems, requirements are no longer merely specified at the outset of the systems development life cycle (SDLC). On the contrary, there is a continuum of requirements levels as more and more details are added throughout the SDLC, which can roughly be divided into two categories in terms of high-level and low-level requirements [2]. High-level requirements describe what features the proposed system has (i.e. features hereafter) and low-level requirements state how to develop such a system (i.e. requirements hereafter). Studies have revealed that most of the anomalies discovered in late development phases can be traced back to hidden flaws in the requirements [9] [11], such as contradictory or missing requirements, or requirements that are discovered to be impossible to satisfy features at the late phase of development. For this reason, requirements validation is playing a more and more significant role in the development process, which confirms the correctness of requirements, in the sense of consistency and completeness [20]. In details, consistency refers to situations where a specification contains no internal contradictions in the requirements, while completeness refers to situations where the requirements must possess two fundamental characteristics, in terms of neither objects nor entities are left undefined and the requirements can address all of the features.

L. George and T. Vardanega (Eds.): Ada-Europe 2014, LNCS 8454, pp. 43–57, 2014.

In order to increase the confidence in the correctness of the requirements, model-based *formal methods* techniques have been to a large extend investigated into the field of requirements validation [7] [10]. In these techniques, the system design derived from requirements is often specified in terms of analyzable models at a certain level of abstraction. Further, features are formalized into verifiable queries or formulas and then fed into the models to perform model checking and/or theorem proving. In this way, the requirements are reasoned about to resolve contradictions, and it is also verified that they are neither so strict to forbid desired behaviors, nor so weak to allow undesired behaviors. However, such *formal methods* techniques also suffer from some limitations, such as how to ease the demand of heavy mathematics background knowledge to perform theorem proving, and how to model the target without having the state explosion problem of model checking occurred.

To tackle with the aforementioned limitations, we propose an approach to requirements validation using an extended version of the formal language Timed Abstract State Machine (TASM), which contains new constructs *TASM Event* and *TASM Observer*. Additionally, TASM has shown its success in the area of systems verification in [18] [19], with some distinctive features: 1) TASM supports the formal specification of both functional behaviors and non-functional properties of safety-critical systems w.r.t. timing and resource consumption and, 2) It is a literate language being understandable and usable without requiring extensive mathematical training, which avoids obscure mathematics formulae and, 3) TASM provides a toolset [16] to execute the pertaining TASM models for the purposes of analysis. The *Observer* technique [4] has an origin in the model-based testing domain where it has been used to specify and observe coverage criteria as well as verify such observable properties, but without changing the system's behaviors. The applications and advantages of using the *Observer* technique inspire us to exploit it to perform requirements validation, which makes a detour on the state explosion issue of model checking by not adding new states in the analysis. To be specific, our approach consists of three main steps:

- **Requirements modeling** models requirements by using various constructs in TASM.
- **Features modeling** translates features into our newly defined TASM observers that are used for the later analysis.
- **Requirements validation** contains four kinds of validation checking on focus, i.e. *Logical Consistency Checking*, *Auxiliary Machine Checking*, *Coverage Checking*, and *Model Checking*, as in the consistency and completeness checking of requirements.

The main contributions of this work are three-fold: 1) We extend the TASM language with two newly defined constructs in terms of *Event* and *Observer* and, 2) We propose a novel approach to requirements validation by using the extended TASM language and, 3) We demonstrate the applicability of our approach through a case study. The remainder of this paper is organized as follows: An introduction to the TASM language and its extension is presented in

Section 2. Section 3 introduces the Brake-by-Wire (BbW) system and its requirements. Our approach to requirements validation is described and demonstrated by using the BbW system in Section 4. Section 5 discusses the related work, and finally concluding remarks and future work are drawn in Section 6.

2 TASM Language and Its Extension

Figure 1 shows the meta-model of the extended TASM language in UML class diagram. The constructs included in the dashed rectangle are the new TASM constructs defined in this work. Section 2.1 gives an overview of the TASM language and Section 2.2 presents the extension of TASM.

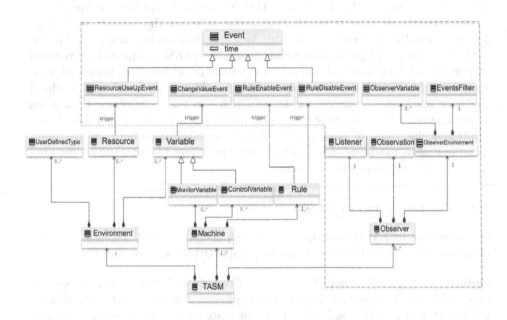

Fig. 1. The Meta-model of the extended TASM language

2.1 Overview of TASM

TASM [16] is a formal language for the specification of safety-critical systems, which extends the Abstract State Machine (ASM) [5] with the capability of modeling timing properties and resource consumption of applications in the target system. TASM inherits the easy-to-use feature from ASM, which is a literate specification language understandable and usable without extensive mathematical training [8]. A TASM model consists of two parts – an environment and a set of main machines. The environment defines the set and the type of variables, and the set of named resources which machines can consume. The main machine is made up of a set of monitored variables which can affect the machine execution, a set of controlled variables which can be modified by machines, and a set of machine rules. The set of rules specify the machine execution logic in the form of "if *condition* then *action*", where *condition* is an expression depending on the monitored variables, and *action* is a set of updates of the controlled variables. We can also use the rule "else then *action*" which is enabled merely when no other rules are enabled. A rule can specify the annotation of the time duration and resource consumption of its execution. The duration of a rule execution can be the keyword *next* that essentially states the fact that time should elapse until one of the other rules is enabled.

TASM describes the basic execution semantics as the computing steps with time and resource annotations: In one step, it reads the monitored variables, selects a rule of which *condition* is satisfied, consumes the specified resources, and after waiting for the duration of the execution, it applies the update set instantaneously. If more than one rules are enabled at the same time, it non-deterministically selects one to execute. As a specification language, TASM supports the concepts of parallelism which stipulates TASM machines are executed in parallel, and hierarchical composition which is achieved by means of auxiliary machines which can be used in other machines. There are two kinds of auxiliary machines - *function* machines which can take environment variables as parameters and return execution result, and *sub* machines which can encapsulate machine rules for reuse purpose [16]. Communication between machines, including main machines and auxiliary machines, can be achieved by defining corresponding environment variables.

2.2   The Extension to TASM

Our extension to TASM consists of two main parts, i.e. *TASM Event* and *TASM Observer* (Event and Observer hereafter, respectively) as shown in Figure 1.

Definition 1 *TASM Event (EV). TASM Event E defines the possible types of an event instance, including ResourceUsedUpEvent, ChangeValueEvent, RuleEnableEvent, and RuleDisableEvent. An event instance e is triggered by the corresponding TASM construct, which is a tuple $< E, t >$, where E is the type of the event instance, and t is the time instant when the instance occurs.*

The events of *ChangeValueEvent* type is triggered by a specific TASM environment variable whenever its value is updated,, which can be referenced in the form of *VariableName->EventType*. The *ResourceUsedUpEvent* is triggered by the case whenever the resource of the application is consumed totally, which can be referenced in the form of *ResourceName->EventType*. The *RuleEnableEvent* and *RuleDisableEvent* are triggered whenever a specific TASM rule is enabled or disabled, respectively, which can be referenced in the form of *MachineName->RuleName->EventType*.

Definition 2 *TASM Observer. An observer is a tuple $<$ ObserverEnvironment, Listener, Observation $>$, where:*

- *ObserverEnvironment is a tuple < ObserverVariable, EventsFilter >,
  where ObserverVariable is a set of variables that can be used by both Listener
  and Observation, and EventsFilter can be configured to filter out events irrelevant to the observer.*
- *Listener specifies the observer execution logic in the form of "**listening**
  condition **then** action", where the condition is an expression describing the
  sequence of the occurrence of events and the action is a set of actions updating the value of observer variables when the condition evaluates to be true.*
- *Observation is a predicate of the TASM model, which can evaluate to be
  either true or false, depending on the value of corresponding observer variables.*

In this work, we only introduce the informal execution semantics of *Observer*,
as depicted in Figure 2, and the formal semantics is considered as part of our
future work. Basically, in the runtime, the TASM model often produces massive
events according to the modeled application. After the *EventsFilter* removes
the irrelevant events, the remaining events will be logged in the local database,
namely *EventsLog*. Next, the *Listener* defined in *Observer* will evaluate its
condition based off of the sequence of logged events. Since *regular expression*
is usually used as a sequential search pattern, the specification of the event
sequence follows the syntax and semantics of regular expression. If the *condition*
is satisfied, then the *action* will start to update the observer variables. Once all
of the updates are executed, the *Observation* will be concluded based on the
updated observer variables. A running TASM model (representing the target
system) can be observed by several observers at the same time.

For a better understanding, we give an example of *Observer* as shown in Figure 3,
where *eventA* and *eventB* are *RuleEnableEvent* type, and *eventC* and *eventD* are
RuleDisableEvent type. The observer variables include a Boolean variable *ov* (initiated as false) and a Time variable *time* (initiated as zero). *ChangeValueEvent*
and *ResourceUsedUpEvent* are regarded as irrelevant events and removed by the
EventsFilter, the *RuleEnableEvent* and *RuleDisableEvent* events are logged
in the *Eventslog* database. As shown in line 9 in Figure 3, the expression of the
Listener condition in regular expression, represents the event sequence that begins
with *eventA*, followed by arbitrary events (represented by ".*") in the middle, and
ends with two events in terms of either *eventB and eventD*, or *eventC and eventD*.
If the condition evaluates to be satisfied, the observer variable *ov* will be assigned
as true, and *time* as the interval between *eventA* and *eventD*. In this example, if
the events sequence in the condition is detected and the interval *time* is larger than
100, the *Observation* will be concluded as a true predicate.

3   Case Study

Our case study is a Brake-by-Wire (BbW) system which is a demonstrator at a
major automotive company [13]. The BbW system aims to replace the mechanical linkage between the brake pedal and the brake actuators. Further, the BbW

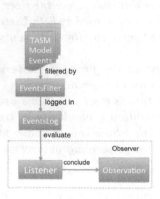

```
1  ObserverVariables:{
2    Boolean ov := false;
3    Time time := 0;
4  }
5  EventsFilter:{
6    filter out: ChangeValueEvent,
                ↪ResourceUsedUpEvent;
7  }
8  Listener:{
9    listening eventA.*(eventB | eventC)
                ↪eventD then
10     ov := true;
11     time := eventD.t - eventA.t;
12 }
13 Observation:{
14   ov == true and time > 100;
15 }
```

Fig. 2. The workflow of the Observer execution

Fig. 3. An example of the TASM Observer

system consists of micro-controller units, sensors, actuators and communication bus, which interprets driver's operation and operating conditions, through sensors, to decide on the desired brake torque of the brake actuators for appropriate brake force on each wheel.

The features that the BbW system should possess are described as follows:

- **Req H1**: The system shall provide a base brake functionality where the driver indicates that she/he wants to reduce speed so that the braking system starts decelerating the vehicle.
- **Req H2**: When the brake pedal is not pressed, the brake shall not be active.
- **Req H3**: The time from the driver's brake request till the actual start of the deceleration should be no more than 300 ms.

The list of requirements for the BbW system in our work is as follows:

- **Req L1**: The brake torque calculator shall compute the driver requested torque and send the value to the vehicle brake controller, when a brake pedal displacement is detected.
- **Req L2**: The vehicle brake controller shall decide the required torque on each wheel and each of the required wheel torque values is sent together with the sensed vehicle velocity to the Anti-lock Braking System (ABS) function on respective wheel.
- **Req L3**: The ABS function shall decide appropriate braking force on each wheel, based on the received torque request, current vehicle velocity and wheel angular velocity.

4 The TASM-Based Approach to Requirements Validation

In this section, we will introduce our approach that addresses the issue of formalizing and validating requirements specifications written in natural language.

Further, our approach is based on the use of the extended TASM language to formalize both requirements and features. We will go into details about each step by introducing the adhering sub-steps and show an illustration by using the BbW system. Specifically, Section 4.1 and Section 4.2 discuss modeling of the requirements and features respectively, and Section 4.3 presents the analysis and results of requirements validation of the BbW system.

4.1   Requirements Modeling

The first step of our approach is to analyze the low-level requirements (i.e. , requirements) in natural language and formalize them by using the corresponding TASM models. This step contains five sub-steps, as shown in Figure 4:

Fig. 4. The sub-steps of requirements modeling

- **Step 1: Requirements Preprocessing** distinguishes functional requirements from non-functional requirements.
- **Step 2: Components Identification** extracts the possible software components of the system referred in the functional requirements and maps them onto TASM main machines.
- **Step 3: Connections Identification** identifies the connections between different software components, according to a certain type of interactions.
- **Step 4: Behavior Specification** specifies the behaviors of components, which implement different system functionalities.
- **Step 5: Property Annotation** adds timing and resource consumption annotations to the relevant TASM model.

Requirements Preprocessing. At this step, we need to distinguish functional requirements from non-functional requirements. The functional requirements will be formalized into executable TASM models, and non-functional requirement in terms of timing and resource consumption requirements can provide useful information for property annotation. In the BbW system, all the requirements, i.e. *ReqL1*, *ReqL2* and *ReqL3*, are functional requirements.

Components Identification. The identification of the system components and the mapping of each component onto a TASM main machine is of importance in the process. In order to do so, we recommend the following two tasks:
- *Identification of the external (or environmental in other words) components that interact with the system.*
- *Identification of the internal components that compose of the system.*

At this step, a list of main machines will be defined for the BbW system, as shown in Table 1.

Table 1. The TASM main machines model the entire Brake-by-Wired system

Main Machine	Quantity	Category	Description
DRIVER	1	External Entity	model the driver's behavior
VEHICLE	1	External Entity	model the behavior of the vehicle
TORQUE_CALC	1	Micro-controller	calculate the driver's requested torque
BRAKE_CTRL	1	Micro-controller	calculate the requested torque per wheel
ABS_CTRL	4	Micro-controller	calculate the brake force on each wheel
BRAKE_ACTU	4	Actuator	perform the brake force on each wheel
WHLSPD_SENSOR	4	Sensor	sense the rotating speed of each wheel
VCLSPD_SENSOR	1	Sensor	sense the moving speed of the vehicle
PEDAL_SENSOR	1	Sensor	sense the position of the brake pedal
COMMU_BUS	1	Bus	the communication bus

Connections Identification. In the TASM model, asynchronous communication between different main machines can be implemented by using a set of variables, which ignores the transmission delay between machines. On the contrary, the common form of inter-process communication (IPC) is message-passing, which considers the transmission delay and bandwidth consumption as unavoidable. To this end, we define a main machine with the annotation of time and bandwidth as a means of modeling the communication bus. In our case study, the sensors in the BbW system communicate with the corresponding controllers through ports using signals, where transmission delay can be ignored. Further, a specific TASM main machine i.e. COMMU_BUS (in Table 1) models the communication bus, which is responsible for the communication between the brake controller and the ABS controllers.

Behavior Specification. There is no silver-bullet to model the behaviors of various components in TASM. Based on our experiences, we recommend the following steps:

- *Identification of possible states of the target system*: A user-defined type is used to represent the possible states, and a state variable is defined to denote the current state of the system.
- *Identification of the transition conditions of states*: The conditions of a certain machine rule are given, according to the corresponding value of the state variable and the transition conditions.
- *Identification of the actions when the system enters a specific state*: The actions of machine rules are specified, based on the behaviors of a component and the next possible state.

In the BbW system, all of the identified components (i.e. TASM main machines) are divided into five categories according to different functionalities: external entity, micro-controller, actuator, sensor, and bus. For reasons of space, we do not list all the rules used by the identified TASM main machines. Instead, we list the rules of four typical templates in our case study, i.e. micro-controller, actuator, sensor, and bus. In order to have a better understanding on the proposed sub-steps, we discuss the specification of a micro-controller component in detail.

A micro-controller component is activated by an event, and it reads a set of variables and performs a sequence of computation after being activated. When it finishes execution, the result will be used by other components. Therefore, the micro-controller component typically has three possible states – WAIT (initial state), COMPUTE, and SEND: The WAIT sate denotes that the micro-controller is waiting for activation and, the COMPUTE state represents that the micro-controller is performing computation. The SEND state introduces that the micro-controller is sending the results to other components. Figure 5 shows the rules of the TASM main machine, which models the micro-controller. PERFORM_COMPUTATION() and SEND_RESULT() are sub machines.

Figure 6 shows the machine rules that model an actuator, and PERFORM_ACTUATION() is a sub machine. Figure 7 shows the rules of the TASM main machine, which models a sensor. Measure_Quantity() is a function machine. Figure 8 shows the machine rules, which models the communication bus. Get_Message() is a function machine and TRANSMITTING_MESSAGE() is a sub machine.

```
1 R1:Activation{
2   if ctrl_state=wait and new_event=
        ↪True then
3     ctrl_state := compute;
4     new_event  := False;
5 }
6 R2:Computation{
7   t:=computation_time;
8   if ctrl_state = compute then
9     PERFORM_COMPUTATION();
10    ctrl_state := send;
11 }
12 R3:Send{
13   if ctrl_state = send then
14     SEND_RESULT();
15     ctrl_state := wait;
16 }
17 R4:Idle{
18   t := next;
19   else then
20     skip;
21 }
```

```
1 R1:Trigger{
2   if actu_state=wait and new_event=
        ↪True then
3     new_event  := False;
4     actu_state := actuate;
5 }
6 R2:Actuation{
7   t:=actuation_time;
8   if actu_state=actuate then
9     PERFORM_ACTUATION();
10    actu_state := wait;
11 }
12 R3:Idle{
13   t := next;
14   else then
15     skip;
16 }
```

Fig. 5. The TASM main machine models the micro-controller component

Fig. 6. The TASM main machine models the actuator component

Non-functional Property Annotation. The accurate estimation of the pertaining non-functional properties of the target system is playing a paramount role in performing non-functional requirements validation. The Property Annotation step can be carried out in the following ways:
- The estimates can be determined based upon the non-functional requirements specified in the low-level requirements.
- The estimates can be obtained by using existing well-known analysis methods, e.g. Worst-Case Execution Time (WCET) Analysis [12] for time duration of rules.

```
1  R1:Sample{
2    if sensor_state = sample then
3      sensor_value :=
           ↪Measure_Quantity();
4      sensor_state := send;
5  }
6  R2:Send{
7    if sensor_state = send and
         ↪sensor_value >= threshold
         ↪then
8      observer_value  := sensor_value
         ↪;
9      new_sample_value:= True;
10     sensor_state    := wait;
11 }
12 R3:Wait{
13   t := period;
14   if sensor_state = wait then
15     sensor_state := sample;
16 }
```

```
1  R1:Transmit{
2    if bus_state=idle and new_message
         ↪=True then
3      bus_message := Get_Message();
4      bus_state := engaged;
5  }
6  R2:Send{
7    t:=bus_delay;
8    band:= bandwidth;
9    if bus_state = engaged then
10     TRANSMITTING_MESSAGE();
11     bus_state := idle;
12 }
13 R3:Wait{
14   t := next;
15   else then
16     skip;
17 }
```

Fig. 7. The TASM main machine models the sensor component

Fig. 8. The TASM main machine models the communication bus component

- The estimates can be determined based upon the information in the related hardware specifications, e.g. the time duration and power consumption of a communication bus transferring one message.
- However, in some cases, the estimates can also be given by the experiences of domain experts, if the accurate estimation is not possible.

We annotate the aforementioned TASM models with time duration and resource consumption, and the annotation terms *computation_time, actuation_time, period, bus_delay* and *bandwidth* are either a specific value or a range of values, which are given by our domain knowledge for simplicity.

4.2   Features Modeling

Our approach proceeds with the formalization of high-level requirements, i.e. , features. At this step, each feature will be translated into corresponding TASM observer(s). The formalization consists of the following sub-steps:

- **Step 1: Listener Specification** specifies the possible events sequence which represents the observable functional behaviors or non-functional properties required by the feature, and the corresponding actions taken on observer variables when the sequence is caught by the Listener.
- **Step 2: Observation Specification** formalizes a predicate depending on the observer variables. If the predicate of the Observation holds, i.e. evaluates to be true, it implies that the satisfaction of the feature can be observed in the system.
- **Step 3: Events Filtering** identifies the interesting events and filters out the irrelevant events by specifying *EventsFilter*.
- **Step 4: Traceability Creation** links the specified Observer to the textual requirements. The link is used for requirements traceability from the

formalization to natural language requirements in order to perform coverage checking.

In the BbW system, there are three features i.e. *ReqH1*, *ReqH2* and *ReqH3*. The specification of *Observer* is illustrated by applying the proposed steps to *ReqH1*. To be specific, *ReqH1* states "The system shall provide a base brake functionality where the driver indicates that she/he wants to reduce speed so that the braking system starts decelerating the vehicle", and the interesting events sequence consists of three parts. The first part "PEDAL_SENSOR->Send->RuleEnableEvent" denotes the event that is triggered when the Send rule of the PEDAL_SENSOR main machine is enabled, which models the behavior that the brake pedal is pressed by the driver. The second part ".*" has the same semantic with the counterpart defined in *regular expression*, which means an arbitrary number of events regardless of their type. The last part "BRAKE_ACTU->Actuation->RuleEnableEvent" represents the event that is triggered after the Actuation rule of the BRAKE_ACTU main machine is executed, i.e. disabled, which models the behavior that the brake actuator acts on the wheels i.e. decreases the speed of the vehicle. When the events sequence is detected, the Observation "ov == true" evaluates to be true, which indicates that the satisfaction of *ReqH1* can be observed in the TASM model.

```
1  ObserverVariables:{
2    Boolean ov := false;
3  }
4  EventsFilter:{
5    filter out: ChangeValueEvent, ResourceUsedUpEvent, RuleDisableEvent;
6  }
7  Listener:{
8    listening PEDAL_SENSOR->Send->RuleEnableEvent .* BRAKE_ACTU->Actuation->
        ↪RuleEnableEvent then
9      ov := true;
10 }
11 Observation:{
12   ov == true;
13 }
```

Fig. 9. The Observer of Req H1

4.3   Requirements Validation

Validation of the formalized requirements aims at increasing the confidence in the validity of requirements. In this work, we assume that there is a semantic equivalence relation between the requirements and TASM models, and between features and observers. This is built upon the fact that the TASM models and observers are derived from the documented requirements and features, by following the proposed modeling steps based on our thorough understanding of the BbW system. The validation goal is achieved by following several analysis steps, based on the use of the derived TASM models and observers which may help to pinpoint flaws that are not trivial to detect. Such validation steps in our approach are:

- **Logical Consistency Checking**. The term of logical consistency can be intuitively explained as "free of contradictions in the specifications". In our work, the logical consistency checking can be performed on the executable TASM models, i.e. requirements, by our developed tool TASM TOOLSET. Two kinds of inconsistency flaws can be discovered. One kind of flaw is that two machine rules are enabled at the same time, which is usually caused by the fact that there exist unpredictable behaviors in the requirements. The other is that different values are assigned to the same variable at the same time, which is usually caused by the fact that there exist hidden undesired behaviors in the requirements.

- **Auxiliary Machine Checking**. Auxiliary machines include function machine and sub machine. When the TASM TOOLSET starts to execute the TASM model, if there exists any undefined auxiliary machine, the tool will detect this situation, stop proceeding, and generate an error message. The existence of undefined auxiliary TASM machines, in terms of functions and sub machines, violates the completeness of TASM model specifying requirements. The undefined auxiliary TASM machines are usually caused by the lack of detailed descriptions of the proposed system's behaviors.

- **Coverage Checking**. Coverage checking corresponds to checking whether the desired behaviors specified in features can be observed in the TASM model, which is an important activity of requirements completeness checking. To perform the coverage checking, all of the features are translated into observers which observe the execution of TASM models at runtime. If the *Observation* holds, the corresponding feature can be regarded as covered by the requirements.

- **Model Checking**. The TASM machines can be easily translated into timed automata through the transformation rules defined in [16]. The transformation enables the use of the UPPAAL model checker to verify the various properties of the TASM model. This check aims at verifying whether the TASM model is free of deadlock and whether an expected property specified in a feature is satisfied by the TASM model. It is necessary to stress that the essential difference between *Model Checking* and *Coverage Checking* is whether a property is exhaustively checked against a model or not. Although a sound property checking is desired, in some cases *Model Checking* will encounter state explosion problem, which limits its usefulness in practice.

We follow the validation steps to check the validity of the requirements of the BbW system. First, we use the TASM TOOLSET to perform *Logical Consistency Checking* on the formalized TASM model. As in the fact that there are no inconsistency warnings reported by the tool, we therefore proceed the validation steps with *Auxiliary Machine Checking*. As shown in Figure 5, 6, 7 and 8, there exist some undefined auxiliary machines in the TASM models of those typical components, which also have been detected by our TASM TOOLSET. For instance, in the *ABS_CTRL* main machine (a micro-controller component), the *PERFORM_COMPUTATION* sub machine is not defined, which implies that the requirements need to specify in more details about how *"The ABS function shall decide appropriate braking force on each wheel"*. Next for *Coverage Checking*, since the observations are determined to be held according to the results of the TASM observers in the runtime, the satisfaction of requirements towards features is therefore reached. On the note about *Model Checking*, we first translate the TASM model into timed automata, and then check the deadlock property as well as the *ReqH3* requirement via the UPPAAL model checker. The corresponding results are: 1) *Deadlock free* is *satisfied* and, 2) the *ReqH3* is *satisfied*. Although the case study is a demonstrator, it is an illustrative example to show how to follow our proposed approach to perform requirements validation at various levels.

5 Related Work

In addition to the aforementioned related work, there are some other interesting pieces of work deserved to be mentioned as follows. Event-B [1] is a formal state-based modeling language that represents a system as a combination of states and state transitions. Iliasov [10] showed how to use Event-B for systems development, where the system constraints are formalized as a set of visualized proof obligations which can be synthesized as use cases. Such proof obligations are then reasoned about their satisfaction in the corresponding Event-B model. Mashkoor et al. [14] proposed a set of transformation heuristics to validate the Event-B specification by using animation.

Cardei et al. [6] presented a methodology that first converts SysML requirements models into a requirements model in OWL, and then performs the rule-based reasoning to detect omissions and inconsistency. Becker et al. [3] provided a formalization for self-adaptive systems and the corresponding requirements, which enables a semi-automatic analysis of performance requirements for self-adaptive systems. Cimatti et al. [7] introduced a series of techniques that have been developed for the formalization and validation of requirements for safety-critical systems. Specifically, the methodology consists of three main steps in terms of informal analysis, formalization, and formal validation. Scandurra et al. [17] proposed a framework to automatically transform use cases into ASM models, which are used to validate the requirements through scenario-based simulation. MARTE [15] is a UML profile for modeling and analysis of RTES, covering both functional and non-functional properties of the system. Nevertheless, to our best knowledge, there has not been any work about using MARTE for the purposes of requirements validation.

6 Conclusions and Future Work

In this paper, we have proposed a novel TASM-based approach to requirements validation. The approach 1) uses the extended TASM language to model the documented requirements and, 2) performs the requirements validation by using two tools in terms of the TASM TOOLSET and the model checker UPPAAL. Our case study using a Brake-by-Wire (BbW) system developed by a major automotive company, has shown that our approach can achieve the goal of requirements validation via *Logical Consistency Checking*, *Auxiliary Machine Checking*, *Coverage Checking*, and *Model Checking*. Even if limited in complexity, the BbW system consists of a number of parts presenting the real world safety-critical systems, such as micro-controllers, sensors, actuators, and communication buses.

In this work, the validity of our TASM model towards requirements and features is built upon our thorough understanding of the BbW system, and hence TASM models are semantic preserving. Moreover, we have observed model validation issue as a common problem with model-based approaches. This is getting more complicated when the system's non-functional properties are considered. To address the situation, as future work, we will combine our proposed modeling approach with a set of assistant techniques, such as rule/pattern-based algorithm to semi- or fully-automatically transform natural languages into TASM models. The future work also includes a wider industrial validation of our approach, and the improvement of our current TASM TOOLSET. Such improvement will not only facilitate our evaluation but also power up our analysis with statistical methods [12] and probabilistic modeling patterns.

References

1. Abrial, J.-R.: Modeling in Event-B - System and Software Engineering. Cambridge University Press (2010)
2. Bahill, A.T., Henderson, S.J.: Requirements development, verification and validation exhibited in famous failures. Syst. Eng. (2005)
3. Becker, M., Luckey, M., Becker, S.: Performance analysis of self-adaptive systems for requirements validation at design-time. In: Proceedings of QoSA 2013, pp. 43–52. ACM, New York (2013)
4. Blom, J., Hessel, A., Jonsson, B., Pettersson, P.: Specifying and generating test cases using observer automata. In: Grabowski, J., Nielsen, B. (eds.) FATES 2004. LNCS, vol. 3395, pp. 125–139. Springer, Heidelberg (2005)
5. Börger, E., Stärk, R.F.: Abstract State Machines. A Method for High-Level System Design and Analysis. Springer (2003)
6. Cardei, I., Fonoage, M., Shankar, R.: Model based requirements specification and validation for component architectures. In: 2008 2nd Annual IEEE Systems Conference, pp. 1–8 (2008)
7. Cimatti, A., Roveri, M., Susi, A., Tonetta, S.: From informal requirements to property-driven formal validation. In: Cofer, D., Fantechi, A. (eds.) FMICS 2008. LNCS, vol. 5596, pp. 166–181. Springer, Heidelberg (2009)
8. Clarke, E.M., Wing, J.M.: Formal methods: state of the art and future directions. ACM Comput. Surv. 28(4), 626–643 (1996)
9. Ellis, A.: Achieving safety in complex control systems. In: Proceedings of SCSC 1995, pp. 1–14. Springer, London (1995)
10. Iliasov, A.: Augmenting formal development with use case reasoning. In: Brorsson, M., Pinho, L.M. (eds.) Ada-Europe 2012. LNCS, vol. 7308, pp. 133–146. Springer, Heidelberg (2012)
11. Leveson, N.G.: Safeware: System Safety and Computers. ACM, NY (1995)
12. Lu, Y.: Pragmatic Approaches for Timing Analysis of Real-Time Embedded Systems. PhD thesis, Mälardalen University (2012)

13. MAENAD (2013), http://www.maenad.eu
14. Mashkoor, A., Jacquot, J.-P., Souquières, J.: Transformation Heuristics for Formal Requirements Validation by Animation. In: Proceedings of SafeCert 2009, York, United Kingdom (2009)
15. OMG (2013), http://www.omgmarte.org/
16. Ouimet, M.: A formal framework for specification-based embedded real-time system engineering. PhD thesis, Department of Aeronautics and Astronautics. MIT (2008)
17. Scandurra, P., Arnoldi, A., Yue, T., Dolci, M.: Functional requirements validation by transforming use case models into abstract state machines. In: Proceedings of SAC 2012, pp. 1063–1068. ACM, NY (2012)
18. Yang, Z., Hu, K., Ma, D., Pi, L.: Towards a formal semantics for the AADL behavior annex. In: Proceedings of DATE 2009, pp. 1166–1171 (2009)
19. Zhou, J., Johnsen, A., Lundqvist, K.: Formal execution semantics for asynchronous constructs of aadl. In: Proceedings of ACES-MB 2012, pp. 43–48 (2012)
20. Zowghi, D., Gervasi, V.: The three cs of requirements: Consistency, completeness, and correctness. In: Proceedings of REFSQ 2002 (2002)

Towards a Runtime Verification Framework for the Ada Programming Language

André de Matos Pedro[1], David Pereira[1],
Luís Miguel Pinho[1], and Jorge Sousa Pinto[2]

[1] CISTER/INESC TEC, ISEP, Polytechnic Institute of Porto, Portugal
{anmap,dmrpe,lmp}@isep.ipp.pt
[2] HASLab/INESC TEC & Universidade do Minho, Portugal
jsp@di.uminho.pt

Abstract. Runtime verification is an emerging discipline that investigates methods and tools to enable the verification of program properties during the execution of the application. The goal is to complement static analysis approaches, in particular when static verification leads to the explosion of states. Non-functional properties, such as the ones present in real-time systems are an ideal target for this kind of verification methodology, as are usually out of the range of the power and expressiveness of classic static analyses. In this paper, we present a framework that allows real-time programs written in Ada to be augmented with runtime verification capabilities. Our framework provides the infrastructures which is needed to instrument the code with runtime monitors. These monitors are responsible for observing the system and reaching verdicts about whether its behavior is compliant with its non-functional properties. We also sketch a contract language to extend the one currently provided by Ada, with the long term goal of having an elegant way in which runtime monitors can be automatically synthesized and instrumented into the target systems. The usefulness of the proposed approach is demonstrated by showing its use for an application scenario.

1 Introduction

Real-time embedded systems are usually large and complex, continuously interacting with the external environment. A single real-time system is usually made of several sub-components concurrently competing for the system's resources. Many, if not all, of these sub-components are not produced in-house, and are assembled together from diverse sources, being these sometimes black-boxes to the system integrator. Some parts may also be *Commercial Off-The-Shelf* (COTS) components that, although being economic, have the drawback of introducing safety concerns, as are usually not accompanied with their source-code and/or complete specification.

Given the critical role of many of the real-time systems developed, their source code is subject to exhaustive testing efforts, which may be extremely expensive. In particular, in what the context of this work relates to, some static analysis

L. George and T. Vardanega (Eds.): Ada-Europe 2014, LNCS 8454, pp. 58–73, 2014.
© Springer International Publishing Switzerland 2014

tools have been developed to check the correctness of this class of systems, in some cases applied with success. *Model Checking* [5] is among the most well-known static analysis approaches, but it has the drawback of quickly exploding due to state space search. Other alternative static analysis approaches have strong drawbacks as well [12], therefore in the last years *Runtime Verification* (RV) [1,12] has emerged in order to complement the existing limitations. RV is concerned with providing theories, languages, and procedures that allow developers to improve programs with specifications of properties to be checked upon execution time. In a nutshell, the idea of RV is to transform the extra specifications and synthesize them into *monitors* which are added to the system. A monitor is a computational element that is responsible for observing (part of) the system and make *verdicts* about its correct execution.

A real-time system is a paradigmatic case to show what RV can bring in terms of safety for software. It is easy to identify, at least, two of the more relevant reasons for such approach: it is very hard to verify during design all the properties that real-time system must exhibit, which requires that some properties are verified only during execution; and non-functional properties such worst-case execution time are extremely hard to *prove* statically. With a runtime approach we can have direct access to the states of the tasks of interest and determine if their conditions hold, thus being able to detect erroneous execution and act accordingly. The introduction of monitors can be handled by a static automatic generation tool, from the properties which are to be checked, and can be time-bounded, since monitors are scheduled as any other task executing in the system.

Most of the RV frameworks developed so far are for Java, and were designed to address software development in that programming language. They are based on formal approaches such as temporal logics [2] and regular expressions [17] and are directed towards ensuring functional correctness. These formal approaches provide expressive languages for writing contracts, and for which their synthesis and implementability are feasible and efficient. Although, ideally, the theory and tools that resulted from this effort should be used for embedded systems (possibly exhibiting real-time characteristics), only a couple of works have addressed this kind of systems. One of these is PathFinder [11], for critical systems written in Java; the other is CoPilot [14,13], a functional specification language and toolchain for the safe runtime monitoring of ultra-critical software.

In this paper, we present the RMF4Ada framework that aims at complementing the available developments as follows: first, it is an RV framework that intends to use the safety properties and expressiveness of the Ada programming language, which we consider very relevant to implement real-time systems; secondly, we target the specification and synthesis of monitors that are capable of verifying important non-functional properties, such as meeting deadlines, respecting worst-case execution times, among others. The focus of this paper is in the structure of the code that allows synthesizing monitors and the management of events and sequences of events. We also describe an extension to the Ada 2012 specification of contracts so that in the future, it can support contracts for non-functional properties and that can be verified using frameworks such as this proposal. In order to show the potential of our proposal, we present an Ada implementation of a *mine-drainage controller* enriched with RV behavior using this framework.

2   The RMF4Ada Runtime Verification Framework

In this section we introduce and describe the details of a novel RV framework for the Ada programming language. RMF4Ada combines aspects of *Runtime Monitoring* (RM) (the field that studies ways to define, implement, and control monitors), formal languages, and software architecture methods to provide the infrastructure that is needed to equip an Ada program with RV functionality. The core of RMF4Ada is a set of Ada packages that provide schemas for monitors (possibly executing in different patterns), data structures to represent formal languages and the evaluation of their formulas/terms, and components to represent and manage the events of the system that one might be interested in verifying. It is not simply yet another RM framework, since the properties to be verified or enforced are generated from timed specifications written in the supported formal languages, in a correct-by-construction way.

The architecture of RMF4Ada is depicted in Figure 1. It is divided into two sub-components: an Instrumentor and a Creator. The Instrumentor is a tool which manages the environment for system instrumentation, and that couples monitors that are automatically synthesized *a priori* by some built-in mechanism of the framework, or by some third-party tools; the Creator is a tool that synthesizes monitors based on the specification written in the contracts of the original program; the output is the corresponding Ada executable code. The Creator also contains mechanisms to generate monitors according to different modes of operation. The generic dynamics of RMF4Ada is as follows: the Instrumentor generates an event manager (among other things, responsible for keeping an execution trace of the system with the correct order, and inform monitors of available events for consuming), and in-lines instructions in the original source-code that create the symbolic representation of the events and communicates them to the event manager; afterwards, the Creator generates the monitors and adds them to the source-code already instrumented as a new package, in order to produce the final program with the RV layer working according to the specifications in the original system.

As we have pointed out earlier, the monitors that are added to the target system do not need to follow a single execution behavior. RMF4Ada provides support for two different *modes* of operation for monitors: *time-triggered* monitoring and *event-triggered* monitoring. In the time-triggered mode, monitors run periodically; the time period is calculated beforehand in order to avoid higher detection delays for the events of interest as we propose in [9,10]. In the event-triggered mode, monitors execute when events occur, are considered sporadic tasks, and consume the available events respecting a given execution pattern.

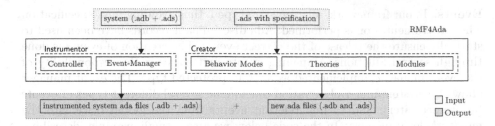

Fig. 1. RMF4Ada Architecture

2.1   The Runtime Monitoring Library

We begin with an overview of the library's structure, and then we introduce library settings such as events, monitor modes, and monitor context-switches.

Structure. The runtime monitoring library (RML) of RMF4Ada is composed of three modules: one that encodes the formal systems used to allow the specification and verification of contracts, other responsible for providing the abstract data types fundamental to construct monitors, and another for building instances of monitors that can be added to the program under consideration. These modules are named *Theories*, *Abstract Data Types*, and *Monitors*.

Theories. This module provides an hierarchy of objects that allow to implement the inductive nature of the sentences of the formal languages that we have adopted to specify contracts as well as to provide the semantical evaluation functions for these sentences, which are the functions responsible for giving verdicts when the target system is executing. Currently, we have considered two formal systems: *Timed Regular Expressions* (TRE) [15], and *Restricted Metric Temporal Logic with Durations* (RMTL-$\int$) [10,9].

Abstract Data Types. This module provides a set of well-known abstract data types that are fundamental to architect the rest of the framework. Among these are included an array-based *first in first out* (FIFO), a circular FIFO, and an array-based stack. The abstract data structures themselves are not covered in this paper, since they are not interesting from the point of view of runtime monitoring.

Monitors. This module includes the types defining *events* and *event traces*. These are the primitive notions where the activity of the system under consideration are stored. Another building-block provided is the protected *event manager type*, responsible for keeping the events in an internal FIFO. Finally, this library offers the type for monitors, which is specialized according to its operations mode, *i.e.*, its either a task type implementing a periodic (time-triggered) or a sporadic (event-triggered) behavior.

Events. In our framework, all events are typed, thus avoiding miss-specification when instrumentation is performed. Ada discriminant records have been used to statically ensure the release of the correct events. The creation of events is done through several functions. Managing events and traces is the responsibility of the event manager, implemented as an Ada protected type. The event manager allows the system under observation to enqueue several different types of events (as we see later), and to pop relevant events from the global trace into the monitor's local memory. In the code below we give a small example, describing how the release of an event can be performed:

```
-- Generate an event meaning a task_release of Task_A
 Ev_A: Events_Concrete.Event :=
 Events_Concrete.Generate_Event_Task_Release_Structure (
   Name => Task_A,
   Monitor_Identifier_List => (Monitor_FormulaOne_Id => true),
   Time => Time_Unit_Type(TIME_STAMP)
 );
```

In the code above, we use the `Generate_Event_Task_Release_Structure` function to construct a release event. `TIME_STAMP` is a value in accordance with the type `Time_Unit_Type`, and `Monitor_Identifier_List` is a binary map that indicates that the event `Ev_A` could be used by the monitor identified by the value of `Monitor_FormulaOne_Id`. The other monitors, if available, need to be assigned to false, since `Monitor_Identifier_List` is a static list that contains a Boolean assigned for each available monitor. The value of `Task_A` is the identifier of the event task release.

Monitoring Modes. Different monitor modes correspond to different task types. For a monitor of type event-based we use the synchronous task control to suspend the task until the Boolean flag `Event_Based_Is_Sporadic` is true. The code to handle the event and read the event from the event manager with corresponding operations on the memory of the monitor, is the following:

```
-- Use of Timming Events for waiting order
Ada.Synchronous_Task_Control.Suspend_Until_True (
  Event_Based_Is_Sporadic
);

-- Get event from event manager
Event_Manager_For_Monitor.Protected_Event_Manager.readEvent (
  Id => Monitor_Id,
  E => Event_Manager_For_Monitor.Trace_For_Event_Manager.
     Trace_Elements.Event(Tmp_Event)
);

-- Set event to the dedicated trace structure of the monitor
Object.Assign_Event_To_Trace(Event_Manager_For_Monitor.
    Trace_For_Event_Manager.Trace_Element_Type(Tmp_Event));
```

`Tmp_Event` is the event that has been read from the event manager, and `object` the monitor object that contains a trace structure. Note that pushing and popping event from event manager are protected operations that avoid simultaneous concurrent accesses. We use the protected type `Protected_Event_Manager` to ensure these operations. In time-triggered monitors identified by type `Time_Based_Mode_Type` we use a periodic task with the delay until sentence. The code to define this behavior is the following:

```
-- if there are events to consume discard the new ones
if Event_Manager_For_Monitor.Trace_For_Event_Manager.
   Get_Number_Elements(Object.Trace) < 1 then

  -- Get list of events
  Event_Manager_For_Monitor.Protected_Event_Manager.
     readListOfEventsBounded (
   Id => Monitor_Id,
   List => Temporary_Trace
  );

  -- Set list of events to trace structure of the monitor object
  Event_Manager_For_Monitor.Trace_For_Event_Manager.
     Push_ListOfEventsBounded (
   Trace => Object.Trace,
   Trace_Tmp => Temporary_Trace
  );

end if;
```

`Monitor_Id` is the identifier used to get the relevant events from the event-manager, and `Temporary_Trace` is a temporary local variable used in transferring events. The if statement maintains the `Push_ListOfEventsBounded` correct, since it does not issue any array out of bounds access. In the worst-case scenario, the `Temporary_Trace` array list may have the same size, and if one or more elements exist in the local monitor trace, then the same number of events cannot be fitted. The procedure `Monitor_Function` that is recursively defined is called in both modes by the instruction:

```
Object.Monitor_Function;
```

`Object` variable includes all available data structures to store the inputs and outputs of the function. After establishing the monitor modes a piece of code need to be coupled for time-triggered mode after the monitor invocation. The code remaining for this is the following:

```
if Object.Mode = Time_Based_Mode_Type then
  Next_Time := Next_Time + Release_Time;
  delay until Next_Time;
end if;
```

`Next_Time` is a clock value. The above code block intends to establish the behavior of the periodic tasks inducing the system to a sleep state until a certain time is reached to wake-up.

Monitor Context-Switches. Monitors employ high level software context switches based on one stack data structure to be incrementally evaluated. As we understand high level context switches are the ones that are implemented by software with the aid of memory RAM instead of processor registers. The stack allows us to encode recursive call into a loop, and to control the execution using some control conditions. We introduce this approach as the *subtractive-based abstraction* for runtime monitoring. Our abstraction begins by popping the generic structure that contains the tuple and the verdict, which are the inputs and the outputs of a monitor function, respectively. The procedure that performs a pop operation is invoked using the following code:

```
-- get tuple from stack
Monitor_Stack.Pop(
  Item => Input_Output_Par,
  From => Object.Stack_For_Arguments
);

-- subdivide state to recall monitor function
Tuple := I_O_Par.Tuple;
Verdict := I_O_Par.Verdict;
```

The context-switch restores the previous outcome values from variables `Tuple` and `Verdict` to be able to call the `Procedure_For_Monitor` procedure with a certain trace. The actual tuple represents the last global state of the monitor, and the last verdict that has been saved, respectively. In Ada the monitor is called according to the procedure:

```
Procedure_For_Monitor( Object.Trace, Tuple, Verdict );
```

One cycle of execution or a step is executed by this instruction, which we denote as the `One_Step` restriction. This step may keep the `Trace` structure intact, indicating that no symbols have been consumed. By the way some executions cannot consume any event symbol of the trace and a buffer overrun of the local monitor trace can occur. To tackle this we assume that the execution is progressive and the monitor execution is recursively defined.

To manage the context-switches we consider four conditional statements.

1. Step-based condition – The evalution of the monitor ends when one step of the recursive function `Procedure_For_Monitor` is executed. After each execution step the state is stored for a further resume of the monitor execution. The Ada code for this restriction is as simples as follows:

```
I_O_Par.Tuple := Tuple;
I_O_Par.Verdict := Verdict;

Monitor_Stack.Push (
  Item => I_O_Par,
  Onto => Object.Stack_For_Arguments
);
```

2. Symbol-based condition – A symbol consumption is the necessary condition to suspend the monitor execution, and proceed with the context-switch. `One_Step_Until_Symbol_Is_Consuming` is the Boolean variable that activates

this condition in the RML. Any external feedback is required for the procedure `Procedure_For_Monitor` since the re-execution only continues if the trace is unchanged. We also assume that the procedure `Procedure_For_Monitor` is progressive, which indicates that eventually some event is consumed. The Ada code that we use to re-evaluate the monitor procedure is the following one:

```
while not Trace_Has_Been_Changed(Object.Trace) loop
  Procedure_For_Monitor( Object.Trace, Tuple, Verdict );
end loop;

I_O_Par.Tuple := Tuple;
I_O_Par.Verdict := Verdict;

Monitor_Stack.Push (
  Item => I_O_Par,
  Onto => Object.Stack_For_Arguments
);
```

`Procedure_For_Monitor` procedure ends with the push of the `I_O_Par` into the `Monitor_Stack` (accordingly with the restriction `One_Step`), and the function `Trace_Has_Been_Changed` establishes a comparison between two traces (new and old ones). To be an efficient search over both traces labels are used to indicate when a trace is equipped with a new event.

3. Time-bounded condition – A temporal bound for the evaluation of a monitor is used to decide the suspension instant of a context-switch. `One_Step_- Until_T_Time_Units` is the Boolean flag used to activate this condition in the RML. The evaluation is made until the time elapsed exceeds the time allowed for the monitor execution. To describe such behavior we use the execution time timers [18]. Such timers allow us to force a monitor to execute in a stipulated constant time by triggering an interruption when the available time expires. In that point the last execution is rejected if a step of the monitor's execution is not completed. The excerpt of Ada code establishing such behavior is the following one:

```
Ada.Execution_Time.Timers.Set_Handler
  ( ETT_Timer,
    Ada.Real_Time.To_Time_Span(CONSTANT_TIME),
    Object.Control.Budget_Expired'Access );

while not Object.Control.Budget_Is_Expired loop
  Procedure_For_Monitor( Object.Trace, Tuple, Verdict );
end loop;

I_O_Par.Tuple := Tuple;
I_O_Par.Verdict := Verdict;

Monitor_Stack.Push (
  Item => I_O_Par,
  Onto => Object.Stack_For_Arguments
);
```

`Object.Control.Budget_Expired` is a protected procedure that waits for the end of the step execution of the monitor, `Object.Control.Budget_Is_Expired` is the function that returns true if the execution time timer expires or false otherwise, and `CONSTANT_TIME` is the constant that indicates the allowed duration for monitor execution.

4. Step-bounded condition – One step of a monitor's execution is performed n times. `One_Step_N_Times` is the condition available in the RML. We tackle this restriction by a simple for loop, as follows:

```
for I in 1..Object.Counter-1 loop
  Procedure_For_Monitor( Object.Trace, Tuple, Verdict );
end loop;

I_O_Par.Tuple := Tuple;
I_O_Par.Verdict := Verdict;

Monitor_Stack.Push (
  Item => I_O_Par,
  Onto => Object.Stack_For_Arguments
);
```

`Object.Counter` defines how many steps the monitor shall execute before a context-switch is performed. The remaining code has the same meaning as described before.

2.2 Library Usage

RML is the support library of RMF4Ada and is available in [7]. Our library encourages developers to make constraints using strong type checking instead of condition-based tests. This abstraction allows the software designers to make less-mistakes when library is used as well as to maintain the integrity of the instrumentation process. In some cases the memory space can be reduced due to the message pass using strings is avoided, the registration of monitors avoids any registration in the event-manager, and the event-manager and monitors discard any filters since the unexpected types of events cannot take place. An overview of library's interconnection is depicted in the Figure 2, including the main blocks, such as, the static instrumentation, the event-manager protected type, and the set of tasks representing the monitors generated automatically by some theory.

A program to be instrumented should be designed following the hierarchy of Ada packages. The main package should be the point where initializations of RML are made, and the remain packages are necessarily extensions of the root package. The instrumentation is made using the push procedures of the event-manager positioned at certain points in program code. We have been included in our library three types of events each one with several sub-types such as

– task release, task begin, task sleep, task resume, and task end;
– pre and post procedures, protected pre and post procedures, pre and post functions, and protected pre and post functions; and
– pre and post assignments, and protected pre and post assignments.

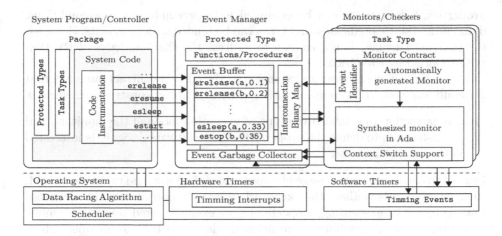

Fig. 2. Illustration of the interconnection of the element blocks provided by the RML

Other manually specified events are discarded in this paper but will be addressed for further phases. The integrity of the event sequences that our framework supplies also should be enforced.

Schedulability analysis can be enforced online using runtime monitoring techniques as well as offline in the development phase. The integrity of the system schedulability analysis requires that events triggered by tasks are correctly pointed and instrumented for each available Ada task type. For instance, this is enough for online schedulability analysis of periodic resource models as proposed in [9]. In the case of the preemptive fixed priority scheduler allowed in Ada by Ravenscar rules, we need to instrument all system tasks in order to provide the events correctly for event monitoring. Our framework should be able to identify if a higher priority task trigger an event task begin, then some time units ago an event task sleep may have occurred. To do it, the framework only needs to select the last event that has occurred in the event trace provided by event-manager. This avoids any instrumentation of events at the operating system level (more precisely at the internals of the scheduler).

We have described a subtractive-based abstraction that leaves us to couple diverse monitoring models in our framework as well as aiding to ensure finite execution segments for each execution cycle. The monitor should be fitted into these abstractions after the synthesis process. A garbage collector also provided by the event-manager allows us to dynamically remove unnecessary events while the system is executing. All events are managed by the event-manager entity, and the interconnection binary map is established to identify the relevant events for each monitor.

3 Contract Language Extension for Runtime Verification

Currently, the newest version of the Ada programming language – Ada 2012 – provides a language of contracts for the dynamic verification of functional properties. Subprograms can be equipped with preconditions, postconditions, dynamic and static predicates, and types can be binded with invariants. However, the contract language is not enough to address the characteristics of RV that are supported by RMF4Ada.

In this section, we propose an extension to the current contract language that is mainly composed of a couple of new syntactic contract constructions such as

1. a construction to establish the type of execution mode of the monitors, and
2. a construction to define the property that the software designer is interested in checking at runtime.

Our extension proposes the usage of a contract of the form `Monitor_Mode =>` $\mathcal{M}$, such that $\mathcal{M}$ is either the keyword `Event_Triggered` or the keyword `Time_Triggered` representing, respectively, an even-triggered monitoring mode or a time-triggered monitoring execution mode. Once the modus operandi of monitors is stated, we will establish formal languages for enforcement of non-functional properties such as temporal order, and durations. Each monitor specification is enforced by the usage of the contract `Monitor_Case =>` $(\mathcal{T}, \mathcal{C})$, such that $\mathcal{T}$ is the formal language of the contract chosen for property specification, and $\mathcal{C}$ is a sentence of this language that specifies some property of interest for runtime enforcement. The pair $(\mathcal{T}, \mathcal{C})$ has one of the following types:

1. a pair (`TRE`, α) for runtime contracts based on TREs with α being inductively defined by

$$\alpha ::= 0 \,|\, 1 \,|\, a \in \Sigma \,|\, \alpha + \alpha \,|\, \alpha\alpha \,|\, \alpha^\star \,|\, \langle \alpha \rangle_I,$$

where Σ is the set of all events, and I is a time interval of the form $[a..b]$ with $a, b \in \mathbb{R}_0^+$, or

2. a pair (`RMTLD`, φ) for runtime contracts based on RMTL$-\int$ with φ being inductively defined by

$$\beta ::= c \in \mathbb{R}_0^+ \,|\, x \in \mathcal{L}v \,|\, \mathsf{duration}[\beta]\,\varphi,$$

$$\varphi ::= p \in \mathcal{P} \,|\, \beta\,\mathsf{op}\,\beta \,|\, \mathsf{not}\,\varphi \,|\, \varphi\,\mathsf{or}\,\varphi \,|\, \varphi\,\mathsf{U}_n\,\varphi \,|\, \varphi\,\mathsf{S}_n\,\varphi \,|\, \mathsf{Ex}\,x\,\varphi,$$

where $\mathcal{P}$ is the set of propositions for all available events, $\mathsf{op} \in \{<, \leq, >, \geq\}$, $\mathcal{L}v$ is the set of logic variables, and n is a constant time in $\mathbb{R}_0^+$.

Note that each monitor specification uses the pre-defined mode of operation, until a new mode of operation is specified.

An event is defined by the introduction of the attribute `Event` in Ada. We use the shortcut `object'Event(e)` for the meaning of the sentence **for** `object'Event` **use** e. All events are previously defined, including the event `ANY`, which dictates that any event can occur. Moreover, we also add the attribute `Time` to define timing settings of the task types dealing with periods and WCET that have been assigned prior to execution.

As we have described, RMF4Ada provides computational support for these formal systems. There are object hierarchies to represent the (mutually) inductive

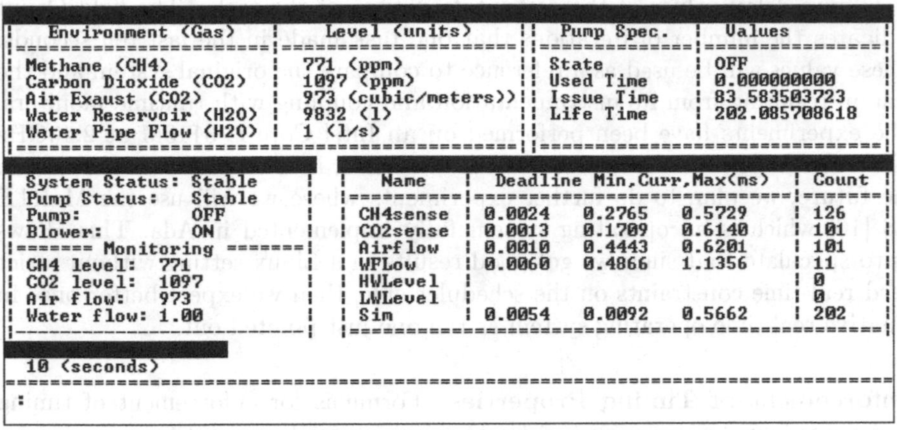

```
:-----------------------------------------------------------------------------:
:  Environment (Gas)    :    Level (units)    ::  Pump Spec.  :  Values        :
:======================:=====================::=============:================:
: Methane (CH4)         : 771 (ppm)           :: State        : OFF            :
: Carbon Dioxide (CO2)  : 1097 (ppm)          :: Used Time    : 0.000000000    :
: Air Exaust (CO2)      : 973 (cubic/meters)) :: Issue Time   : 83.583503723   :
: Water Reservoir (H2O) : 9832 (l)            :: Life Time    : 202.085708618  :
: Water Pipe Flow (H2O) : 1 (l/s)             ::              :                :
:======================:=====================::=============:================:

:--------------------------------:    :------------------------------------------------------:
: System Status:  Stable         :    :  Name    : Deadline Min,Curr,Max(ms)  :  Count  :
: Pump Status:    Stable         :    :=========:===========================:=======:
: Pump:            OFF           :    : CH4sense : 0.0024  0.2765   0.5729   : 126     :
: Blower:          ON            :    : CO2sense : 0.0013  0.1709   0.6140   : 101     :
:======= Monitoring =======:    :    : Airflow  : 0.0010  0.4443   0.6201   : 101     :
: CH4 level:   771               :    : WFLow    : 0.0060  0.4866   1.1356   : 11      :
: CO2 level:   1097              :    : HWLevel  :                           : 0       :
: Air flow:    973               :    : LWLevel  :                           : 0       :
: Water flow: 1.00               :    : Sim      : 0.0054  0.0092   0.5662   : 202     :
:--------------------------------:    :=========:===========================:=======:

: 10 (seconds)
:=============================================================================
:
```

Fig. 3. Command Line Interface of the Mine Drainage Simulator

structure of the terms and the formulas of the two formal systems. Moreover, evaluation functions for the statements are also included. In the rest of this paper, we will describe the implementation of a safety-critical real-time system in Ada with the support of RMF4Ada, and we will use the extension of contracts presented in this section. However, the synthesis of the monitors has been obtained manually, because the tool for doing it automatically is not yet available at the present time.

4   Experimental Scenario

In this last section, we describe the implementation of a real-time program that models a mine-drainage scenario in Ada. This scenario has been proposed by Burns *et al.* in [4,3]. The authors propose a mine drainage controller, and a station for employers to control and monitor the mine state. The system contains a water pump that drains the water into the ground, which needs to be switched off when a critical level of methane is reached. The implementation is available in [8], and employs our idealized contract extension to the RV. The evaluation of RMF4Ada for this particular scenario has been performed as follows: first, we have implemented the mine-drainage scenario guided by the case study presented by the authors [3]; afterwards, we specified the necessary contracts and synthesized them into monitors by hand, due to the lack of the Creator tool. Since the Instrumentor is not currently ready as well, we also performed the instrumentation by hand. After these steps have been completed successfully, we have compared the performance of the original implementation with the monitor-enriched one in order to measure the overhead imposed by the constructions provided by RMF4Ada.

The graphical interface of the simulator is presented in Fig. 3. We can observe in the table depicting the monitoring of tasks in Fig. 3 the minimum and maximum delay values of the computation time of the tasks. The field Count indicates the number of iterations that one task made in the last ten seconds. These values will be used as a reference to compare the original system and the system resulting from its instrumentation and coupling with runtime monitors. The experiments have been performed on an Intel Core i3-3110M at 2.40GHz CPU, and 8 GB RAM running on Fedora 18 x64, in a uniprocessor setting. In the future, we plan to do further experiments where we will use the MaRTE OS [16] which is an operating system fully implemented in Ada. This allows us to speculate that since we got good results in a Linux setting without strict hard real-time constraints on the scheduler side, then we expect better ones in a native real-time operating system as the one just pointed out.

Enforcement of Timing Properties. Formulas for enforcement of timing properties have been established for task timing analysis, and for a particular execution sequence of the simulation environment. Both formulas will be synthesized, producing two monitors in Ada language that can be coupled manually into the simulator. As a first example of our development, we introduce a contract specification that states that a given task named task T_Simulation always has a duration smaller than the pre-defined worst-case execution time. It allows us to monitor a task without using *execution time timers*, which are highly dependent on the operating system API. However, our approach may contain more overhead than one using execution time timers since it has been implemented at a source-level instead of a level closer to the hardware. We are also concerned by the fact that the behaviors supported by execution time timers are stricter than the behaviors supported by our monitors, and the expressiveness is incomparable: on the one hand, the time isolation is a positive point of our framework since we can establish that a set of tasks has a certain budget to execute in a certain period; on the other hand, the overhead is only the big disadvantage when systems have very strict hardware resources. The task specification using our contract language for this duration limited task execution case is the following:

```
task type T_Simulation (period: integer; deadline: integer)
  with
        Monitor_Mode => Event_Triggered,
        Monitor_Case => ( RMTLD ,
      T_Simulation'Event(Task_Release) next implies
      duration[T_Simulation'Time(period)]
      T_Simulation'Event(ANY) < T_Simulation'Time(wcet)
      );
```

The Monitor_Case contract defines a RMTL-$\int$ formula to be evaluated in event-triggered mode, 'Event is an attribute that identifies the event or events to be used, ANY identifies all the events assigned to a certain structure, and **a next implies b** is a shortcut to the logic formula $\neg a \vee a \cup_{\leq n} b$ with a n greater than the size of the observation as defined in [10]. The synthesis of this monitor can be found in [6]. A second example is a protected type Protected_Environment executing a certain timed order. Calls for the protected environment are made beginning with the release event pre of the function read_CH4 and are followed by any combination of events with duration of at most twenty milliseconds. Finally, it ends with the return of the function read_CO2 value identified by the event *post*. The specification for this second example is the following:

```
protected type Protected_Environment
  with
  Monitor_Mode => Time_Triggered
     Monitor_Case => ( TRE,
  ( Protected_Environment.read_CH4'Event(pre) .
    <(Protected_Environment'Event(ANY))*>[0..20] .
    Protected_Environment.read_CO2'Event(post))*
  ) ,
  is
     function read_CO2 return CO2_Level_State;
     function read_CH4 return CH4_Level_State;
     function read_Air_Flow return Air_Exhaust_State;
     function read_WaterPipe_Flow return WaterPipe_Flow_State;
  end;
```

The interval [0..20] assumes the time unit of milliseconds, and pre and post are the events that occur before and after the execution of a function, respectively. The code resulting from synthesizing both the previous examples can be found in [8], particularly in the specification files monitor_function_formulaone.ads and monitor_function_formulatwo.ads, respectively.

Time Isolation. It is important to note that time isolation can be ensured using our framework by applying directly the established formalization in [9,10]. In this work we only need to assume that a task release a certain set of events. Our Instrumentor tool should be capable to correctly instrument these events. The time isolation is a major advantage when several systems should be merged in order to reduce hardware costs, but the level of criticality is ensured and mixed.

4.1   Verdicts

The Instrumentor tool generates four files that are the monitoring.ads, the monitoring.adb, the spec.ads, and the spec.adb. The Spec package contains the definition of events used to analyze the *system under observation* (SUO), and the trace type. The Monitoring package instantiates the generic packages provided by RML to be included into the SUO at the instrumentation phase. The package includes the event-manager definition, the both monitor assignments for execution using the monitor collection, and a controller to initialize and finalize the instrumentation before execution begin and end, respectively.

The results are surprisingly positive. The monitor generated by the first formula introduces a maximum overhead of $11\mu s$ for every task iteration of the task T_Simulator. Considering that a wake up from an absolute delay until the operation, including one context switch, in Marte OS is $8.8\mu s$ [16] in a Pentium III at 500mhz, the results are satisfactory. We are using one core of an Intel i3 at 2.4GHz. The monitor generated by the first formula has an estimated *worst case execution time* (WCET) of $53\mu s$ for one step execution in event-triggered mode. We can conclude that we have maximum overhead of $11+53\mu s$ for runtime monitoring. This value has been estimated for 202 iterations of the task T_Simulator or the first ten seconds of one execution.

5 Conclusions

In this paper, we have presented a framework for enabling the instrumentation of Ada programs with monitors that enforce RV behavior. The evaluation of our framework shows that the overhead is minimal when compared to the original system, and that it could even be decreased by making our framework constructs more efficient and implementing them in an operation system with actual real-time behavior. Moreover, we have introduced a small extension to the current Ada contract language for enabling the specification of contracts to be checked by monitors. Finally, we provided the general structure of the complete framework, which will include a Creator tool for performing the automatic synthesis of monitors from contracts, and an Instrumentor tool that will automatically instrument a target program with event notification and adequate monitor operation.

Currently, we use two formal systems to support the construction of contracts, namely, TREs and the RMTL-$\int$ timed temporal logic. In the future we plan to explore further formal systems, and to generalize our current implementation in order to allow the integration of such new formal systems in a modular approach, without needing to recompile the framework. Another interesting point to investigate will be the adequacy of RMF4Ada in a multi-core environment, which raises new interesting and hard challenges, such as how to deal with simultaneous events occurring in the different cores, and ways to combine cores solely for monitoring while having the rest of the cores for executing the code of the actual application. Finally, we also want to explore the adequacy of the framework for COTS as internal black-box components, without source-code or rigorous specification for those components.

Acknowledgments. The authors would like to thank the anonymous reviewers for their comments that helped improve the manuscript. This work was partially supported by Portuguese National Funds through FCT (Portuguese Foundation for Science and Technology) and by ERDF (European Regional Development Fund) through COMPETE (Operational Programme 'Thematic Factors of Competitiveness'), within projects FCOMP-01-0124-FEDER-037281 (CISTER), FCOMP-01-0124-FEDER-015006 (VIPCORE) and FCOMP-01-0124-FEDER-020486 (AVIACC); and by FCT and EU ARTEMIS JU, within project ARTEMIS/0003/2012, JU grant nr. 333053 (CONCERTO).

References

1. Bauer, A., Leucker, M., Schallhart, C.: Runtime Verification for LTL and TLTL. ACM Trans. Softw. Eng. Methodol. 20(4), 14:1–14:64 (2011)

2. Bellini, P., Mattolini, R., Nesi, P.: Temporal logics for real-time system specification. ACM Comput. Surv. 32(1), 12–42 (2000)
3. Burns, A., Lin, T.M.: An engineering process for the verification of real-time systems. Form. Asp. Comput. 19(1), 111–136 (2007)
4. Burns, A., Lister, A.M.: A framework for building dependable systems. Comput. J. 34(2), 173–181 (1991)
5. Clarke Jr., E.M., Grumberg, O., Peled, D.A.: Model checking. MIT Press, Cambridge (1999)
6. de Matos Pedro, A., Pereira, D., Pinho, L.M., Pinto, J.S.: Monitors provided for the Mine Drainage System Simulator, http://webpages.cister.isep.ipp.pt/~anmap/adaeurope14/examples/mine_drainage/monitors/ (accessed: December 15, 2013)
7. de Matos Pedro, A., Pereira, D., Pinho, L.M., Pinto, J.S.: Runtime Monitoring Library for RMF4Ada, http://webpages.cister.isep.ipp.pt/~anmap/adaeurope14/ (accessed: December 15, 2013)
8. de Matos Pedro, A., Pereira, D., Pinho, L.M., Pinto, J.S.: The Mine Drainage Simulator Code, http://webpages.cister.isep.ipp.pt/~anmap/adaeurope14/examples/mine_drainage/system/ (accessed: December 15, 2013)
9. de Matos Pedro, A., Pereira, D., Pinho, L.M., Pinto, J.S.: Logic-based Schedulability Analysis for Compositional Hard Real-Time Embedded Systems. In: Proceedings of the 6th International Workshop on Compositional Theory and Technology for Real-Time Embedded Systems, CRTS 2013 (2013)
10. de Matos Pedro, A., Pereira, D., Pinho, L.M., Pinto, J.S.: A Compositional Monitoring Framework for Hard Real-Time Systems. In: Badger, J.M., Rozier, K.Y. (eds.) NFM 2014. LNCS, vol. 8430, pp. 16–30. Springer, Heidelberg (2014)
11. Havelund, K., Rosu, G.: Monitoring Java Programs with Java PathExplorer. Electronic Notes in Theoretical Computer Science 55(2), 200–217 (2001)
12. Leucker, M., Schallhart, C.: A brief account of runtime verification. J. Log. Algebr. Program. 78(5), 293–303 (2009)
13. Pike, L., Niller, S., Wegmann, N.: Runtime verification for ultra-critical systems. In: Khurshid, S., Sen, K. (eds.) RV 2011. LNCS, vol. 7186, pp. 310–324. Springer, Heidelberg (2012)
14. Pike, L., Wegmann, N., Niller, S., Goodloe, A.: Copilot: Monitoring embedded systems. Innovations in Systems and Software Engineering: Special Issue on Software Health Management (2012)
15. Pucella, R.: On equivalences for a class of timed regular expressions. Electr. Notes Theor. Comput. Sci. 106, 315–333 (2004)
16. Aldea Rivas, M., González Harbour, M.: MaRTE OS: An Ada Kernel for Real-Time Embedded Applications. In: Strohmeier, A., Craeynest, D. (eds.) Ada-Europe 2001. LNCS, vol. 2043, pp. 305–316. Springer, Heidelberg (2001)
17. Sen, K.: Generating optimal monitors for extended regular expressions. In: Proc. of the 3rd Workshop on Runtime Verification (RV 2003). ENTCS, vol. 89, pp. 162–181 (2003)
18. Zamorano, J., Alonso, A., Pulido, J.A., de la Puente, J.A.: Implementing execution-time clocks for the ada ravenscar profile. In: Llamosí, A., Strohmeier, A. (eds.) Ada-Europe 2004. LNCS, vol. 3063, pp. 132–143. Springer, Heidelberg (2004)

Reliable Handling of Real-Time Scheduling Attributes on Multiprocessor Platforms in Ada 2012

Sergio Sáez, Jorge Real, and Alfons Crespo

Instituto de Automática e Informática Industrial
Universitat Politècnica de València
Camino de vera, s/n, 46022 Valencia, Spain
{ssaez,jorge,alfons}@disca.upv.es

Abstract. The real-time attributes of a concurrent task define the parameters that will determine when the task can be allocated the required resources. Typical examples are the task's priority, the deadline, and the CPU (or CPUs) on which it must be executed. Since the 2012 revision, Ada is prepared for handling all these attributes. But the handling is per-attribute: it is not possible to change several attributes at a time, in a single call. Instead, they have to be changed one by one, which poses scheduling issues especially in multiprocessor platforms.

This paper proposes and discusses approaches for implementing atomic changes of multiple scheduling attributes, thus mitigating or eliminating those issues.

Keywords: Real-time systems, multiprocessor scheduling, Ada 2012.

1 Introduction

The scheduling attributes of a concurrent, real-time task define how resources are allocated to that task. Typical scheduling attributes are *priority*, *deadline* (in EDF-scheduled systems) and *CPU* of the task (in multiprocessor systems). Using Ada 2012 [1], a programmer can access these attributes and modify them according to changing application needs.

The package `System.Multiprocessors.Dispatching_Domains` supports the concept of dispatching domains for multiprocessor platforms, i.e., the set of processors on which a task can be executed. The package offers subprograms for querying and setting the current CPU for a task. It also provides the subprogram `Delay_Until_And_Set_CPU` to perform an atomic delay and change of CPU. The calling task will be assigned the new processor when the delay expires. This avoids the task taking too long to move to the destination CPU, when it has a relatively low priority in the original CPU.

The package `Ada.Dispatching.EDF` supports the concept of deadline and provides subprograms to query and set a task's deadline. Similarly to the CPU case, the package also provides one subprogram, `Delay_Until_And_Set_Deadline`, for

L. George and T. Vardanega (Eds.): Ada-Europe 2014, LNCS 8454, pp. 74–90, 2014.

atomically executing an absolute delay and setting a new relative deadline for the task. This atomicity is needed so that the calling task can wake up from the delay at the priority level dictated by its new deadline, and not the previous one.

The package `Ada.Dynamic_Priorities` provides subprograms for querying and setting a task's priority at run time. As opposed to the cases of deadline and CPU, there is no subprogram provided for atomically changing the priority at the end of a delay (a hypothetical `Delay_Until_And_Set_Priority`). Hence it is possible that scheduling anomalies occur when a task needs to wake up from a delay with a changed priority. For example, if the task wakes up with an old low priority and then it wants to raise its priority to high, then it can suffer interference from mid-priority tasks in the interim. This issue can however be worked around by using a timing event rather than a delay statement. The timing event handler would change the task's priority from a high interrupt priority, hence reducing the scheduling error to an interference glitch to higher-priority tasks during the execution of the timing event handler.

So CPU and deadline can be separately changed with immediate or deferred effect, and priority can be immediately changed. But there is no functionality in Ada, however, that allows the programmer to change several scheduling attributes at a time, either immediately or right after a delay. Such scheme would be very useful for applications using prevalent multiprocessor techniques such as:

Job partitioning which alternates *jobs* of a task (execution instances) in different CPUs at possibly different priorities and/or deadlines. Here the task needs to change several of its attributes, and have them enforced by the next job activation.

Task splitting and dual-priority systems where a task may need to change CPU, priority, deadline or a combination of them after a programmed amount of real time or execution time [2,3,4].

Multimoded systems that potentially require changes to several attributes of tasks after a mode change request [5,6].

The need for language changes to support this functionality is a current subject of discussion in a part of the Ada community [7,8,9]. One argument against changes or additions to the language is that, presumably, the programmer could use timing events to obtain a sufficiently effective solution [9]. Since the timing event executes at a very high priority, and it acts upon another task, the handler can change the priority or deadline of the target task, and then awake it from suspension, possibly in a different CPU. In this paper, we explore and implement this idea as well as other approaches. We then analyse different aspects of the implementations obtained, from system requirements to run-time behaviour. Our conclusion is that, although effective to a certain extent, approaches such as timing events are not absent from certain scheduling artefacts. These artefacts however, are shown to disappear in an alternative scheme based on the use of a server task for enforcing the attribute changes. The server task approach is a working solution in Ada 2012, although less efficient than it could be if the programmer could enforce the affinity of timing event handlers.

The paper is organised as follows. Section 2 motivates our study by showing the issues around the operation of changing scheduling attributes at run time, especially on multiprocessor platforms. Section 3 discusses design alternatives of safe mechanisms for handling multiple scheduling attributes in multiprocessors, either with immediate or delayed effect. Section 4 describes and discusses implementations of those design alternatives. Finally, Section 5 summarises our conclusions.

2 Motivation

Before we propose alternatives for properly handling task scheduling attributes in multiprocessor platforms, we will visit some scenarios that justify the need for a controlled mechanism. We will show how the order in which several attributes are changed is relevant for proper execution of the real-time schedule at run time, especially when the CPU is one of the changing attributes. Failing to apply changes in the correct order leads to scheduling errors. Even if the order is correct, failing to change them atomically will cause scheduling artefacts (short, bounded situations of priority inversion).

Consider Scenario A in figure 1, where we want to change both the priority and CPU[1] of a task τ in a 2-processor system, with CPU1 and CPU2. Task τ is running at priority 20 on CPU1. We want to move task τ to processor CPU2 with priority 10. If the change of CPU and priority is not atomic, then they must be done in some sequential order.

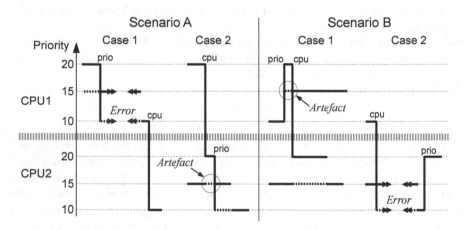

Fig. 1. Scenarios described in Section 2. Thick lines represent task execution. Dotted thick lines represent intervals of interference. Intervals between two double arrows are arbitrarily large. Errors affect the changing task τ. Artefacts affect tasks of priority 15.

---

[1] The same discussion applies for the case of changing deadline and CPU of deadline-scheduled tasks. We limit ourselves to priority and CPU for simplicity.

Case 1. If the priority is changed first, then τ will have its priority lowered to 10 while in CPU1. This would make τ suffer a potentially large amount of interference from all tasks with priority higher than 10 in CPU1. The change to CPU2 will not occur until all tasks with a priority higher than 10 are idle on CPU1. This delay can be unacceptably large and it would break the assumptions of any static real-time scheduling analysis. The impact on the schedule would be especially notorious if the new priority of τ was the highest in CPU2.

Case 2. Let's now consider the reverse order. If the CPU is changed before the priority, then τ will move to CPU2 with priority 20, rather than 10. This will preempt any tasks with priority lower than 20, when τ should execute at priority as low as 10 on CPU2. The duration of this interference will however be bounded to the time between the change of CPU and the change of priority from 20 to 10. If that time is short and bounded, then this particular order (CPU, then priority) will cause only a scheduling artefact.

Consider now the reverse Scenario B: task τ has a priority 10 in CPU1 and wants to move to CPU2 with a priority 20. If we first change the priority, then we will cause interference in CPU1 to all tasks with priorities between 10 and 20. This interference will however last only the time it takes to move from CPU1 to CPU2. A situation similar to Case 2 above, but the artefact will occur in the original CPU1 rather than in the destination CPU2. In symmetry with the previous scenario, if we first change the CPU, then τ is moved to CPU2 with a priority 10 rather than 20, so it will not be able to raise its priority to 20 until all tasks with priorities between 20 and 10 are idle. This corresponds to Case 1 above, but the unbounded interference on τ would occur while in CPU2, rather than CPU1.

In the rest of this paper, we will explore design alternatives to remove the scheduling errors described in this Section. Note that if the scheduling artefacts can not be removed, at least they will only cause limited interference.

3   Design Alternatives

The situations described above suggest that the change of several attributes of a target task, especially when the CPU attribute is involved, needs be done atomically. At an application level (i.e., not considering the implementation of the underlying system services to change task scheduling attributes) there are four Ada mechanisms we want to explore for pursuing the required atomicity:

- A protected object with the highest ceiling changes the target task attributes.
- The target task performs the changes of its own attributes using the highest priority to avoid interference from other tasks during the sequence of changes.
- A timing event is programmed to change the attributes of the target task.
- A server task changes the attributes of the target task using rendezvous at the highest priority.

In the following subsections, we explore the properties of these approaches to correctly solve the problem of changing several scheduling attributes at a time.

3.1   Using Protected Objects

Changing the priority, deadline or CPU of an Ada task are task dispatching points. However, all these operations are deferred if they occur within a protected action. This seems to give a chance to atomicity if all attribute changes are done within a protected action. By choosing the right ceiling priority for the protected object, the programmer can avoid priority inversions leading to scheduling errors such as those described in Section 2. In the most extreme case, the ceiling can be as high as System.Interrupt_Priority'Last, so that the attribute changes will never be pre-empted by any other application task or interrupt handler.

Taking Case 1 of Scenario A in Figure 1, if the change of priority and CPU was atomic, then task τ would travel to CPU2 without spending a potentially large amount of time suspended in CPU1, with a relatively low priority that would delay its migration. In Case 2 of Scenario B, the task would migrate to CPU2 with the correct priority 20, and hence it would not suffer priority inversion from lower-priority tasks in CPU2.

The deferred setting of multiple scheduling attributes (à la Delay_Until_-And_Set_Scheduling_Attributes) can also be dealt with by requeuing the calling task in a private entry of the protected object, with a closed barrier, and programming a timing event for the required delay time. The timing event handler would then open the barrier of that private entry and release the waiting task with the new attributes.

Unfortunately, this analysis fails because we must also take into account how the underlying combination of operating system (OS) and run-time system actually implements the change of several attributes at the end of a protected action. When the task abandons the protected action it must have its priority and CPU changed. The original problem arises again: if the OS/runtime is requested to change the priority before the CPU, then the task will be inserted in the scheduling queue corresponding to its new priority. Since the change of CPU is still pending, then the error described for Scenario A Case 1 will happen again. If the OS/runtime is commanded to perform the changes in the reverse order, first CPU and then priority, then we would repeat the situation and scheduling error shown in Case 2 of Scenario B in Figure 1.

A solution to these problems can only come from the particular runtime implementation of how protected actions are completed. A safe design choice is to have the completion of the protected action executed at the maximum priority and follow the order: change CPU, then priority. But that falls out of the control of an application programmer.

3.2   Self Change of Attributes from the Highest Priority

A second approach is to have the changing task applying the changes to itself but after rising its priority to the highest possible (Interrupt_Priority'Last) so that it cannot be pre-empted in the middle of the changes. The sequence of operations in the task would be: (1) Set my own priority to the highest, where I cannot be pre-empted; (2) Call Delay_Until_And_Set_CPU to change to the target CPU at the specified absolute time (it could be immediately if Set_CPU is used instead); Finally (3) enforce my new scheduling attributes, in an order such that the last attribute changed is my priority, so that all changes are done from Interrupt_Priority'Last.

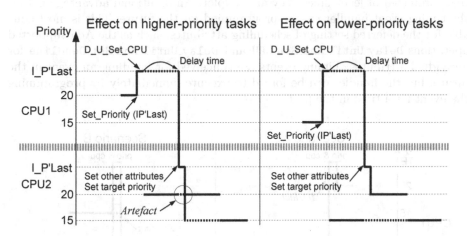

Fig. 2. Scenarios for the self-change approach and their impact on higher- and lower-priority tasks in the destination processor CPU2

Figure 2 shows this approach and the impact it may have on other higher- and lower-priority tasks. On the left hand side, the task executes on CPU1 at priority 20 and wants to move to CPU2 with priority 15. At the time given in Delay_Until_And_Set_CPU, the task wakes up in CPU2, still with the highest priority. This may cause bounded interference on all tasks in CPU2. In particular, this will even preempt tasks with a priority higher than the destination priority of the changing task. This is marked as an artefact in the left-hand side of Figure 2.

On the right-hand side of Figure 2, the changing task executes on CPU1 at priority 15 and then migrates to CPU2 with priority 20. The impact on lower-priority tasks in CPU2 is just regular pre-emption.

We note however that any task running on CPU2 (below Interrupt_Priority'Last) could be subject to pre-emption bursts in the case of multiple tasks migrating to CPU2 in a short interval during its execution. And it would not matter whether the target priorities of the pre-empting tasks were higher or lower than that of the pre-empted task (or tasks) in CPU2. This is an important drawback of this approach since it ruins the assumptions of schedulability analysis: any task on CPU2 could suffer interference from any other task potentially migrating to CPU2 from any other CPU.

3.3 Using Timing Events

For our purpose, and in terms of scheduling, the timing event mechanism has similar properties to using a protected action with the highest possible ceiling priority. Furthermore, timing events are amenable to more efficient implementations than protected objects, since they are simpler. An additional advantage is that the timing event handler can be programmed for the future. This is most suitable for the deferred setting of scheduling attributes, such as the Ada supported operations `Delay_Until_And_Set_CPU` and `Delay_Until_And_Set_Deadline` for individual attributes. Timing events are conceived for handling an event in the future, but the handler can be forced to execute immediately by programming the event for a time in the past.

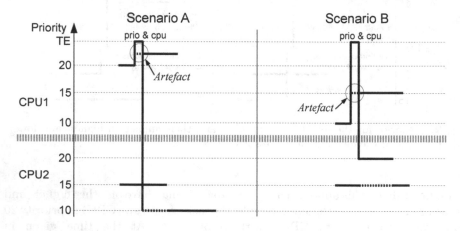

Fig. 3. An implementation based on a timing event prevents the scheduling errors shown in Figure 1. TE represents the priority at which the timing event handler is executed. In practice, under the Ceiling Locking policy, this priority is `Interrupt_Priority'Last`.

But perhaps the principal advantage of using a timing event (*vs.* a protected object) is that the timing event handler will apply the attribute changes to *another task*. It can therefore change the task's priority without forcing a reschedule (since the handler is still executing at the highest priority) and then change the task's CPU before completing the execution of the handler. This eliminates the issue mentioned above with protected objects: even though the OS does not support the atomic change of several scheduling attributes of a task, since the changes are done from a timing event handler, there will be no other application tasks interfering the whole operation. Figure 3 shows how the scheduling errors described in Section 2 disappear and only the artefact glitches remain. Since the changes of priority and CPU are enforced from the timing event handler, with no possible pre-emption, the order in which they are performed is not relevant, hence the absence of cases 1 and 2 in Figure 3.

In summary, an implementation based on timing events effectively eliminates the scheduling errors described in section 2, but not the artefacts. We note that, unfortunately, it is unknown to the programmer in which CPU the artefact will occur, given that the underlying OS/runtime could choose any CPU to execute the timing event handler[2]. This poses a challenge to schedulability analysis and motivates us to explore how the hypothetical ability to set the affinity for timing events, would help solve this issue and determine precisely where the artefacts occur, which would provide invaluable information for schedulability analysis. We will develop this idea in Section 4.4.

3.4   Using Rendezvous with a Server Task

We now explore an alternative approach whereby a server task is used for servicing requests of immediate and deferred changes of the scheduling attributes.

Assume one server task is in charge of applying the attribute changes to another calling (client) task. The server task has the highest priority, `Interrupt_ Priority'Last`. A client task calls the appropriate server entry (for immediate or deferred change) and then it becomes blocked during the execution of the handled sequence of sentences of the corresponding accept statement on the server side. According to the Ada standard [1], the execution of the rendezvous occurs at the priority of the calling task. Since we do not want to reproduce the scheduling errors described above for the protected object scheme, we want the rendezvous to occur at the highest priority. To this end, the calling task will rise its priority to the highest before issuing the actual entry call to the server.

Consider first the immediate setting of scheduling attributes by means of a procedure `Apply_Scheduling_Attributes`. Within this procedure, the calling task first rises its priority to `Interrupt_Priority'Last` and then calls an entry in the server task to enforce the new scheduling attributes. Upon completion of the entry call, the server task goes back to accepting new calls and the client task is released from the rendezvous blocking with the new attributes applied. The effect on the schedule is a bounded interference at the highest priority in the origin CPU, that can easily be accounted for in the schedulability analysis as blocking time for all tasks of a priority higher than the client task in the origin CPU. This is because the whole operation starts at the client's original priority in the origin CPU.

Figure 4 shows the process for both immediate and deferred changes. In the immediate case (left side of Figure 4), a task in CPU1 with priority 20 wants to change its priority to 10 and CPU to CPU2. The task first rises its priority to the highest and then calls the appropriate entry in the server task. During the rendezvous (represented by a grey box) the server task enforces the changes of priority and CPU with no possible interference from other tasks. Note that, as opposed to what occurs with timing events, the artefacts depicted in Figure 4 will

---

[2] In Figure 3 we have represented the timing event executing in the same CPU where the calling task executes, but nothing prevents the runtime system to execute the handler in CPU2 or even in a third CPU, if it exists.

always occur in the origin CPU, so although they exist, they can be predictably accounted for in the schedulability analysis. We have represented the continuous execution of a second task of priority 15 in CPU2 to show that there are no glitches caused by this approach.

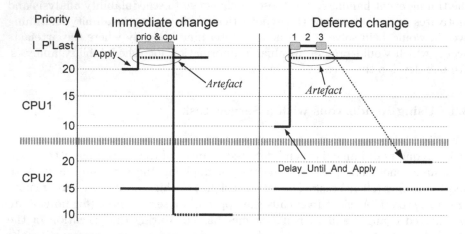

Fig. 4. Execution examples for immediate and deferred change of scheduling attributes using an implementation based on server tasks. Gray boxes represent execution of the server task. The explanation for marks 1, 2 and 3 is given in Section 3.4.

Consider now the deferred change of attributes, enabled by a procedure Delay_Until_And_Apply_Scheduling_Attributes. The right hand side of Figure 4 shows the case of a task running on CPU1 at priority 10, that wants to migrate to CPU2 with priority 20 at a given time in the future. As in the immediate case, the first thing to do is to rise the priority of the task to the highest. Then the entry call is issued and the rendezvous starts. In this case, the rendezvous only copies the parameters of the call to apply them at a later stage. This is marked as step 1 on the right hand side of Figure 4. After step 1 the rendezvous completes and we have both server and client at the highest priority, since we have not yet changed any of the task's attributes. We now want to make sure that the client task goes on and executes a delay until sentence to suspend itself until the requested time. This is marked as step 2 in Figure 4. Having the client task suspended, the server task now executes step 3, where it simply enforces the new attributes to the (suspended) client task. The result is that no scheduling errors can occur, and the artefacts are actually only short blocking times. The whole operation of changing the priority and CPU of a task can be accounted as blocking time for tasks of a higher priority than the changing task in the origin CPU. And this situation of priority inversion always occurs in the origin CPU. This is a clear advantage with respect to the timing event alternative described in Section 3.3, where it can't be predicted in which CPU the priority inversion will occur.

To ensure that the steps will occur exactly in the order described here (1, then 2, then 3), the server task has to yield the processor after the rendezvous (step 1), so that the client task executes the delay statement (step 2) and is placed at the tail of the ready queue of Interrupt_Priority'Last. After that, the server task gains the CPU again to perform the change of attributes on the suspended client – this is because the only two tasks executing at the highest priority level are the client and the server. Indeed, this protocol causes two context switches between server and client, but the important benefit is that the associated overhead is bounded and predictable.

4   Implementation

This section discusses implementation details of the design alternatives described so far. After briefly restating the implementation goals, we will first look at the details of a data type to capture all the scheduling attributes of tasks, and its related primitive operations. We will then show the most relevant implementation aspects of the alternatives proposed in sections 3.2, 3.3 and 3.4, that is, having the attributes changed by the target task itself, or by a timing event or by a server task, respectively. We are not considering the implementation details of the protected object approach described in Section 3.1 because the way it behaves is heavily dependent on the underlying combination of OS and runtime support.

4.1   Goals

The goal of the software under design is to provide an abstraction to capture the set of scheduling attributes (priority, deadline, CPU, or other user-defined attributes...) individually associated to each task in the system. The programmer must be allowed to query these attributes, and to atomically change one or more individual attributes at a time. The change of these attributes can either have immediate or deferred effect, at a certain specified absolute time in the future. The type representing the set of attributes shall be extendable, so that application-specific scheduling attributes can be added at a later time.

4.2   Representation of Scheduling Attributes

Listing 1 shows the specification of the tagged type Scheduling_Attributes, that captures the scheduling attributes of a task. An instance of this type (or a type derived from it) is associated with each task so that the whole set of attributes can be passed to a changer subprogram in a single call. The type was already proposed in [8], and extended with a derived type for including a deadline attribute for deadline-scheduled tasks. We show here only the two attributes defined in the root type, priority and CPU.

The implementation details in the private part show that the type is simply an extensible record with the proper fields, one for each attribute. The class-wide type Any_Scheduling_Attributes is needed for the class-wide operations Apply_Scheduling_Attributes and Delay_Until_And_Apply_Scheduling_Attributes.

These subprograms internally use the private subprogram `Enforce_Scheduling_Attributes`, which is in charge of ultimately setting the attributes. It has to be implemented for each extension of the type, since the parameters to change will vary between those extensions. Listing 2 shows the implementation of the corresponding root operation.

The type is simple enough, and the operations are common setters and getters. The subprogram `Retrieve_Scheduling_Attributes` allows the programmer to read the attributes of a task. This is needed when we only need to change a subset of the attributes and leave the rest intact.

Listing 1. Data type for scheduling attributes and primitive operations

```
-- with clauses omitted
package Ada_Real_Time.Scheduling_Attributes is
   -- Data type to represent scheduling  attributes
   type Scheduling_Attributes  is tagged private;
   procedure Set_Priority  (SP : in out Scheduling_Attributes ; Prio:  Any_Priority );
   function  Get_Priority  (SP :  Scheduling_Attributes ) return  Any_Priority ;
   procedure Set_CPU (SP : in out Scheduling_Attributes ; CPU_Nr: CPU_Range);
   function  Get_CPU (SP :  Scheduling_Attributes) return  CPU_Range;
   procedure  Retrieve_Scheduling_Attributes  (SP : in out Scheduling_Attributes ;
                                          T_Id :  Task_Id := Current_Task);
   type Any_Scheduling_Attributes  is access all  Scheduling_Attributes ' Class;

   -- Class-wide procedures
   procedure  Apply_Scheduling_Attributes  (SP :  Any_Scheduling_Attributes ;
                                       T_Id :  Task_Id := Current_Task);
   procedure  Delay_Until_And_Apply_Scheduling_Attributes  (SP :  Any_Scheduling_Attributes ;
                                               Delay_Until_Time  : Time);
private
   type  Scheduling_Attributes  is tagged
      record
         Prio      :  Any_Priority  :=  Default_Priority ;
         CPU_Nr :  CPU_Range :=  Not_A_Specific_CPU;
      end record;

   procedure  Enforce_Scheduling_Attributes (SP :  Scheduling_Attributes ; T_Id : Task_Id );

end Ada_Real_Time.Scheduling_Attributes ;
```

Listing 2. Root subprogram in charge of ultimately changing the attributes

```
procedure  Enforce_Scheduling_Attributes (SP :  Scheduling_Attributes ; T_Id : Task_Id) is
begin
   Set_Priority ( Priority  => SP.Prio, T => T_Id);
   Set_CPU (CPU => SP.CPU_Nr, T => T_Id);
end  Enforce_Scheduling_Attributes ;
```

The implementation of a particular approach to handle the attributes will be fully contained in the subprograms `Apply_Scheduling_Attributes` and `Delay_Until_And_Apply_Scheduling_Attributes`. The following subsections illustrate the implementations of the three viable design alternatives discussed in Section 3.

4.3   Implementation Based on Self Changing the Attributes

Listing 3 shows the implementation of the deferred change of attributes contained in subprogram `Delay_Until_And_Apply_Scheduling_Attributes`. The key aspect of this approach (as described in Section 3.2) is that the changing task has the highest priority before it changes to the target CPU (line 5 of Listing 3). This ensures that it will continue to execute at the highest priority when it arrives in the destination CPU. Then we change the other attributes (all but CPU and priority, if any) and finally, we change the priority.

Note that the last two sentences (lines 8 and 9) will be executed on the target CPU, thus interfering with tasks that may have a higher priority than the final priority of the changing task.

Listing 3. Deferred change of attributes in the self-change approach

```
1   procedure Delay_Until_And_Apply_Scheduling_Attributes  (SP : Any_Scheduling_Attributes ;
2                                                            Delay_Until_Time : Time) is
3   begin
4       Set_Priority ( Interrupt_Priority 'Last);  -- Rise caller's priority to highest
5       Delay_Until_And_Set_CPU(Delay_Until_Time,SP.CPU_Nr);
6       -- Caller wakes up from delay in the  destination  CPU and still with the highest  priority
7       SP. Enforce_Scheduling_Attributes (Current_Task);  -- Update other attributes
8       Set_Priority (SP.Prio);  -- Decrease caller's  priority  down to the target  priority
9   end Delay_Until_And_Apply_Scheduling_Attributes ;
```

4.4 Implementation Based on Timing Events

As discussed in Section 3.3, timing events could lead to a more efficient implementation than the self-changing and server task approaches. However, the interference caused by a timing event handler cannot be bound to a particular CPU, since the affinity of timing events cannot be enforced.

Listing 4 shows a hypothetical, extended specification of the Set_Handler subprogram (for programming a timing event handler). This extension adds the parameter CPU_Nr to set the handler's affinity. At the low level, the operation hides the complexity of adding timed events to the timer queue of a different CPU. If we had this in Ada, then we could remove the most important drawback of the timing-event approach to handling scheduling attributes.

Listing 4. A proposed signature for timing events with CPU affinity

```
procedure Set_Handler (Event :  in out Timing_Event; At_Time : Time; Handler :  Timing_Event_Handler;
                       CPU_Nr : CPU_Range := Get_CPU);
```

The use of this hypothetical feature could be as follows. Assume a *Scheduling Manager* abstraction is declared for each task whose scheduling attributes may be changed. This scheduling manager maintains the scheduling attributes of the task and enables their enforcement when the timing event expires. Listing 5 shows a part of the implementation of a protected object supporting the scheduling manager abstraction.

The immediate change of scheduling attributes, implemented within the entry body of Apply_Scheduling_Parameters, programs an already expired timing event to force the execution of the handler as soon as the calling task completes the entry call. In the case the calling task is also the target task, it also forces the task to wait until the handler is executed. The deferred setting of attributes is implemented in Delay_Until_And_Apply_Scheduling_Attributes. It is similar to the immediate case, but using an expiration time in the future.

Listing 5. Timing Event handler and protected operations

```
-- Scheduling Manager specification
protected type Scheduling_Manager with Interrupt_Priority => Interrupt_Priority 'Last is
   entry  Apply_Scheduling_Attributes (SP: Any_Scheduling_Attributes );
   entry  Delay_Until_And_Apply_Scheduling_Attributes  (SP : Any_Scheduling_Attributes ;
                                                        Delay_Until_Time :  Time);
private
   entry Wait;
   procedure Handler (Event :  in out Timing_Event);

   Task_Waiting : Boolean := false ;
   Sched_Params : Any_Scheduling_Attributes ;
   Timing_Ev : Timing_Event;
end Scheduling_Manager;

-- Scheduling Manager body
protected body Scheduling_Manager is

   entry Wait when not Task_Waiting is
   begin
      null ;
   end Wait;

   procedure Handler (Event :  in out Timing_Event) is
   begin
      Sched_Params. Enforce_Scheduling_Attributes (Owner_Task);
      Task_Waiting := false ;
   end Handler;

   entry  Apply_Scheduling_Attributes (SP: Any_Scheduling_Attributes ) when True is
   begin
      if not Task_Waiting then
         Sched_Params := SP;
         if Scheduling_Manager. Apply_Scheduling_Attributes ' Caller  /= Owner_Task then
            -- A task wants to change another task's  attributes
            Timing_Ev.Set_Handler(Time_First,  Handler'Access, SP.Get_CPU);
         else
            -- A task wants to change its own scheduling  attributes
            Task_Waiting := True; -- Barrier for entry  Wait
            -- An immediate timing event is programmed...
            Timing_Ev.Set_Handler(Time_First,  Handler'Access, SP.Get_CPU);
            -- ... and the task is requeued to Wait until  Handler updates its  attributes
            requeue Wait;
         end if ;
      end if ;
   end  Apply_Scheduling_Attributes ;

   entry  Delay_Until_And_Apply_Scheduling_Attributes  (SP : Any_Scheduling_Attributes ;
                                                        Delay_Until_Time :  Time) when True is
   begin
      Sched_Params := SP;
      Task_Waiting := True;
      -- Program a TE for Delay_Until_Time ...
      Timing_Ev.Set_Handler(Delay_Until_Time, Handler'Access, SP.Get_CPU);
      -- ... and wait until  Handler wakes me up with the new attributes
      requeue Wait;
   end  Delay_Until_And_Apply_Scheduling_Attributes ;

end Scheduling_Manager;
```

4.5 Implementation Based on Server Tasks

In the approach described in Section 3.4, a server task is used to atomically change the scheduling attributes of a client task. Listing 6 shows an implementation of the server task type, from which server objects can be instantiated. We may need up to one server task per CPU. The function Next_CPU, used as the initial value for the discriminant CPU_Nr of the task type, is just a global function that returns one distinct CPU number upon each call, all within the range of CPUs available in the execution platform.

Each server task offers two entries that will be used by the class-wide operations to implement the immediate and deferred changes. When a call is accepted to the entry Apply_Attributes_Immediately, the server simply calls the procedure that enforces the new attributes. As Listing 7 shows, the entry call is sent to the particular server task that is attached to the CPU where the changing task is executing. We have omitted the implementation of the function Current_CPU, which is dependent on the particular underlying operating system.

Listing 6. Server task that atomically enforces the scheduling attributes

```
task type Scheduling_Manager_Type(CPU_Nr : CPU := Next_CPU) with
    Interrupt_Priority  => Interrupt_Priority 'Last,  CPU => CPU_Nr is
    -- entries omitted
end Scheduling_Manager_Type;

task body Scheduling_Manager_Type is
    Sched_Param : Any_Scheduling_Attributes;
    Target_Task: Task_Id;
begin
  loop
     select
        accept Apply_Attributes_Immediately  (SP :  in  Any_Scheduling_Attributes;
                                              T_Id :  Task_Id) do
            -- Change task's attributes
            SP. Enforce_Scheduling_Attributes (T_Id);
        end Apply_Attributes_Immediately;
     or
        accept Apply_Attributes_On_Suspend (SP :  in  Any_Scheduling_Attributes;
                                            T_Id :  Task_Id) do
            -- Stores the target task and new attributes (Fig. 3 step 1)
            Target_Task := T_Id;
            Sched_Param := SP;
        end Apply_Attributes_On_Suspend;
        -- Forces client task to execute the delay until (Fig. 3 step 2)
        delay  0.0;
        -- Change the sched. attributes of the suspended client task (Fig. 3 step 3)
        Sched_Param.Enforce_Scheduling_Attributes (Target_Task);
     or
        terminate;
     end select;
  end loop;
end Scheduling_Manager_Type;
```

The second entry in Listing 6, Apply_Attributes_On_Suspend, implements steps 1 and 3 shown at the right-hand side of Figure 4. The sentence delay 0.0 after the *accept* forces the server task to move to the tail of the Interrupt_Priority'Last ready queue[3]. This allows the client task, that has the same highest priority, to execute the statement delay until Delay_Until_Time, within subprogram Delay_Until_And_Apply_Scheduling_Attributes shown in Listing 7 (labelled as step 2 in Figure 4).

---

[3] The Yield operation is not supported in our platform.

Once the client task is suspended, the server task resumes execution (it is the highest-priority active task) and changes the scheduling attributes of the suspended client task. When the client task wakes up, it will be inserted in the corresponding ready queue of the target CPU, but with the new scheduling attributes already applied. Therefore, no scheduling interferences at application level will occur[4].

Listing 7. Class-wide operations of the scheduling attributes

```
-- Class-wide procedures
procedure Apply_Scheduling_Attributes (SP : Any_Scheduling_Attributes ;
                                       T_Id : Task_Id := Current_Task) is
begin
    Set_Priority ( Interrupt_Priority 'Last);
    Scheduling_Manager(Current_CPU).Apply_Parameters_Immediately(SP, T_Id);
end Apply_Scheduling_Attributes ;

procedure Delay_Until_And_Apply_Scheduling_Attributes (SP : Any_Scheduling_Attributes ;
                                       Delay_Until_Time : Time) is
begin
    Set_Priority ( Interrupt_Priority 'Last); -- Rise its priority to IP'Last
    Scheduling_Manager(Current_CPU).Apply_Parameters_On_Suspend(SP,
                                       Current_Task);
    -- Sched. attributes will be change on suspension (Fig. 3 step 2)
    delay until Delay_Until_Time; -- It will wake up with new attributes applied
end Delay_Until_And_Apply_Scheduling_Attributes ;
```

5   Conclusions

The ability to safely change several scheduling attributes of a task in a single operation, is a useful feature for real-time systems, especially on multiprocessor platforms. It is on these platforms that the operation poses the biggest challenges, since there are multiple opportunities for scheduling issues to occur at run time. This is especially true when the CPU is one of the changing attributes. In this paper, we have described those issues and explored four ways to solve them in Ada. We conclude that:

- A solution based on protected objects does not guarantee, at the language level, the required atomicity in the change of several scheduling attributes. Even if the protected action was executed at the highest possible ceiling. This is because we ultimately depend on how the OS/runtime implements the lower-level services to actually enforce the scheduling attributes.
- Self-changing the attributes from the highest priority level, introduces remote interference in the destination CPU. Although this interference is presumably short (just the time it takes to call the OS/runtime support to have the changes enforced, plus a task context switch in and out the destination CPU), a task in the destination CPU may suffer bursts of interference when many tasks are migrating to the CPU where it is running.

---

[4] The possible scheduling interferences that a task activation produces at kernel level depend ultimately on the implementation of the underlying operating system.

– Delegating on a timing event handler for the change of attributes, while the changing task is safely blocked awaiting for the handler to execute. This approach produces one interference glitch, presumably shorter than in the previous case since no task context switch is strictly necessary here. However, it is impossible for the programmer to determine in which CPU the interference will occur (unless it is very precisely documented in the language implementation). Moreover, at least one implementation that we know of uses a task for servicing timing events, hence the efficiency argument does not necessarily hold in all cases. We note that the main weakness of this approach (namely, ignoring which CPU is affected by the handler glitch) could be overcome by adding a new language feature that enabled the programmer to set the affinity of timing event handlers.

– Using a server task to change the attributes of client tasks has proven to be the most reliable implementation in our experience. This approach requires up to one server task per CPU and produces interference only in the origin CPU, where it can be accounted for as interference from the highest priority level. Since all attribute changes are applied to a non-running task, they will be actually enforced at the next task activation. There is no need for further operations that are susceptible of causing additional interference. Our own criticism to this approach is that we need a double context switch between the server and the client tasks in order to apply all the changes in a controlled manner.

Acknowledgements. This work has been partially supported by the Spanish Government's projects COBAMI (DPI2011-28507-C02-02) and Hi-PartES (TIN2011-28567-C03-01-02-03) and the European Commission's MultiPARTES project (FP7-ICT-2011.3.4, Contract 287702).

References

1. ISO/IEC JTC1 SC22 WG9 Ada Rapporteur Group: Ada Reference Manual - Language and Standard Libraries - ISO/IEC 8652:2012(E), http://www.ada-europe.org/manuals/LRM-2012.pdf
2. Davis, R., Wellings, A.: Dual priority scheduling. In: Proceedings of the 16th IEEE Real-Time Systems Symposium, pp. 100–109 (1995)
3. Kato, S., Yamasaki, N., Ishikawa, Y.: Semi-partitioned scheduling of sporadic task systems on multiprocessors. In: 21st Euromicro Conference on Real-Time Systems, ECRTS 2009, pp. 249–258. IEEE Computer Society, Los Alamitos (2009)
4. Lakshmanan, K., Rajkumar, R., Lehoczky, J.P.: Partitioned fixed-priority preemptive scheduling for multi-core processors. In: 21st Euromicro Conference on Real-Time Systems, ECRTS 2009, pp. 239–248. IEEE Computer Society (2009)
5. Tindell, K., Burns, A., Wellings, A.: Mode changes in priority preemptively scheduled systems. In: Real-Time Systems Symposium, pp. 100–109 (1992)

6. Real, J., Crespo, A.: Mode Change Protocols for Real-Time Systems: A Survey and a new Proposal. Real-Time Systems 26(2), 161–197 (2004)
7. Sáez, S., Crespo, A.: Deferred setting of scheduling attributes in Ada 2012. Ada Letters 33(1), 93–100 (2013)
8. Sáez, S., Real, J., Crespo, A.: Deferred and atomic setting of scheduling attributes for Ada. Ada Letters 33(2), 97–108 (2013)
9. Vardanega, T., White, R.: Session summary: Improvements to Ada. Ada User Journal 34(4), 239–241 (2013)

Parallelism in Ada: Status and Prospects

Luís Miguel Pinho[1], Brad Moore[2], and Stephen Michell[3]

[1] CISTER/INESC-TEC, ISEP, Polytechnic Institute of Porto, Portugal
lmp@isep.ipp.pt
[2] General Dynamics, Canada
brad.moore@gdcanada.com
[3] Maurya Software Inc, Canada
stephen.michell@maurya.on.ca

Abstract. Recently, a semantic and runtime model for parallel programming was proposed for addition to Ada. The proposal uses program annotations (expressed as Ada 2012 aspects) to inform the compiler of opportunities for parallel computation, and also offers the ability to specify details of parallel execution. The proposal includes support for specialized behaviors via dedicated libraries and a runtime environment that builds on pools of worker tasks. This paper extends that work by adding notations for data types and parallel blocks, simplifying some of the parallel notations and eliminating obstructions to the implementation of efficient parallel algorithms.

1 Introduction

Recently a fine-grain parallel model for Ada has been proposed [1], based on the notion of *tasklets*, which are non-schedulable computation units (similar to Cilk [2] or OpenMP [3] "tasks"). This model is based on annotating Ada code with new aspects that guide the compiler on how sequential code can be parallelized, where the compiler is responsible for transforming the source for parallel execution.

Unlike Ada tasks, tasklets are not nameable or directly visible in a program, and may exist only as a logical entity. A tasklet carries the execution of a subprogram or of a code fragment in parallel with other tasklets executing the same or complementary code fragments (with different state) and possibly in parallel with other tasklets executing code fragments from other Ada tasks. This work is also similar to what is being proposed in other languages such as C++ [4] and C [5].

Tasklets do not replace tasking as the unit of concurrency but rather complement tasks. Programmers declare an intent that code fragments be executable in parallel, but do not necessarily concern themselves with the details of the parallelism itself, or how it interoperates with other tasks. To the programmer, each tasklet execution looks like a very lightweight task that briefly comes into existence and then terminates at the end of its execution. In order to make tasklets integrate smoothly with the tasking mechanism, priority, and real-time bounds, tasklets can be executed by worker tasks. The Ada tasking model is then used to express the concurrency since tasks in Ada already have a computationally sound model.

L. George and T. Vardanega (Eds.): Ada-Europe 2014, LNCS 8454, pp. 91–106, 2014.
© Springer International Publishing Switzerland 2014

A proposal for an extensible underlying library is presented at [6], based on tasklets being executed by pools of worker Ada tasks. The work at [6] considers that tasking must carry the load in sharing cores when parallelization occurs in homogenous parallel cores and the underlying runtime already maps tasks to threads. Nevertheless, it is recognized that there is a need for the programmer to be able to provide more control of the parallelism when necessary. Examples of the need to tightly control how the parallelism is implemented include huge data sets on massively parallel machines, general purpose GPU's, and real-time systems. In such cases, the allocation of resources may need to be tightly controlled and managed. Furthermore, for the case where tasks are not mapped to threads, a different approach can be used altogether for executing the tasklets. Therefore, the proposal defines the semantics as well as an interface, which can be used by an implementer to add libraries specific to particular domains or platforms.

The proposal incorporates logical units of parallelism into the semantic model of the language, allowing potential parallelism to be expressed both for task/control and data parallelism notations [7]. In the former, the control structures of the code (e.g. for loops [1], blocks and subprograms) which are amenable to parallelization are identified (syntax to annotate for loops and subprograms is presented at [1]), while in the latter it is the primitive operations of data types (arrays or records) that are annotated to be potentially performed in parallel (a preliminary syntax is presented in [8]). Both are based on the same notion of the tasklet as the logical unit of parallelism.

Concerning the behavior model, the programmer identifies potential *Parallel OPportunities* (POPs) in the code, guiding the compiler in generating code that creates the logical tasklets. During execution, the runtime executes the tasklets in parallel, if the load of the system and the underlying architecture allows it. Note that this model also allows the compiler to integrate vectorization, as logically the compiler can decompose parallel processing in several tasklets which are directly executed in hardware. If programmers have a clear understanding of the specific target hardware they may optimize parallelism controls such as size of parallel chunks, etc. Nevertheless, we consider that in the majority the cases the compiler is better able to perform that control.

In this paper we provide the current status of this proposal, as well as how it is extended for supporting data parallelism notation and how parallelism is handled in expressions. We extend our previous syntax model by allowing programmers to express parallelism via a parallel block syntax, which can provide an easier approach for the programmer to specify parallel algorithms, and also serve as a useful building block for parallelism implementation. Finally, we discuss some open issues.

2   Proposal Model and Status

The work in [1] introduced the notion of a *Parallel OPportunity* (POP). This is a code fragment that appears sequential but which can be executed by processing elements in parallel. This could be by-element operations on an array, parallel iterations of a for

---

[1]   A *loop* is a control structure of the code. Nevertheless, a *for loop* is widely used for iteration on array data types. Therefore, a *for loop* can also be seen as a way to express data decomposition.

loop over a structure or container, parallel executions of subprograms, and so on. That work also introduced the notion of a *tasklet* to capture the notion of a single execution trace within a POP, which we allow the programmer to express with special syntax.

Conceptually, each Ada task is seen as a graph of execution of multiple control-dependent tasklets (Figure 1), with a fork-join model. At least one (implicit) tasklet exists in each task, to execute the body of the task. Tasklets can be spawned by other tasklets (fork), and need to synchronize with the spawning tasklet (join).

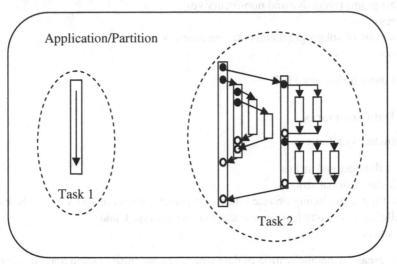

Fig. 1. Task 1 denotes the current model of an Ada task where a single thread of control is executing the body of the task. Task 2 denotes the new model, where an Ada task can execute a graph, where rectangles denote tasklets, dark circles fork points, and white circles join points.

The basic approach to the syntax is to use the Ada *aspect* mechanism

```
with parallel => [True| False]
```

to denote a POP. The goal is to place this aspect on specifications, such as function declarations and data type declarations so that individual statements do not require annotation. Adding these annotations is less laborious and less error prone than achieving equivalent parallelism from scratch, in the absence of syntax, and library support, neither of which Ada has built into the standard. It also allows integration with the compiler, as the annotations do not need to provide the exact breakdown of parallel execution. As a bare minimum, the annotations only need to indicate the places where parallelization can be performed. The compiler is then able to perform suitable transformations.

Nevertheless, in some cases, such as hard real-time systems or specialized massively parallel machines, the programmer may need to provide finer control of the parallel behavior. These further controls are provided in the form of additional aspects to guide mapping and reduction of algorithms, to select work strategies (such as work-sharing or work-stealing), and to provide explicit control of user-provided task pools for workers. When these finer controls are needed, the programmer is specializing for a particular architecture, achieving predictability or performance at the expense of decreased portability. The compiler then, together with the runtime (which can be architecture-specific), generates the code required for parallelization.

We have identified the need for explicit syntax to guide the compiler in the generation of tasklets to execute the following:

— Data structures
— Parallel for loops (also over containers)
— Subprograms (recursive and non-recursive)
— Expressions
— Evaluation of subprogram and entry parameters
— Blocks

Each of these is discussed below.

2.1   Data Structures

Data structures include:

— single dimensional arrays,
— multi-dimensional arrays,
— record types (including private types, and private extensions as well as the explicit parallelization of any primitive operations on the type), and
— containers.

Obvious areas for parallelization of data structures are initialization and copying large structures, but also operations that can operate by-element or by-slice if the structure of the type and of the operation can be partitioned for parallel execution.

The new proposal for parallelism notations within data types is discussed in section 3. We do not have a proposal for tagged types at this time. The issues involved in the overriding of parallel subprograms with non-parallel overridden subprograms (or vice-versa) need further discussion.

2.2   Parallel for Loops

The basic syntax for a parallel for loop is given by [1]:

```
for I in 1 .. N
   with Parallel => True
loop
   --...
end loop;
```

Because the cost of scheduling a worker for parallel execution or of setting up the data to be processed by that worker may be many times the cost of the operation itself, syntax may be needed to guide the implementation in the number and mapping of tasklets for the loop. For example, by-element addition on a loop over a set of integers could be broken into N tasklets, where N is the number of cores or 1/10, 1/100 or 1/1000 of the set size.

Our proposal includes [6] an aspect `Chunk_Size` that lets the programmer provide a fixed chunk size or guides the compiler in choosing one. Note that if fine control is not needed, the aspect may be left unspecified in which case the compiler can typically choose a reasonable chunking value by using an algorithmic approach. The proposal also includes an aspect `Work_Plan` that lets the programmer select the approach to use on management of load balancing. This can be either by selecting an object provided by the library, or even, if supported, selecting an option provided by the compiler. Other aspects are also presented in section 3.

2.3 Parallel for Loops over Containers

Iteration over containers using a `for loop` can also be made in parallel in several cases, as for example, in a search or reduction. This mechanism can be supported in two complementary, non exclusive approaches.

The first approach is to provide a new interface `Ada.Parallel.Iterator_Interfaces`, extending `Ada.Iterator_Interfaces`, that provides new iterator types supporting parallel iteration (e.g. providing a set of iterators to different parts of the container). The `First` and `Next` operations of these iterators would guarantee non-overlapping processing.

A different, complementary, solution involves the compiler transforming the code and iterating through the container spawning parallelism as needed. This would force at least one sequential iteration to determine the start elements of the parallel execution, but it would allow applying parallelism to existing containers. Both approaches can coexist, with the compiler using the latter if the container does not provide support for parallel iterators.

2.4 Subprograms

For the case of subprograms, we propose the ability to specify the execution of a subprogram in parallel with subsequent code in the enclosing block or scope where the subprogram is called.

This work extends our earlier papers in that the semantics for parallel subprogram calls in standalone statements also applies to parallel blocks (when we discuss them in section 3) and complex expressions: the aspect *Parallel* on the subprogram specification means that each call to the subprogram will be executed by a new tasklet, thus may execute in parallel with the following statement(s) (if in a standalone statement such as a procedure call) or with the following subexpression(s) (if used in a complex expression).

When a subprogram or a block executes in parallel with following statements, the synchronization point for the parallel computations is the earlier of:

— either the end of the enclosing scope, or
— the first point where an object updated by the parallel call or block is read or written by the following statements.

For parallel subprogram calls or parallel blocks, the enclosing scope is the end of the containing block or subprogram. While compilers can usually work out where such dependencies exist, human intervention is also possible by nesting scopes with the use of blocks to force such synchronization.

Note that, for recursive subprograms that are called recursively two or more times at each level, the definition of the parallel model means that the earlier invocations of the recursive call execute in parallel with later invocations. For example

```
function Fib( Left : Natural)
   return Natural with Parallel is
begin
   return              -- Expression is the enclosing scope
      Fib(Left-1)  -- Tasklet spawned to execute parallel
                       -- with following sub-expressions
      +                -- consumes results, so sync
                       -- happens before "+"
      Fib(Left-2);-- Nothing left for parallel execution
                       -- in the expression hence no spawning
end Fib;
```

Parallel recursive functions are thus a simple extension of parallel subprograms.

Placing **with** Parallel => False on a subprogram specification guarantees that all calls to the subprogram will be executed by the tasklet that executes the enclosing scope of the call. It does not, however, prevent parallelism from being initiated within the body of the subprogram itself (for example, a subprogram may contain a data type that has a **with** Parallel on it). It also does not prevent parallelization at levels above the immediately enclosing scope of a call to the subprogram. Also, other subprograms in the same enclosing scope may be executing in parallel with that scope, and hence with the subprogram under consideration.

2.5 Expressions

We consider that complex expressions should be parallelizable, if the parallel execution can be made safely, and/or efficiently.

Our previous work allowed for programmers to introduce aspects within expressions in order to control the actual spawning of parallelism, however, we now consider that this is a very complex, error prone, and "inelegant" mechanism, which should not be used. Instead, we now propose that expressions are parallelized by the compiler using the knowledge on parallel operations on data types and function calls, which is given by programmers through the aspects in the specification of the types and functions. This is later described in subsection 3.1.

2.6 Subprogram and Entry Parameters

Where one or more parallel functions serves as a parameter to a subprogram or entry call X, the synchronization of the function parameters must be before invoking the call on the subprogram or entry X (the invocation of X consumes its parameters, which are the return values of the parallel functions, hence synchronization of the parallel functions is required).

Since the order of evaluation of parameters is not defined, the programmer cannot rely upon order of execution to determine parallel/sequential behaviours. When one cares about the order and potential parallelization, programmers need to evaluate the functions in statements before the subprogram call.

2.7   Blocks

In the proposal of [1], we had dismissed adding parallelism notation to blocks, since we considered that the syntax required to make them effective would be similar to declaration of "anonymous" subprograms (controlling the modes and scope of variables through notations similar to in and out parameters), so we decided to propose that programmers specify parallel subprograms in these cases.

However, further work demonstrated that the use of blocks allows for an easy structuring of parallel regions of code, particularly if synchronization is required between the parallel executions. A concept similar to these blocks is the task construct of OpenMP [9]. The new proposal for parallelism notations in blocks is provided in section 4.

3   Data Parallelism and Expressions

One of the areas where Ada excels is in the use of type declarations together with primitive operations on the type to create classes of objects (in the pure sense of the term, as well as the object-oriented sense). It is thus important to also provide capabilities for the programmer to annotate data types which can be processed in parallel.

In this proposal, an (optional) Parallel aspect can be added to data types to inform the compiler that some of its primitive operations can be parallelized. In addition, two new aspects are introduced; Parallel_By_Element, and Parallel_By_Component. Parallel_By_Element applies to arrays and Parallel_By_Component applies to composite types. These aspects can be added to the data type operations to specify how the operation on the data type is to be performed based on the composition of its individual elements [2]. Note that these operations could be built based on specifying parallelism within them by coding new subprograms. However, for simple operations the extra syntax involved in such explicit parallel statements becomes cumbersome. The following example describes notations for a simple parallel array:

```
type Par_Arr is array (1..100) of Some_Type
   with Parallel => true;

function "+"(Left, Right: Par_Arr) return Par_Arr
   with Parallel_By_Element => "+";
   -- the full specification of the individual by element
   -- "+" operation is known to the compiler so it is
   -- only the operation name that is required
```

---

[2]   The compiler is free to optimize and use SIMD hardware when available (as it already can), and this is outside of the aspects we are specifying.

With this notation, the compiler knows that in expressions the sum of two parallel arrays (or array slices) can be performed by composing parallel execution of Some_Type sums. Note that the compiler may generate the code to perform 100 parallel individual sums, or aggregate in some chunk size (e.g. creating 10 tasklets each one performing 10 sums). Continuing with the spirit that the programmer for some specific reason may want to have a finer control of this chunking, a Chunk_Size aspect is allowed in the Parallel_By_Element notation:

```
function "+"(Left, Right: Par_Arr) return Par_Arr
   with Parallel_By_Element => "+",
        Chunk_Size          => 10;
```

Note that some operations cannot be performed by element, but in this case, the capabilities provided for primitive functions and *for loops* can be used instead. For instance, the dot product of two Par_Arr variables can be specified as:

```
function "*"(Left, Right: Par_Arr) return Some_Type is
   Result: Some_Type := Identity_Value;
begin
   for I in 1 .. 100
      with Parallel => True, Accumulator => Result
   loop
      Result := Result + Left(I) * Right(I);
   end loop;
   return Result;
end "*";
```

Or, if reduction and/or identity is also needed, then reduction aspects may also be specified [3]:

---

[3] Note the extension to [1] as we have identified the need to group the accumulator with the reducing operation and identity value, for the case where the same loop may be determining multiple results simultaneously. The following example illustrates determining the sum and the product of a range within the same loop:

```
   S: Integer := 0;
   P: Integer := 1;
begin
   for I in 1 .. 100
      with Parallel => True,
           Accumulator =>(S, Reduction =>"+", Identity =>0),
           Accumulator =>(P, Reduction =>"*", Identity =>1)
   loop
           S := S + I;
           P := P * I;
   end loop;
   -- ...
end;
```

```ada
function "*"(Left, Right: Par_Arr) return Some_Type is
   Result: Some_Type := Identity_Value;
begin
   for I in 1 .. 100
       with Parallel => True,
            Accumulator => (Result,
                            Reduction => "+",
                            Identity => Identity_Value)
   loop
      Result := Result + Left(I) * Right(I);
   end loop;
   return Result;
end "*";
```

Multi-dimensional arrays can be treated the same way:

```ada
type Par_MArr is array (1..100,1..10) of Some_Type
   with Parallel => true;

function "+"(Left, Right: Par_MArr) return Par_Marr
   with Parallel_By_Element =>   "+";
```

However, in this case programmers may wish to perform operations within a single dimension, therefore the "+" operation could then be written instead as:

```ada
function "+"(Left, Right: Par_MArr) return Par_MArr is
   Result: Par_Marr;
begin
   for I in 1 .. 100
      with Parallel => True, Chunk_Size => 10
   loop
      for J in 1 .. 10
         with Parallel => False -- forces sequential
      loop
          Par_Marr (I,J) := Left (I,J) + Right (I,J);
      end loop;
   end loop;
   return Result;
end "+";
```

We can, nevertheless, take the concept further, and create aspects for by-dimension operations. This is a topic for further investigation.

For composite types, the model would be the same; however, `Parallel_By_Component` would be used instead (operations may be different in each component) [4]:

```
type Par_Rec is record
   with Parallel => True
   A: Some_Type_A;
   B: Some_Type_B;
end record;
function "+"(Left, Right: Par_Rec) return Par_Rec
   with Parallel_By_Component => (A => "+",
                                  B => Some_Op);
```

It should also be possible to parallelize the assignment of variables of a parallel data type. In the following code excerpt, the compiler can perform the assignment to the individual components of Z "in place" within the parallel addition of the same components of X and Y:

```
   X, Y, Z: Par_Rec;
begin
   Z := X + Y;
   -- ...
```

Using these basic mechanisms, it is also possible to create libraries of parallelizable containers. Note that recursive structures and any general container may in cases be only amenable to parallelization through the development of parallel-aware and context-aware operations (in the sense that two inserts need to know if they are operating on the same structure or the container is built in a way that they can be concurrent). In some cases, it may be safe to process some existing container types in parallel (e.g. searching in a vector). The basic mechanism provided here, together with the possibility of parallel iterators, can be used to build such containers.

3.1   Parallelism within Expressions

By specifying potentially parallel operations and potentially parallel spawning of subprogram calls, expressions can now be performed in parallel. Consideration needs to be given to ensure that ordering and safety are preserved.

When a data object or operation on such an object (such as "+") is part of an expression and that operation is a data-parallel operation, then potentially many tasklets may be used to perform the execution. When an expression contains calls to

---

[4] Visibility rules would likely prevent the use of `Parallel_By_Component` aspect in the public part of a package declaration for a data type which is private to the package (the aspect requires access to the individual components of the record). Statements of parallelism declared only in the private part, would hide potential parallelism from users of the type; this is the same as the implementer of the primitive operations of the type specifying parallelism internally to the operation, in the hidden body of the package. To address this, partial parallel notations could be added to the public part, and later completed in the private part.

potentially parallel functions connected by operators, then the execution of a subprogram can execute in parallel with other parts of the expression on the proviso that each operator cannot execute until functions that satisfy its parameters have synchronized (as specified in the synchronization rules of section 2). The Ada rule on precedence and left-to-right evaluation of operators within precedence must be preserved. The compiler is nevertheless permitted to order the evaluation of expressions to optimize the opportunities for parallelism.

However, programmers may want to apply different parallel execution criteria to individual function calls in an expression. In this case, the programmer can create parallel and sequential variants of the same subprogram to use to control the use of parallelism. For example, for function Foo, we can specify a Parallel => False aspect, thus preventing a call to Foo to spawn a tasklet:

```
function Foo( Left, Right : Some Type)return Some_Type
   with Parallel => False;
```

and provide a variant which would allowing the spawn of a tasklet:

```
function Foo_Par(Left, Right: Some Type) return Some_Type
   with Parallel => True is (Foo(Left, Right));
```

or

```
function Foo_Par(Left, Right: Some Type) return Some_Type
   with Parallel => True renames Foo(Left, Right);
```

Then we could write

```
Y := Foo_Par(X,Z) + (Foo(G,F) + Some_Other_Func);
```

to ensure that the first part is executed in a separate tasklet but the last Foo is not. Note that if Some_Other_Func was not there, then the call to Foo would not be in a separate tasklet anyway, because of the rules presented in section 2.

4   Parallel Blocks as a Building Block for Easier Parallelism Specification

A block that is declared parallel (using the **with** Parallel aspect notation) executes in parallel with the statements immediately following the block end statement. A synchronization point for the parallel block and subsequent statements is the end of the immediately enclosing scope.

```
begin -- this is the main task
   declare with Parallel => True
      -- types and variables here
      Foo: ... := Outer_foo;
      Result: ...;
```

```
begin
   Some_Code;
   -- Here whatever is inside is executed by one
   -- tasklet (or more if nested parallelism)
   -- but can execute in parallel with other code in
   -- the enclosing scope.
   -- Should only be used when there is no risk that
   -- the data elements being read or written require
   -- co-ordination with code outside the block.
   -- The programmer is hinting the compiler that
   -- this is safe.
   end; -- end of parallel region
   Some_other_code; -- executed in parallel with the
                    --  block above
end;  -- end of enclosing scope: join of parallel
      -- execution
```

The **with** Parallel notation could be applied to the begin construct, in case a declare region was not required:

```
begin -- this is the main task
   begin with Parallel => true
      Some_Code;
   end; -- end of parallel region
   Some_other_code; -- in parallel with the block above
end; -- end of enclosing scope: join of execution
```

Similar to the implicit synchronization of the return results of functions, it is possible that an implicit join is forced when, in the enclosing scope, the programmer reads a variable being updated by a block in an inner scope. This is as if a variable is treated as a future [10]:

```
   Result: Integer;
begin -- Main Task
   Code; -- Sequential
   declare with Parallel -- the parallel block
   begin
      Result := Foo + Bar;
   end;
   Other_Work; -- done in parallel with the
               -- block just above
   Put_Line ("Result = " &
             Integer'Image (Result)); -- Implicit
                                      -- join here before
                                      -- Result is read
end;
```

We can view the futures analysis as simply the compiler introducing further implicit blocks. It would be as if the above code could get transformed by the compiler into an intermediate step which resembles:

```
Result: Integer;
begin -- Main Task
   Code; -- Sequential
   begin -- implicit block for synchronization
      begin with Parallel -- the parallel block
         Result := Foo + Bar;
      end;
      Other_Work; -- done in parallel with the block
   end; -- for the join
   -- sequential again
   Put_Line ("Result = " & Integer'Image (Result));
end;
```

Note also that `Other_Work` can be also seen as another implicit block. So the final transformation of the above code to the implementation level could look like the following (compiles currently in Paraffin [11]):

```
with Ada.Parallel.Blocks; use Ada;
declare
   Result: Integer;
   Manager : Parallel.Blocks.Parallel_Manager;
   procedure Block1 is
   begin
      Result := Foo + Bar;
   end Block1;
   procedure Block2 is
   begin
      Other_Work;
   end Block2;

begin
   Manager.Execute_Parallel_Blocks (A => Block1'Access,
                                    B => Block2'Access);
   -- Synchronization occurs before returning from
   -- Execute_Parallel_Blocks
   Put_Line ("Result = " & Integer'Image (Result));
end;
```

A final note for the use of parallel constructs inside the declarative region of a block (or subprogram): it is our proposal that the scope of parallelism execution can include both the declaration and the body of the block/subprogram, if the compiler is able to determine that the semantics are the same as if elaboration of the declarative region was complete before the `begin` statement.

5   Open Issues

The current proposal outlines to the semantic model of parallelism opportunities, tasklets and "syntactic sugar". However, several issues are still open.

One important question is whether implicit joins generated by the compiler for parallel variable updates should be allowed. In section 4 we described how a model similar to futures could be used to allow for a parallel block to update a variable being read in the enclosing scope. In this model the compiler would either detect the potential race condition and insert an implicit synchronization point, or would insert the required check at runtime. An alternative which we are considering is to forbid such race condition, which is a safer although less flexible approach. In this case, the compiler would reject any code where a potential race condition occurs (following the rules for concurrent access to objects as specified in the Language Reference Manual [12, section 9.10]), only allowing it if objects are guarantee to be independently addressable. If not detectable at compile-time it could be detectable at run-time.

Another issue is the underlying runtime. A runtime model based on execution of tasklets on top of Ada tasks has been presented in [6], but this model is not complete as it is currently silent about the issue of synchronization and communication between tasklets. It is clear that this is required either because multiple tasklets may be accessing the same variable (e.g. an accumulator) or needing to execute in phases (e.g. to solve a matrix using Gauss Jordan Elimination [13]). One approach is to let tasklets communicate via protected operations, however, the use of protected objects and barriers is only possible if tasklets are executed by full-fledged Ada tasks, and in some cases (e.g. barriers and entries) only if the mapping between tasklets and tasks is 1-to-1. Allowing the programmer to explicitly use those constructs in potentially parallel code would require forcing this underlying model.

We note that simple tasklet communication and synchronization mechanisms can be provided as a standard library interface that the runtime implementer can provide based on protected objects and barriers if the implementation is task based, or some other form (atomics, signals, etc.) if otherwise. This would also allow for a shared parallel runtime between language domains. On the other hand, executing Ada code not as part of an Ada task is currently outside the semantic model of Ada, and presents problems of its own, including the additional complexity of having to define synchronization primitives that are similar to primitives already in the language.

A second issue is that some modern many-core architectures can be seen as truly distributed systems [14]. The model proposed here can be extended so that tasklets can execute in different partitions, however analysis is needed to determine if a different distribution execution model is required.

Finally, by introducing parallel notations, the cases where the code may be updating the same variable simultaneously increases. Although compilers can detect many cases of unsafe behavior, it is not guaranteed (as it is not today with tasking) that these situations are detectable. Introducing real *pure* subprograms in Ada, without side effects, could potentially make for much safer parallelism.

6   Conclusion

This paper provides the current status of a proposal to augment Ada with support for parallelism notations, based on a semantic model of a *tasklet*, a logic unit of parallelism. The work expanded the places where tasklets can be used to execute code in parallel, both for data types and blocks. The extension to data type specifications and primitive operations will significantly extend the abstraction and reduce placing parallel aspects in package and subprogram bodies. The parallelism notation in data types as well as blocks, together with a new form of specifying when subprogram calls generate new tasklets, also allowed simplifying the proposal, removing the need for controlling tasklet spawning within expressions and parameters.

Acknowledgements. The authors would like to thank Tucker Taft and the anonymous reviewers for the valuable comments and suggestions that helped improve the manuscript. This work was partially supported by Portuguese National Funds through FCT (Portuguese Foundation for Science and Technology) and by ERDF (European Regional Development Fund) through COMPETE (Operational Programme 'Thematic Factors of Competitiveness'), within project FCOMP-01-0124-FEDER-037281 (CISTER); by FCT and EU ARTEMIS JU, within project ARTEMIS/0003/2012, JU grant nr. 333053 (CONCERTO), and European Union Seventh Framework Programme (FP7/2007-2013) under grant agreement n° 611016 (P-SOCRATES).

References

[1] Michell, S., Moore, B., Pinho, L.M.: Tasklettes – A Fine Grained Parallelism for Ada on Multicores. In: Keller, H.B., Plödereder, E., Dencker, P., Klenk, H. (eds.) Ada-Europe 2013. LNCS, vol. 7896, pp. 17–34. Springer, Heidelberg (2013)

[2] Frigo, M., Leiserson, C.E., Randall, K.H.: The implementation of the Cilk-5 multithreaded language. SIGPLAN Not. 33, 212–223 (1998)

[3] Marowka, A.: Parallel computing on any desktop. Communications of the ACM 50, 74–78 (2007)

[4] Halpern, P.: Strict Fork-Join Parallelism, JTC1/SC22/WG21 N3409 (September 2012)

[5] CPLEX, C Parallel Language EXtensions study group, archives at http://www.open-std.org/mailman/listinfo/cplex

[6] Moore, B., Michell, S., Pinho, L.M.: Parallelism in Ada: General Model and Ravenscar. In: 16th International Real-Time Ada Workshop, York, UK (April 2013)

[7] The Multicore Association, Multicore Programming Practices Guide, http://www.multicore-association.org/

[8] Michell, S., Moore, B., Pinho, L.M.: Real-Time Programming on Accelerator Many-Core Processors. In: Proceedings of the High-Integrity Language Technologies Conference, HILT 2013 (November 2013)

[9] OpenMP Architecture Review Board, OpenMP Application Program Interface, Version 4.0 (July 2013)

[10] Ali, H., Pinho, L.M.: A parallel programming model for Ada. In: Proceedings of the ACM SIGAda Annual Conference, SIGAda 2011 (November 2011)
[11] Moore, B.: Paraffin libraries, http://sourceforge.net/projects/paraffin/
[12] ISO/IEC, Ada Reference Manual, ISO/IEC 8652:2012(E) (2012)
[13] Squire, J.: Parallel implementation of the gauss-jordan elimination using maximum element for pivot (October 2008),
http://www.csee.umbc.edu/~squire/download/psimeq.adb
[14] Pinho, L.M., Michell, S., Moore, B.: Ada and Many-core Platforms. In: 16th International Real-Time Ada Workshop, York, UK (April 2013)

Deadline-Aware Programming and Scheduling

Alan Burns and Andy Wellings

Department of Computer Science,
University of York, UK
{alan.burns,andy.wellings}@york.ac.uk

Abstract. Deadlines are the most important events in real-time systems. Real-time programs must therefore be aware of deadlines, and be able to identify and react to missed deadlines. Moreover, Earliest Deadline First (EDF) is the most widely studied optimal dynamic scheduling algorithm for uniprocessor real-time systems. In this paper we explore how a resource sharing protocol (called the DFP – Deadline Floor inheritance Protocol), which has been proposed for languages such as Ada, can be incorporated into the language's definition. We also address the programming of systems that have mixed scheduling (e.g. fixed priority and EDF). The incorporation of the DFP into Ada requires some changes to the current predefined packages. These changes are also of use in supporting the programming of deadline-aware systems even when not scheduling by EDF.

1 Introduction

The correctness of an embedded real-time system depends not only on the system's outputs but also on the time at which these outputs are produced. The completion of a request after its timing deadline is considered to be of degraded (potentially no) value, and could even lead to a failure of the whole system. Therefore, the most important characteristic of real-time systems is that they have strict timing requirements that must be guaranteed and satisfied. Schedulability analysis plays a crucial role in enabling these guarantees to be provided.

The *Earliest Deadline First* (EDF) algorithm is one of the most widely studied dynamic priority scheduling policies for real-time systems. It has been proved [18] to be optimal among all scheduling algorithms for a uniprocessor; in the sense that if a real-time task set cannot be scheduled by EDF, then it cannot be scheduled by any other algorithm.

The Ada 2005 standard [20] introduced EDF as one of the supported dispatching policies and the *Stack Resource Policy* (SRP) was specified as the protocol for resource sharing among EDF tasks [11]. SRP is a complex protocol, as has been shown by the initial difficulties with its specification and implementation (see Section 3). Recently, a new protocol for resource sharing in EDF has been proposed [7,9]. This new protocol, called the *Deadline Floor inheritance Protocol* (DFP), is simpler to understand and more efficient to implement (while keeping all the useful properties of SRP). At the 16th International Real-Time Ada Workshop, the recommendation was agreed [22] that SRP should be deprecated and be replaced by the DFP for single processor systems. In this paper we further explore the motivation for this change, and consider in more detail the impact on the language's definition.

L. George and T. Vardanega (Eds.): Ada-Europe 2014, LNCS 8454, pp. 107–118, 2014.
© Springer International Publishing Switzerland 2014

We review, in section 3, the current provision of Ada in its support for EDF and SRP. The new protocol is described in Section 4, and the changes needed to incorporate this definition into the language are outlined in Section 5. Coverage of systems that have both fixed priority and EDF scheduling is given in Section 6. In Section 7 the impact of the proposed changes are considered in the context of Ada's approach to programming real-time abstractions. Then, in Section 8 we briefly consider the implications of multiprocessor systems on the protocol. Conclusions are contained in Section 9. First, however, we give a short definition of a system model.

2   System Model

Although not restricting ourselves to the Ravenscar profile [8], the system model assumed in this paper has many similarities to that profile. A system is assumed to consist of N tasks; all of which are defined to have a period (denoted by the symbol T) that is their minimum inter-arrival time, a relative deadline (D) and a worst-case execution time (C). All tasks are executed on a single processor (or are statically partitioned onto a set of processors). For system correctness, any task τ_i arriving at time t must be able to execute for its maximum computation time (C_i) by its deadline which is at time $t + D_i$.

With fixed priority scheduling, each task is assigned a priority (P), and all protected objects are assigned ceiling priorities and a priority ceiling protocol (PCP) [19] is implemented. The form of PCP usually applied is the 'immediate' version (IPCP) in which a task's priority is raised to the resources's ceiling at the point the resource is accessed. For optimal schedulability, a task's priorities is derived from its relative deadline. Two tasks with relative deadlines D_i and D_j, with $D_i < D_j$ will have priorities with the constraint $P_i > P_j$.

The term 'deadline' can be overloaded in scheduling papers. Here we explicitly use *relative* deadline when concerned with the task's D parameter. The use of *deadline* on its own refers to the absolute deadline of the current invocation of the task. It could be argued that Ada fails to fully support deadline-aware programming as relative deadlines for tasks cannot currently be directly represented in the program's code using language defined types and subprograms.

3   Earliest Deadline First Dispatching and SRP in Ada

Baker [3,2] proposed the Stack Resource Policy (SRP) for bounding priority inversion when accessing resources in real-time systems scheduled under EDF. SRP is a generalisation of IPCP.

With SRP, each task is assigned a number called the *preemption level* that correlates inversely to its relative deadline: the shorter the relative deadline the higher the preemption level. Shared resources are also assigned a preemption level that is the highest of the preemption levels of all the tasks that may use that resource. The use of SRP imposes a new rule to basic EDF scheduling: *a task can only be chosen for execution if its preemption level is strictly higher than the preemption levels of the resources currently locked in the system.* The basic rule is, of course, *a task can only be chosen for execution if it has the earliest deadline.*

The most complex part of the EDF dispatching definition in Ada is the integration of the base Ada dispatching model (based on fixed priorities for the tasks and priority ceilings for the protected objects) with the SRP rules and the *preemption level* concept. EDF is defined to work in a given band of priority levels, which may cover the whole range of system priorities, or a specific sub-interval of these priorities. The Ada Reference Manual (ARM) defines a means of integrating preemption levels and priorities: preemption levels of tasks and protected objects are mapped to priorities in the EDF priority band.

The ARM defines that, by default, the active priority of an EDF task is the lowest priority in its EDF priority band. The task will inherit priorities as any other Ada task; in particular, when an EDF task executes a protected operation it will inherit the priority (preemption level) of the protected object. But, for EDF tasks, the ARM defines a further source of priority inheritance (for arbitrary task T): *the highest priority P, if any, less than the base priority of T such that one or more tasks are executing within a protected object with ceiling priority P and task T has an earlier deadline than all such tasks; and furthermore T has an earlier deadline than all other tasks on ready queues with priorities in the given EDF_Across_Priorities range that are strictly less than P.*

This rule has proved difficult to specify correctly (the original definition was shown to be incorrect [24]) and to implement correctly [15] or efficiently [1].

There is one further drawback that is specific to the Ada definition of SRP: the limited number of distinct preemption levels. The number of distinct preemption levels that can be used for tasks in an EDF priority range is the size of the range minus one. In a system with few priority levels or in a narrow EDF range this limitation could jeopardize the schedulability of the system by causing more blocking than is necessary. It could be argued that the implementation should provide more priority levels, but priority levels are expensive because they affect the size and performance of many of the run-time data structures such as the delay queues, ready queues and the entry queues.

4   The Deadline Floor Protocol

Recently, Burns introduced a new protocol for resource sharing in EDF, called the Deadline Floor inheritance Protocol (DFP) [7]. The DFP has all the key properties of SRP; specifically, causing at most a single blocking effect from any task with a longer relative deadline, which leads to the same worst-case blocking in both protocols. In an EDF-scheduled system, the DFP is structurally equivalent to IPCP in a system scheduled under fixed priorities.

Under the DFP, every resource has a relative deadline equal to the shortest relative deadline of any task that uses it. The relative deadline of a resource is called *deadline floor*, making clear the symmetry with the *priority ceiling* defined for the resources in any PCP.

The key idea of the DFP is that the absolute deadline of a task could be temporarily shortened while accessing a resource. Given a task with absolute deadline d that accesses a resource with deadline floor D^F at time t, the absolute deadline of the task is (potentially) reduced according to $d := min(d, t + D^F)$ while holding the resource.

To give a concrete example, assume two tasks (A and B) with relative deadlines of 20 and 30 share a resource. The deadline floor of the resource is therefore 20. Assume task B is released at time 100: its absolute deadline is therefore 130. At time 103 it accesses the resource: its absolute deadline is therefore reduced to 123. While B holds the resource, task A is released at time 105: its absolute deadline is 125, this is not sufficient to preempt B (as $125 > 123$). If B exits the resource at time 107, its absolute deadline will change from 123 to 130; as a result A will preempt as it now has the earlier deadline (i.e. $125 < 130$).

The action of the protocol results in a single block per task, deadlock free execution and works for nested resource usage. Whilst a task accesses a resource its deadline is reduced so that no newly released task can preempt it and then access the resource. See [7] for details and proof of the key properties. This is equivalent to the use of a priority ceiling; again the only tasks that can preempt a task executing within a protected object are tasks that are guaranteed not to use that object (unless there is a program error, which can be caught at run-time).

The DFP does not add any new rule to the EDF scheduling, thus it leads to simpler and more efficient implementation than the SRP [1].

5   Required Language Simplifications and Modifications

To embed the rules for the DFP within Ada, the following issues must be addressed:

- All tasks must have a relative deadline assigned via an aspect/pragma or a routine defined in a library package.
- Protected objects must have also a relative deadline (floor) assigned via an aspect/pragma.
- Default relative deadline values must be defined for tasks and protected objects (and their types).
- Rules for EDF scheduling must be extended to include a new locking policy: `Floor_Locking`.
- Rules for EDF scheduling need simplifying to remove the 'across priorities' feature of the current definition.
- For completeness (and parity with priority ceilings) means of modifying the relative deadline attribute of tasks and protected objects should be defined.

First, however, some changes to library packages are needed to make the notion of deadline (relative and absolute) first class within the tasking model. Currently, relevant definitions are coupled to the specification of EDF scheduling. Whilst deadlines are key to EDF scheduling, they have a wider purpose; deadlines are relevant to all forms of real-time scheduling. Moreover, programs that wish to catch and respond to missed deadlines need to be able to manipulate deadlines directly.

5.1   Changes to Existing Library Packages

The 2005 version of Ada introduced EDF scheduling and the subtype `Deadline`. Unfortunately, we feel, it only introduced this, as we noted above, for the support of EDF scheduling. We feel that *deadline* and *relative deadline* are fundamental concepts in real-time and deadline-aware programming. We therefore propose that the whole package `Ada.Dispatching.EDF` be renamed, repositioned and extended to support relative as well as absolute deadlines. The new package could be as follows.

```
with Ada.Real_Time;
with Ada.Task_Identification;
use Ada;
package Ada.Deadlines is
  subtype Deadline is Real_Time.Time;
  subtype Relative_Deadline is Real_Time.Time_Span;
  Default_Deadline : constant Deadline :=
            Real_Time.Time_Last;
  Default_Relative_Deadline : constant Relative_Deadline :=
            Real_Time.Time_Span_Last;
  procedure Set_Deadline(D : in Deadline;
            T : in Task_Identification.Task_ID :=
            Task_Identification.Current_Task);
  function Get_Deadline(T : in Task_Identification.Task_ID :=
            Task_Identification.Current_Task) return Deadline;
  procedure Set_Relative_Deadline(R : in Relative_Deadline;
            T : in Task_Identification.Task_ID :=
            Task_Identification.Current_Task);
  function Get_Relative_Deadline(T : in Task_Identification.Task_ID :=
                                 Task_Identification.Current_Task)
                                 return Relative_Deadline;
  procedure Delay_Until_And_Set_Deadline(
            Delay_Until_Time : in Real_Time.Time;
            TS : in Real_Time.Time_Span :=
            Get_Relative_Deadline);
end Ada.Deadlines;
```

Key changes are:

- Change of name and library position.
- Introduction of a type for relative deadline and a default value.
- Set and Get routines added for relative deadlines.
- A default relative deadline provided for `Delay_Until_And_Set_Deadline`.

All tasks will have a deadline and a relative deadline; default values being used if the program does not specify specific values. As with priority, where a task has a base and an active priority, a task will also have a base (absolute) deadline and an active (absolute) deadline – see definition of the locking policy below. A call of `Get_Deadline` returns the base deadline of the task.

The existing aspect/pragma `Relative_Deadline` should be redefined to take an expression of type `Relative_Deadline`. Note, although the same name is used here, this is the same situation with subtype `Priority` and aspect/pragms `Priority`. However, the definition of the aspect `Relative_Deadline` should really be moved from D.2.6. We suggest that it be placed, with the above package, in a new section D.8.1. perhaps entitled *Deadline-Aware Programming*.

5.2 New Locking Policy

Initially, when EDF was added to Ada, the existing locking policy `Ceiling_Locking` was modified so that is accounted for EDF dispatching, FP (fixed priority) dispatching and combined EDF and FP dispatching. Although there are some clear advantages in having only a single protocol, it is now considered to have been a mistake [22], due to the complex rules required. Here we propose a new locking policy `Floor_Locking`. We will not attempt to give here a full definition sufficient for the ARM, but the following points define the semantics for this new policy.

- Whenever a task is executing outside a protected action, its active deadline is equal to its base deadline.
- When a task executes a protected action its active deadline will be reduced to (if it is currently greater than) 'now' plus the deadline floor of the corresponding protected object.
- When a task completes a protected action its active deadline returns to the value it had on entry.
- When a task calls a protected operation, a check is made that there is no task currently executing within the corresponding protected object; `Program_Error` is raised if this check fails.

A protected object is given an initial deadline floor value using the `Relative_Dead-line` aspect/pragma. Dynamic deadline floors could be defined in a similar way to dynamic ceiling priorities (see Section D.5.2 of the ARM). We do not consider this here.

With this definition of a new locking policy, the definition of `Ceiling_Locking` can return to its pre-2005 wording.

Note the semantics requires a check on non-concurrent access to the protected object. It is not sufficient to check that the relative deadline of the task is not less than the deadline floor of the object. This points to a difference with `Ceiling_Locking` where a comparison based on priorities is sufficient. To implement the check on inappropriate usage over the corresponding protected object requires only a simple 'occupied' flag to be checked and modified. Usefully, if there is an attempt to gain access to an occupied protected object then the task 'at fault' is forced, on a single processor, to be the second task that is attempting to gain access, and it will therefore be this task that has the exception raised. The correct task will be unaffected.

Interestingly, a simple check on non-concurrent access would also be sufficient for the priority ceiling case. And again the exception is bound to be raised in the task 'at fault'. Of course, checking concurrent access, rather than correct priority/ceiling values will only catch an actual error rather than a potential one. Inappropriate ceiling values will be caught on first usage, inappropriate concurrent access may be very difficult to create during testing. Although not a sufficient test, it might be advisable to also include in the definition of `Floor_Locking` a static check on the relative deadlines of user tasks and the deadline floors of the used protected objects.

To ensure that locking protocols work correctly, the programmer must give the correct values for deadline floors and ceiling priorities. A run-time check prevents concurrent access, but a compiler-based check cannot be undertaken and hence the use of the correct values can only be asserted by code inspection or static analysis.

5.3 New Dispatching Policy

Currently EDF dispatching is supported via the policy `EDF_Across_Priorities`. A range of priorities is needed to account for the different priority ceilings needed for the protected objects. The tasks themselves only execute at the base priority of this range when they are not executing within a protected action. All ready queues are ordered by the (absolute) deadline of the ready tasks.

To prevent confusion, and to emphasis the fact that with the new protocol only a single priority is needed for all EDF dispatched tasks (regardless of the number of protected objects they use), we propose a new dispatching policy. And to accommodate hierarchical dispatching (see Section 6) we define the new policy as `EDF_Within_Priorities`. Again we will not attempt to give a full definition appropriate for the ARM[1].

With `EDF_Within_Priorities`, all tasks with the same priority compete for the processor using the rules for EDF dispatching. The ready queue is ordered by *active* deadline. A collection of EDF dispatched tasks and the set of protected objects they use/share will all have the same priority (and ceiling priority). But they will have different relative deadlines (and deadline floors).

A task that has not been given an explicit deadline or relative deadline will get the default values of `Default_Deadline` (equal to : `Real_Time.Time_Last`) and `Default_Relative_Deadline` (equal to `Real_Time.Time_Span_Last`). The default value for the deadline floor of any protected object is 0 (actually `Time-Span_Zero`). This will have the effect of making all protected actions non-preemptive (as does the default priority ceiling).

5.4 Ravenscar-Like Profile

The facilities provided by the policies `EDF_Across_Priorities` and `Floor_Locking`, and the library package `Ada.Dispatching.EDF` allows a Ravenscar-like profile for EDF scheduling to be defined.

For periodic (time-triggered) tasks the profile would only allow a task to be delayed by the use of `Delay_Until_And_Set_Deadline` using the default parameter for relative delay (which is the task's relative delay). A task would be forced to set its relative deadline using an aspect/pragma and use the default parameter for the above delay statement. It would be unable to use the `Set_Deadline` and `Set_Relative_Deadline` routines.

For sporadic tasks, which are typically released by the action of an interrupt handler, `Set_Deadline` would need to be used, but could be restricted to be allowed only within that context.

To accomplish these restrictions is may be useful to partition `Dispatching.EDF` into the part needed for a restricted profile, and that which is available to all programs.

---

[1] For example, consideration would need to be given to whether deadline inheritance should occur during a rendezvous and task activation, and whether entry queues can be deadline ordered.

6 Hierarchical and Mixed Scheduling

One of the advantages of the new EDF_Within_Priorities policy is that it unifies Ada's use of priority as the primary dispatching policy. It is no longer necessary to reserve a range of priorities for a single EDF domain. If we ignore the non-preemptive policy, we now have a clear means of supporting mixed scheduling in a hierarchical manner:

- At all times, the task at the head of the highest priority non-empty ready queue is the one chosen to be executed.
- Each ready queue has its own discipline to determine which task is at its head.

The disciplines supported are: FIFO, Round Robin (RR) and now EDF; i.e. FIFO_Within_Priorities, Round_Robin_Within_Priorities and now EDF_Within_Priorities.

So, for example, one could have the top 16 priority levels reserved for pure FP tasks, then the next level for EDF and next (lowest) priority level for RR. At the EDF and RR levels there may be many task allocated. For the FP there many be few, perhaps only one task per priority.

If two priority levels are designated EDF then tasks from the higher priority level will always run in preference to tasks at the lower level (irrespective of deadlines). Only if the ready queue at the higher priority is empty will the task with the shortest active deadline from the lower ready queue be chosen for execution.

To allow tasks from any priority level to share their use of protected objects (POs) it is necessary to ensure the locking policies are appropriately defined. First the fundamental priority based dispatching policy must be supported by Ceiling_Locking. If two tasks of different priority use the same PO then the ceiling priority of the PO must be no lower that the highest priority of the client tasks. Within an EDF ordered priority level, the policy Floor_Locking must apply. It follows therefore that when hierarchical dispatching is used both Ceiling_Locking and Floor_Locking will need to be specified. The current definition of Ceiling_Locking must be changed to reflect this.

To further illustrate the behaviour of a mixed dispatching scheme, consider two situations on a single processor system. First, assume the highest priorities are reserved for FIFO (FP) and a single EDF ready queue is at a lower priority. Let an EDF task, τ_e execute and call a PO used by a FP task, τ_f. The following points appertain.

- The priority of τ_f is higher than τ_e.
- If τ_e is executing then τ_f must be suspended.
- When τ_e calls the PO its active priority will be set to the priority of τ_f. Its active deadline may also shorten, but this is irrelevant in this example.
- If τ_f is released, it will not execute (its base priority is not greater than the active priority of τ_e and dispatching at this priority level is FIFO).
- When τ_e leaves the PO its priority will return to its original base level, and if τ_f had been released it would now preempt.

For a second example, consider the EDF tasks at the highest priority level (P_{high}) and a set of FP tasks below. The priority ceiling of the PO will be P_{high}. If an EDF task calls the PO, its active priority will not change but its active deadline may. Now consider the lower priority FP task τ_f accessing the PO:

- Priority of τ_e is higher than τ_f.
- If τ_f is executing then τ_e must be suspended (and no other EDF task will be active).
- When τ_f calls the PO its active priority will be set above its current level to P_{high}; its active deadline will be updated according to the DFP; no further FP tasks will run.
- If τ_e is released it will not execute (its base priority is not greater than the active priority of P_{high} and, because of the DFP it cannot have an earlier absolute deadline).
- When τ_f leaves the PO, its priority will return to its original base level (its base deadline will return to its default value), and if τ_e had been released it would now preempt.

It follows from these examples that *both* Ceiling_Locking and Floor_Locking are needed, but they are not needed together. If a task calls a PO with a higher priority then the ceiling policy applies. And if an EDF dispatched task calls a PO with the same priority then the deadline floor policy applies. Note, of course, that a task cannot call a PO with a lower priority as this would break the priority ceiling protocol.

7   Impact on Real-Time Programming Abstractions

Since its inception, Ada has supported real-time systems' development. Its focus has been on a set of low-level primitive programming mechanisms and support for real-time dispatching policies. The low-level mechanisms (such as the "delay until" statement, the asynchronous select statement, timing events, protected objects etc) have allowed a wide range of real-time programming abstractions to be developed [23]. However, almost paradoxically, up until Ada 2005 the notion of absolute deadline was not explicit in the language. Even at Ada 2005, deadlines were only introduced to support EDF scheduling.

We have shown earlier, that to facilitate integration of the DFP, the notions of absolute and relative deadlines must become more general language concepts that are not confined only to EDF scheduling. Of course, this is correct as even tasks that are being scheduled FIFO within a priority level may have a deadline. Although, this has no effect on the dispatching, the program may need to undertake corrective actions if a task misses its deadline. There are many possible actions (see, for example, Chapter 13 in Burns and Wellings [12]). Below, we illustrate one task template that can be used to illustrate the impact of having deadlines more explicit in the language. The template is for a periodic task that aborts its current release if the deadline is missed, executes some handling code and then waits for its next periodic release. Note the use of the default relative deadline in the Delay_Until_And_Set_Deadline statement.

```
with Ada.Real_Time; use Ada.Real_Time;
with Ada.Deadlines; use Ada.Deadlines;
...

  task type Periodic_Task(Period_In_Milliseconds : Positive;
                          Rel_Deadline_In_Milliseconds : Positive);

  task body Periodic_Task is
    Interval : Time_Span := Milliseconds(Period_In_Milliseconds);
    Rel_Deadline : Time_Span :=
                          Milliseconds(Rel_Deadline_In_Milliseconds);
    Next_Release_Time : Time;
  begin
    Set_Relative_Deadline(Rel_Deadline);
    Next_Release_Time := Clock;
    Set_Deadline(Next_Release_Time + Rel_Deadline);
    loop
      select
        delay until Get_Deadline;
        -- handle deadline miss here
      then abort
        -- undertake the work of the task
      end select;
      Next_Release_Time := Next_Release_Time + Interval;
      Delay_Until_And_Set_Deadline(Next_Release_Time);
    end loop;
  end Periodic_Task;

...
```

Although there is not a significant difference between this and the original template, the programmer's intention is clearer.

8   Multiprocessor Considerations

Ada 2012 [21] supports the notion of a dispatching domain, which consists of one or more processors on which tasks can be globally scheduled. Each processor in the system can only exists in one dispatching domain. A task can only be allocated to a single dispatching domain. In the case where a task is allocated to a multiprocessor dispatching domain, there is an option to fix that task to only be dispatched on a single processor in that domain. Hence, Ada 2012 has the flexibility to support global, partitioned and semi-partitioned systems, as well as algorithms that fix computational intensive tasks to a single processor and schedule less computational intensive tasks globally around them [13].

Dispatching domains in conjunction with the two-level dispatching model in those domains gives the system developer a significant level of control over how tasks are allocated and scheduled in multiprocessor (and multicore) systems.

Although there has been some success in determining the necessary support for scheduling, the issue of how best to support multiprocessor lock-based resource control protocols is still far from clear. New results are emerging [16,4,5,14,6,10], but it is too soon for programming languages/operating systems to adopt a particular approach [17].

This paper has discussed the Deadline Floor Protocol in the context of single processor systems. Just like the Stack Resource Protocol, the desirable properties (mentioned in Section 4) are not maintained when protected objects can be simultaneously accessed from multiprocessors. For example, multiple blocks per task and deadlocks are possible. Furthermore, mutual exclusion is not guaranteed by the protocol itself; hence a lock is required, along with a FIFO spinning-based access mechanism. Until more optimal solutions become available, this approach, in conjunction with the default ceiling and default floor, will ensure that a protected action is implemented non-preemptively with predictable blocking times. The programmer will have to ensure that any nested accesses do not lead to deadlock.

9 Conclusions

Arguably since its inception, Ada has supported a two-level dispatching model. Initially, in Ada 83, this was preemptive priority-based scheduling at the top level, and FIFO at the low level (that is, within a priority). Progressively, over the years, the language has added support for non-preemptive priority-based scheduling (at the top level) and round-robin and EDF (within priority levels). Unfortunately, the introduction of EDF scheduling in Ada 2005 required the support of the Stack Resource Policy and its integration into the two-level scheduling scheme. This corrupted the pure two-level scheduling model and required a range of priorities to support a single EDF secondary dispatching level. Since Ada 2005, better understanding of EDF scheduling has been obtained. One result is a new resource control protocol, the DFP. The integration of this protocol into the Ada dispatching model allows a return to the pure two-level model. With this integration, Ada can support

– preemptive or non-preemptive priority-based dispatching at the top level, and
– a mixture of FIFO, RR or EDF dispatching at the secondary level.

The integration requires that deadlines become a more widely visible concept in the language's definition. This has advantages as even for priority-based systems, the need to recover from deadline misses requires deadlines to be set and manipulated. Having deadlines directly expressible in the language makes deadline-aware programming and scheduling more visible and hence more maintainable.

Acknowledgements. The authors would like to thank Marina Gutierrez, Mario Aldea and Michael González Harbour for useful discussions on the implementation of the DFP.

References

1. Aldea, M., Burns, A., Gutiérrez, M., Harbour, M.G.: Incorporating the deadline floor protocol in Ada. ACM SIGAda Ada Letters – Proc. of IRTAW 16 XXXIII(2), 49–58 (2013)
2. Baker, T.: A stack-based resource allocation policy for realtime processes. In: Proc. IEEE Real-Time Systems Symposium (RTSS), pp. 191–200 (1990)
3. Baker, T.: Stack-based scheduling of realtime processes. Journal of Real-Time Systems 3(1) (March 1991)

4. Block, A., Leontyev, H., Brandenburg, B.B., Anderson, J.H.: A flexible real-time locking protocol for multiprocessors. In: 13th International Conference on Embedded and Real-Time Computing Systems and Applications, RTCSA 2007, pp. 47–56. IEEE Computer Society (2007)
5. Brandenburg, B., Anderson, J.: Optimality results for multiprocessor real-time locking. In: Real-Time Systems Symposium (RTSS), pp. 49–60 (2010)
6. Brandenburg, B., Anderson, J.: Real-time resource sharing under cluster scheduling. In: Proc. EMSOFT. ACM Press (2011)
7. Burns, A.: A Deadline-Floor Inheritance Protocol for EDF Scheduled Real-Time Systems with Resource Sharing. Technical Report YCS-2012-476, Department of Computer Science, University of York, UK (2012)
8. Burns, A., Dobbing, B., Romanski, G.: The Ravenscar tasking profile for high integrity real-time programs. In: Asplund, L. (ed.) Ada-Europe 1998. LNCS, vol. 1411, pp. 263–275. Springer, Heidelberg (1998)
9. Burns, A., Gutiérrez, M., Aldea, M., Harbour, M.G.: A Deadline-Floor Inheritance Protocol for EDF Scheduled Embedded Real-Time Systems with Resource Sharing. IEEE Transaction on Computers (available online, 2014)
10. Burns, A., Wellings, A.: A schedulability compatible multiprocessor resource sharing protocol - MrsP. In: Proceedings of ECRTS, pp. 282–291 (2013)
11. Burns, A., Wellings, A.J., Taft, S.T.: Supporting deadlines and EDF scheduling in ada. In: Llamosí, A., Strohmeier, A. (eds.) Ada-Europe 2004. LNCS, vol. 3063, pp. 156–165. Springer, Heidelberg (2004)
12. Burns, A., Wellings, A.J.: Real-Time Systems and Programming Languages, 4th edn. Addison Wesley Longman (2009)
13. Davis, R., Burns, A.: A survey of hard real-time scheduling for multiprocessor systems. ACM Computing Surveys 43(4), 35:1 –35:44 (2011)
14. Faggioli, D., Lipari, G., Cucinotta, T.: The multiprocessor bandwidth inheritance protocol. In: Proc. of the 22nd Euromicro Conference on Real-Time Systems (ECRTS), pp. 90–99 (2010)
15. Fairbairn, M.L., Burns, A.: Implementing and verifying EDF preemption-level resource control. In: Brorsson, M., Pinho, L.M. (eds.) Ada-Europe 2012. LNCS, vol. 7308, pp. 193–206. Springer, Heidelberg (2012)
16. Gai, P., Lipari, G., Di Natale, M.: Minimizing memory utilization of real-time task sets in single and multi-processor systems-on-a-chip. In: Proc. 22nd RTSS, pp. 73–83 (2001)
17. Lin, S., Burns, A., Wellings, A.: Supporting lock-based multiprocessor resource sharing protocols in real-time programming languages. Concurrency and Computation: Practice and Experience (2012)
18. Liu, C., Layland, J.: Scheduling algorithms for multiprogramming in a hard real-time environment. JACM 20(1), 46–61 (1973)
19. Sha, L., Rajkumar, R., Lehoczky, J.: Priority inheritance protocols: An approach to real-time synchronisation. IEEE Transactions on Computers 39(9), 1175–1185 (1990)
20. Taft, S.T., Duff, R.A., Brukardt, R.L., Ploedereder, E., Leroy, P.: Ada 2005 Reference Manual. LNCS, vol. 4348. Springer, Heidelberg (2006)
21. Taft, S.T., Duff, R.A., Brukardt, R.L., Ploedereder, E., Leroy, P., Schonberg, E.: Ada 2012 Reference Manual. LNCS, vol. 8339. Springer, Heidelberg (2012)
22. Wellings, A.: Session summary: Locking protocols. ACM SIGAda Ada Letters, Proc. of IRTAW 16 XXXIII(2), 123–125 (2013)
23. Wellings, A.J., Burns, A.: Real-time utilities for Ada 2005. In: Abdennadher, N., Kordon, F. (eds.) Ada-Europe 2007. LNCS, vol. 4498, pp. 1–14. Springer, Heidelberg (2007)
24. Zerzelidis, A., Burns, A., Wellings, A.: Correcting the EDF protocol in Ada 2005. Proc. of IRTAW 13, Ada Letters XXVII(2), 18–22 (2007)

Schedulability Analysis for Directed Acyclic Graphs on Multiprocessor Systems at a Subtask Level

Manar Qamhieh and Serge Midonnet

Université Paris-Est, Paris, France
{manar.qamhieh,serge.midonnet}@univ-paris-est.fr

Abstract. This paper addresses the problem of scheduling parallel real-time tasks of Directed Acyclic Graph (DAG) model on multiprocessor systems. We propose a new scheduling method based on a subtask-level, which means that the schedulability decisions are taken based on the local temporal parameters of subtasks. This method requires modifying the subtasks to add more parameters which are necessary for the analysis, such as local offsets, deadlines and release jitters. Then we provide interference and workload analyses of DAG tasks, and we provide a schedulability test for any work conserving scheduling algorithm.

1 Introduction

Recently, the performance of systems has been increased using multiprocessors instead of uniprocessors to overcome processor physical limitations and to produce faster and smaller processors. The use of parallelism in software makes them compatible with multiprocessor hardware, because the calculations of parallel applications are performed on multiple processors simultaneously.

In real-time systems, scheduling parallel real-time tasks on multiprocessor systems is a challenging problem, and the extension of uniprocessor schedulability conditions to parallel multiprocessor systems is not trivial. The need of synchronization between parallel tasks and processors makes the scheduling process more complicated.

In this paper, we are interested in scheduling Directed Acyclic Graph (DAG) tasks on multiprocessor systems. The contribution is to provide schedulability conditions for DAG tasks that take into account subtasks' parameters instead of DAG-level parameters (a solution commonly used in previous researches found in literature).

The remainder of this paper is organized as follows. In Section 2, we present a state-of-the-art of methods relative to real-time parallel task scheduling on multiprocessor systems especially for the DAG model. The considered model and the used terminology are described in Section 3. In Section 4, we explain the subtask-level scheduling process, and we define additional parameters to subtasks in order to be scheduled individually using any work conserving algorithm. A workload analysis is given in Section 5. This workload analysis is used to derive

L. George and T. Vardanega (Eds.): Ada-Europe 2014, LNCS 8454, pp. 119–133, 2014.
© Springer International Publishing Switzerland 2014

a schedulability test for any work conserving scheduling algorithms. Finally, we conclude this study and show future work in Section 6.

2   Related Work

Many hard real-time scheduling algorithms and schedulability analyses on homogeneous multiprocessor systems have been proposed in the literature [1]. They mostly focus on the traditional sequential independent real-time task model.

Regarding parallel tasks, there are different models and each has its own advantages and limitations. First there is the Fork-join model, in which a parallel task is an alternating sequence of parallel and sequential segments, a stretching algorithm to execute parallel segments as sequential as possible was proposed in [2].

A more general model of parallel tasks, called the segment model, has been studied in the literature. The multiprocessor scheduling of periodic tasksets with implicit deadlines with this model has been addressed in [3]. This model represent a task as a sequence of segments, each segment consists of a number of identical threads.

The analysis has been extended to the DAG model and the same results can be applied. Another scheduling approach based on the response time analysis for the multi-threaded segment model has been provided in [4] for soft real-time multi-core systems.

The DAG model has been studied in [5] in the uniprocessor case. The authors considered a hybrid task set of periodic independent tasks and dependent sporadic graph tasks that execute only once. A graph task in this model consists of a set of tasks with precedence constraints and each task has a release time and deadline. They proposed an algorithm based on a modification of task parameters in order to remove the dependencies between the tasks in the analysis. We use a similar technique in Section 4 to modify subtasks with few differences due to the characteristics of the model.

A capacity augmentation bound of $4 - \frac{2}{m}$ and a resource augmentation bound of $2 - \frac{1}{m}$ have been proposed recently for GEDF scheduling of periodic implicit-deadline DAG tasksets in [6], where m is the number of processors in the system. Also, Bonifaci et al. [7] studied the schedulability of a DAG set on multiprocessor systems. They proved that GEDF has a speedup bound of $2 - 1/m$, and Deadline monotonic a speedup bound equal to $3 - 1/m$. It is worth noticing that the above described scheduling methods do not consider the internal structure of DAGs in the analysis. And the parallel DAG tasks are either transformed into a collection of independent sequential tasks or they are scheduled directly while considering the global parameters of the DAGs, such as their total worst-case execution time and the critical path length.

More recently, we proposed in [8] a schedulability test of periodic implicit-deadline DAG tasks when GEDF is used. The schedulability decisions are based on a DAG-level (the global deadline of the DAGs), while the workload analysis of the test considered the internal structure of DAGs. We proved by experimental results that this method reduces analysis pessimism and enhances scheduling performance for DAGs. This paper is an extension of this work, in which we aim at enhancing the scheduling analysis by proposing a DAG scheduling on a subtask-level. To our best knowledge, no similar research exists using the method to address the problem of scheduling parallel DAG tasks.

3   System Model

In this paper, we consider a taskset τ of n real-time Directed Acyclic Graph (DAG) tasks scheduled on m identical processors. Each DAG task τ_i is a sporadic constrained-deadline graph composed of n_i subtasks under precedence constraints.

A DAG task τ_i is characterized by $(n_i, \{1 \leq j \leq n_i | \tau_{i,j}\}, G_i, D_i, T_i)$, where n_i is the number of its subtasks, the second parameter is the set of subtasks, G_i is the set of directed relations between the subtasks, D_i is the relative deadline of τ_i and T_i is the minimum inter-arrival time between the successive jobs.

Let $\tau_{i,j}$ denote the jth subtask of the set of subtasks forming DAG task τ_i, where $1 \leq j \leq n_i$. Each subtask $\tau_{i,j}$ is a single-threaded task that has a single timing parameter which is its worst case execution time (WCET) $C_{i,j}$. The subtasks of a DAG inherit the period and deadline of their DAG.

Let $g_{i,k}^{i,j} \in G_i$ represent a directed link from subtask $\tau_{i,j}$ to $\tau_{i,k}$. A direct link between subtask $\tau_{i,j}$ and $\tau_{i,k}$ means that subtask $\tau_{i,k}$ cannot start its execution unless subtask $\tau_{i,j}$ completes its own. In this case, subtask $\tau_{i,j}$ is called a **parent** subtask of $\tau_{i,k}$ where $\tau_{i,j} \in parents(\tau_{i,k}) \in pred(\tau_{i,k})$, where $pred(\tau_{i,k})$ is the set of all predecessors of subtask $\tau_{i,k}$ from the source of the DAG which have to execute indirectly before $\tau_{i,k}$ (such as parents of $\tau_{i,k}$'s parents). Likewise, subtask $\tau_{i,k} \in children(\tau_{i,j})$ is called a **child** subtask of $\tau_{i,j}$, and the set of all successors of $\tau_{i,k}$ is denoted by $succ(\tau_{i,k})$. Subtask $\tau_{i,j}$ may have zero or more parent/children subtasks. A source subtask has no parent subtasks and a sink subtask is the one without any successors.

Let C_i denote the total WCET of DAG task τ_i, where $C_i = \sum_{k=1}^{n_i} C_{i,k}$. Let L_i denote the length of the critical path of DAG task τ_i, which is defined as the longest execution path in τ_i when it executes on a platform of infinite number of processors.

We assume that each DAG task τ_i generates an infinite sequence of jobs. Let J_i^k be the kth job of DAG task τ_i which is characterized by (r_i, d_i), where r_i is the release time of the job, and d_i is its absolute deadline. Each DAG job J_i^k consists of a collection of subtask jobs each is denoted by $J_{i,j}^k, j \in 1 \ldots n_i$. In the remainder of this paper, the numeration of jobs is removed when it is unnecessary for the clarity of the discussion.

Figure 1(a) shows an example of a DAG task τ_1 which consists of 6 subtasks. Subtask $\tau_{1,1}$ is the source of the DAG and $\tau_{1,6}$ is its sink. The lines in the figure represent the directed precedence constraints between the subtasks. The critical path of τ_1 is $\{\tau_{1,1}, \tau_{1,2}, \tau_{1,6}\}$ and its length is $L_i = 6$. For subtask $\tau_{1,5}$, its parent subtask is $\tau_{1,3}$ while $\tau_{1,1}$ is one of its predecessor.

For any DAG taskset, there are two necessary basic conditions, if at least one of them is false, the taskset is not feasible:

$$\sum_{\tau_i \in \tau} \frac{C_i}{T_i} \leq m$$

$$\forall \{\tau_i \in \tau\} : L_i \leq D_i$$

In the following sections, we provide a schedulability analysis for DAG tasks using any global work conserving scheduling algorithm. A global algorithm allows job migration and preemptions between processors (migration costs and preemption costs are not taken into account in this work), while a work conserving algorithm does not authorize delaying the execution of an active job if there is an idle processor in the system.

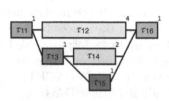

(a) A DAG task τ_1 consists of 6 subtasks with parameters: $D_1 = 8$, $C_1 = 10$, $L_1 = 6$.

(b) Time diagram of each subtask of DAG task τ_1

Fig. 1. Example of DAG model

4   DAG Task Scheduling

When scheduling DAG sets on multiprocessor systems, the interference on each DAG task has the following two sources:

- an external interference from jobs of higher priority DAG tasks, in which some or all of the interfering subtasks can contribute to the interference,
- an internal interference from the subtasks of the same DAG on each other.

For parallel DAG tasks, a DAG-level scheduling algorithm means that the scheduling decisions are based on global parameters of the DAG tasks. According to this scheduling, the priorities are assigned to DAG tasks which are applied then to their respective subtasks. The DAG-level schedulability analysis depends on the global parameters of the DAGs, such as their deadline, period, total WCET and the length of their critical path. Usually, the resulted schedulability tests are pessimistic, and the internal structure of the DAGs is not considered in the performed analysis.

Hence, the interference analysis of DAG-level scheduling is difficult to be calculated and it is harder to identify the exact sources of interference. However, if the scheduling algorithm uses extra knowledge about subtasks and their execution flow, then the interference analysis can be more accurate and precise. In this case the scheduling process is said to be done at a subtask-level. According to this, subtasks will be assigned priorities based on the scheduling algorithm. However, the schedulability analysis requires extra temporal parameters for each subtask other than its WCET provided by the DAG model.

Further in this paper, we will propose a technique to add local temporal parameters to the subtasks based on their dependencies and the precedence constraints between them. As a result, the problem of scheduling parallel DAG tasks on multiprocessor systems will be simplified to scheduling a set of independent sequential subtasks on multiprocessor systems, which is widely studied in the literature.

4.1 Subtask Analysis and Modification

In a previous work [8], we provided algorithms to add two temporal parameters, in addition to the WCET parameter (provided by the model), to each subtask in the DAG set. This was done to improve the interference analysis of DAG scheduling in the case of GEDF scheduling. These two parameters are the local offset and deadline of each subtask, and they were derived from the internal structure of the DAG task and the execution flow of the subtasks in the best case scenario. We consider that this scenario happens when a DAG set executes on an infinite number of processors, all of its subtasks execute in parallel as soon as possible without being delayed due to interference.

Definition 1. *A local offset $O_{i,j}$ of a subtask $\tau_{i,j}$ is defined as the earliest possible activation time of the subtask w.r.t. the release of its DAG task τ_i.*

Definition 2. *A local deadline $D_{i,j}$ of a subtask $\tau_{i,j}$ is the latest time for subtask $\tau_{i,j}$ to complete its execution so as to leave enough time for its successors to execute within their local deadlines.*

For each subtask, the local offset and deadline are calculated using straightforward depth-first search algorithms (a detailed description can be found in [8]). The local offset of a subtask takes into consideration the time needed for its predecessor subtasks to execute in the best case scenario. Respectively, the local deadline of a subtask leaves enough time for its successor subtasks to execute.

Observation 1. *If a subtask $\tau_{i,j} \in \tau_i$ misses its local deadline $D_{i,j}$, then its DAG task τ_i will definitely miss its deadline D_i.*

Based on the definition of the local deadline, when a subtask misses its local deadline, the time remaining until the global deadline of the DAG task is not enough for the successors to execute in the best case. Therefore, an early schedulability failure can be announced based on the subtask's deadline instead of waiting for the DAG's deadline miss.

Figure 1 shows the mapping between the DAG task τ_1 and its subtasks after the modification. The timing diagram of each subtask $\tau_{1,j}$, where $1 \leq j \leq 6$, of the DAG is shown in Figure 1(b). The local offset $O_{1,1}$ of the source subtask $\tau_{1,1}$ equals to 0 because this subtask has no predecessors and it is released at the release time of the DAG task τ_1. Its local deadline $D_{1,1} = 3$ because its successors need at least 5 time units to execute in the best case, which is the longest path from $\tau_{1,1}$ (excluded) to a sink subtask ($\{\tau_{1,2}, \tau_{1,6}\}$ in the example). Then, both subtasks $\tau_{1,2}$ and $\tau_{1,3}$ are released after the completion of $\tau_{1,1}$. As a result, $O_{1,2} = O_{1,3} = 1$. For the rest of the subtasks, their local offsets and deadlines are shown in Figure 1(b).

The local offsets and deadlines of subtasks are calculated based on their best-case activation scenario, in which all the subtasks execute as soon as they are released with no interference or delays, These parameters helps in identifying the longest execution window of each subtask. However, the activation of a subtask job can be delayed due to the interference of higher priority subtasks. Respectively, the latest possible activation of a subtask job occurs when all of its predecessors execute as late as possible (just before their local deadlines). According to this, the activation of a subtask job can happen at any time within this interval, and this can be considered as the maximum release jitter of the subtask.

Definition 3. *A maximum release jitter $\widehat{j}_{i,j}$ of a subtask $\tau_{i,j}$ is defined as the difference between the earliest and latest release time of the subtask with respect to the activation of the DAG task.*

$$\widehat{j}_{i,j} = \max_{\forall \tau_{i,k} \in Parents(\tau_{i,j})} (D_{i,k} - (O_{i,j} - O_{i,k})) \tag{1}$$

Based on the definition of the release jitter of a subtask, all of its jobs are released within the jitter interval, which is shown in the following equation:

$$\forall J_{i,k}^j , \; j \in \mathbb{N}, \tau_{i,k} \in \tau_i : \; r_{i,k}^j \in [O_{i,k}, O_{i,k} + \widehat{j}_{i,j}]$$

Figure 1(b) shows the maximum release jitter values for the subtasks in DAG τ_1 from Figure 1(a). It's worth noticing that the source subtask $\tau_{1,1}$ has no jitter since it has no predecessor subtasks.

From Equation 1 and the example in Figure 1(b), we can notice that the calculation of the release jitter of the subtasks is pessimistic, and it considers always that the predecessor subtasks execute as late as possible. According to this, the critical subtasks of a DAG task (subtasks forming its critical path) will have no slack time[1] if they are activated at their maximum release jitter. In the following sections, we provide an optimization to the release jitter of subtasks based on the interference analysis.

Regarding the period of the subtasks (minimum inter-arrival time for sporadic tasks), each subtask inherits the period of its DAG task, where $\forall \tau_{i,j} \in \tau_i$, $T_{i,j} = T_i$.

As a result, the subtasks of a given DAG task are characterized now by a local offset, a WCET, a local deadline and a release jitter. These parameters will

---

[1] Slack time is the time difference between the deadline of a task and its WCET.

allow us to treat subtasks individually and independently in order to provide a schedulability analysis at a subtask-level.

4.2 Interference Analysis

For the subtask-level scheduling process using any work conserving algorithm, the execution of a subtask can be blocked by higher priority subtasks. The interference on a subtask $\tau_{k,h} \in \tau_k$ is defined as follows:

Definition 4. $I_{k,h}(a,b)$ *is the length of all intervals where subtask $\tau_{k,h}$ is ready to execute but blocked by higher priority subtasks in an interval $[a,b)$.*

Definition 5. $I_{k,h}^{i,j}(a,b)$ *is the length of all intervals where subtask $\tau_{k,h}$ is ready to execute but blocked by subtask $\tau_{i,j}$ which has higher priority in an interval $[a,b)$.*

Since the subtasks are single-threaded sequential real-time tasks, the relation between $I_{k,h}(a,b)$ and $I_{k,h}^{i,j}(a,b)$ is denoted by the following equation:

$$I_{k,h}(a,b) = \frac{1}{m} * \sum_{\forall \tau_{i,j} \in \tau_i \in \tau} I_{k,h}^{i,j}(a,b) \tag{2}$$

Due to the characteristics of the DAG tasks and the precedence constraints between the subtasks, the interference on a subtask $\tau_{k,h}$ is divided into two sources, external and internal interference. Let $Ie_{k,h}(a,b)$ denote the interference from higher priority subtasks of DAG tasks other than τ_k in the set, which is defined as follows:

$$Ie_{k,h}(a,b) = \frac{1}{m} * \sum_{i \neq k, \forall \tau_{i,j} \in \tau_i} I_{k,h}^{i,j}(a,b) \tag{3}$$

Where some or all of the subtasks of DAG task τ_i $(i \neq k)$ can interfere with $\tau_{k,h}$ based on their priorities.

Furthermore, subtasks of DAG τ_k can block the execution of $\tau_{k,h}$ which is defined as the internal interference $Ii_{k,h}(a,b)$. Since we consider constrained deadline DAG tasks, for a given job of subtask $\tau_{k,h}$, one job at most from each subtask contributes to the interference. The internal interference depends on the type of interfering subtasks which are divided into the following categories:

- a predecessor subtask $\tau_{k,x} \in pred(\tau_{k,h})$ of subtask $\tau_{k,h}$: this subtask will delay the activation of $\tau_{k,h}$, but once subtask $\tau_{k,x}$ completes its execution, subtask $\tau_{k,h}$ will start its own and there will be no further effect of $\tau_{k,x}$ on $\tau_{k,h}$,
- a sibling subtask $\tau_{k,x} \in sibling(\tau_{k,h})$ is the subtask that executes in parallel with no dependencies with subtask $\tau_{k,h}$. The $sibling(\tau_{k,h})$ is the set of subtasks that are not predecessors or successors of subtask $\tau_{k,h}$,

- a successor subtask $\tau_{k,x} \in succ(\tau_{k,h})$ has no interference with subtask $\tau_{k,h}$, because both subtasks cannot execute in parallel and subtask $\tau_{k,x}$ starts its execution after $\tau_{k,h}$ completes its own. According to this, $I_{k,h}^{k,x}(a,b) = 0$,
- subtask $\tau_{k,h}$ has no interference on itself since we consider constrained deadline DAG tasks, in which only one job of each DAG task is activated at any time t. Hence, $I_{k,h}^{k,h}(a,b) = 0$.

Based on the above definitions, the internal interference $Ii_{k,h}(a,b)$ on subtask $\tau_{k,h}$ in the interval $[a,b)$ is defined as:

$$Ii_{k,h}(a,b) = \frac{1}{m} * \sum_{\forall \tau_{k,i} \notin succ(\tau_{k,h}); i \neq h} I_{k,h}^{k,i}(a,b) \tag{4}$$

Let $J_{k,h}^*$ be the job of subtask $\tau_{k,h}$ which has maximum interference, and let $I_{k,h}(r_{k,h}^*, d_{k,h}^*)$ denote the worst-case interference for subtask job $J_{k,h}^*$ of $\tau_{k,h}$ in the interval $[r_{k,h}^*, d_{k,h}^*)$. For the sake of clarity, we will use $\widehat{I}_{k,h} = I_{k,h}(r_{k,h}^*, d_{k,h}^*)$ in this document.

Lemma 1. *A taskset τ, of sporadic constrained deadline DAG tasks, is schedulable on m identical processors, for any work conserving algorithm if:*

$$\forall \tau_{k,h} \in \tau_k \in \tau$$
$$\widehat{I}_{k,h} = \widehat{I}e_{k,h} + \widehat{I}i_{k,h} \leq (D_{k,h} - C_{k,h}) \tag{5}$$

Proof. The proof of this lemma is straight-forward. The interference on a subtask job has two main sources; internal and external. In order for any subtask to be schedulable, its execution window (between its activation and deadline) should be enough to execute its execution time plus the interference workload which is identified above.

4.3   Interference from Predecessor Subtasks

As described earlier, a predecessor subtask should complete its execution before its successors are activated. Hence, a successor subtask can only be delayed by its predecessors. In Section 4.1, we assigned a maximum release jitter for each subtask in the DAG. This parameter represents the interval in which the subtask job can be activated and it replaces the dependencies between the subtasks. If we consider that all the predecessors of $\tau_{k,h}$ have executed as late as possible, then the subtask job $J_{k,h}^*$ will be delayed to the end of this interval ($\widehat{j}_{k,h}$ time units after its offset), then the condition in Lemma 1 will be modified as follows:

Lemma 2. *A taskset τ of DAG tasks is schedulable on m identical processors, using any work conserving algorithm, if:*

$$\forall \tau_{k,h} \in \tau_k \in \tau$$
$$\widehat{I}e_{k,h} + \widehat{I}i_{k,h} \leq (D_{k,h} - C_{k,h} - \widehat{j}_{k,h}) \leq (D_{k,h} - C_{k,h} - j_{k,h}) \tag{6}$$

where

$$\widehat{Ii}_{k,h} = \frac{1}{m} * \sum_{\forall \tau_{k,i} \in sibling(\tau_{k,h})} I_{k,h}^{k,i}(a,b)$$

Proof. As shown in Figure 2 and based on the definition of the release jitter in Equation 1, if all predecessors respected their local deadlines, then subtask $\tau_{k,h}$ will be activated no later than $t = (r_k + O_{k,h} + \widehat{j}_{k,h})$. In the interval $[t, d_{k,h})$, predecessors will have no further interference, and only sibling subtasks of $\tau_{k,h}$ will interfere with $\tau_{k,h}$, which should be less than the available slack time ($D_{k,h} - C_{k,h} - \widehat{j}_{k,h}$).

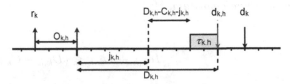

Fig. 2. The interference window excluding interference from predecessor subtasks

We have mentioned earlier that considering the maximum release jitter $\widehat{j}_{k,h}$ of subtask $\tau_{k,h}$ in the interference analysis is too pessimistic, because it considers that the predecessors will execute as late as possible. As a result, the upper bound of interference used in Lemma 2 will be always zero for any critical subtask $\tau_{k,h}$ since their release jitter $\widehat{j}_{k,h} = D_{k,h} - C_{k,h}$.

As shown in Figure 3, it is possible to optimize the jitter of each subtask by knowing that a parent subtask $\tau_{k,i}$ has a response time equal to $(\widehat{I}_{k,i} + C_{k,i})$ when a work conserving algorithm is used. Its latest finish time $f_{k,i}^*$ can be defined as:

$$f_{k,i}^* = C_{k,i} + \widehat{I}_{k,i} \le D_{k,i}$$

The finish time $f_{k,i}$ of any job of a schedulable subtask $\tau_{k,i}$ should not be greater than its local deadline $D_{k,i}$, or a deadline miss will occur.

By using the finish time of each parent subtask of $\tau_{k,h}$, we can calculate an optimized release jitter $j_{k,h}'$ defined by the following equation:

$$\begin{aligned} j_{k,h}' &= \max_{\forall \tau_{k,i} \in parents(\tau_{k,h})} (f_{k,i}^* - (O_{k,h} - O_{k,i})) \\ &= \max_{\forall \tau_{k,i} \in parents(\tau_{k,h})} (C_{k,i} + \widehat{I}_{k,i} - (O_{k,h} - O_{k,i})) \qquad (7) \\ &\le \widehat{j}_{k,h} \end{aligned}$$

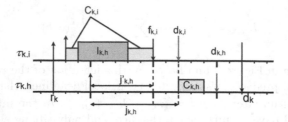

Fig. 3. The optimized release jitter of subtask $\tau_{k,h}$ from its sole parent $\tau_{k,i}$

Corollary 1. *A taskset τ of DAG tasks is schedulable on m identical processors, using any work conserving algorithm, if:*

$$\forall \tau_{k,h} \in \tau_k \in \tau$$

$$\widehat{Ie}_{k,h} + \widehat{Ii}_{k,h} \leq (D_{k,h} - C_{k,h} - j'_{k,h}) \quad (8)$$

where

$$\widehat{Ii}_{k,h} = \frac{1}{m} * \sum_{\forall \tau_{k,i} \in sibling(\tau_{k,h})} I^{k,i}_{k,h}(a,b) \quad (9)$$

The use of the optimized release jitter of a subtask instead of its maximum release jitter improves the schedulability test by considering a more accurate upper bound on interference.

5   Workload Analysis

It is difficult to identify the actual interference from external and sibling subtasks required for the schedulability test in Corollary 1. However, we can use an upper bound on the interference based on the workload computation of an interfering subtask, knowing that the interference of a subtask on another one in a fixed interval cannot exceed the workload of the interfering subtask during the same interval. Let $W_{i,j}(a,b)$ be the amount of work done by the jobs of subtask $\tau_{i,j}$ in the interval $[a,b)$. Then:

$$I^{i,j}_{k,h}(a,b) \leq W_{i,j}(a,b)$$

Within the interference interval $[a,b)$, let a carry-in job of an interfering subtask be defined as the job that is released before the start of the interval and has a deadline within the interval. While a body job is the job that is released within the interval $[a,b)$ and its deadline can be within or after the end of the interval.

5.1   Workload from Sibling Subtasks

A sibling subtask $\tau_{k,i}$ of $\tau_{k,h}$ is the subtask from the same DAG task τ_k that can execute in parallel with $\tau_{k,h}$. Moreover, subtask $\tau_{k,i}$ has no precedence relations with $\tau_{k,h}$ and it cannot be among its predecessors or successors.

For a given subtask job, one job at most from each sibling subtask will interfere with it, because the jobs of sibling subtasks belong to the same DAG job, and the release of their DAG job is considered as their activation reference. In other words, one job from each sibling subtask $\tau_{k,h}$ is released in the interval $[r_k + O_{k,h}, r_k + O_{k,h} + \widehat{j}_{k,h}]$. For any work conserving algorithm, the interference $\widehat{Ii}_{k,h}^{k,i}$ of a subtask $\tau_{k,i}$ on its sibling $\tau_{k,h}$ is calculated by identifying the maximum interfering interval $L_{k,h}^{k,i}$ of $\tau_{k,i}$ on $\tau_{k,h}$. This interval is defined as the longest interval in which subtasks $\tau_{k,h}$ and $\tau_{k,i}$ can execute in parallel. It is calculated as follows:

$$L_{k,h}^{k,i} = min(D'_{k,i}, D'_{k,h}) - max(O_{k,i}, O_{k,h}) \qquad (10)$$

For the sake of clarity, we considered $D'_{k,h}$ to be the relative deadline of subtask $\tau_{k,h}$ from the release of the DAG task, where $D'_{k,h} = O_{k,h} + D_{k,h}$.

Lemma 3. *The maximum internal interference $\widehat{Ii}_{k,h}^{k,i}$ of subtask $\tau_{k,i}$ on a job of its sibling subtask $\tau_{k,h}$ is*

$$\widehat{Ii}_{k,h}^{k,i} \le min(C_{k,i}, L_{k,h}^{k,i}) = \widehat{Wi}_{k,i} \qquad (11)$$

Proof. Based on the definition of the interference interval $L_{k,h}^{k,i}$, the maximum possible workload of subtask $\tau_{k,i}$ in the interval happens when $\tau_{k,i}$ executes as long as possible in this interval. From here comes the *min* in the Equation 11.

5.2 Workload Analysis for External Subtasks

For any work conserving algorithm, Bertogna et al. identified, in their paper [9], the worst-case activation scenario of jobs of an interfering task in a fixed interval (a, b) which generates the maximum possible workload. They considered a task model of independent sequential single-threaded tasks. As shown in Figure 4, this scenario happens when the carry-in job of the interfering task starts its execution at the beginning of the interference window and executes as late as possible. The following body jobs then execute as soon as possible until the end of the window. This scenario is proved in [9] to generate the maximum workload in the interval.

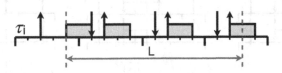

Fig. 4. The densest possible packing of jobs in interval pf length L for traditional task using any work conserving algorithm

We use this scenario to calculate the workload of each external subtask in order to be used as an upper bound of its interference on a given subtask in the system. Since each external subtask $\tau_{i,j}$ has no precedence constraints with $\tau_{k,h}$ (where $k \neq i$), then this scenario can be applied to each subtask independently. As shown in Figure 5, the subtasks of an interfering DAG task τ_i will interfere on subtask job $J^*_{k,h}$. Assume that subtask job $J^*_{k,h}$ has an activation window $[r^*_{k,h}, d^*_{k,h})$ as shown in Figure 5(b), while Figure 5(a) shows the DAG task τ_i and its internal structure. In order to calculate the worst-case workload of its subtasks on $j_{k,h}$, the worst-case activation scenario is applied to each subtask $\tau_{i,j}$. As shown in Figure 5(b), the first job of each subtask starts its execution as late as possible at the beginning of the interference interval, and the following job executes as soon as possible. Based on this scenario, the maximum workload done in the interference interval is 10.

However, applying this scenario on each subtask of the same DAG task independently is pessimistic. Because in reality, these interfering subtasks have precedence constraints that define their execution flow. For example, subtask $\tau_{i,1}$ in Figure 5(b) cannot execute in parallel with its children subtasks $\tau_{i,2}$ and $\tau_{i,3}$. But still, the workload in this activation scenario can be used as an upper bound for workload. Using the following example, we will show that it is not trivial to find a worst-case activation scenario of jobs adapted to DAG tasks that generates the maximum workload.

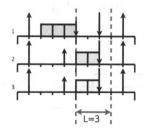
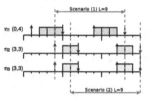

(a) Example of a DAG task τ_i.

(b) The worst workload activation scenario for subtask jobs of τ_i for any work conserving algorithm.

(c) The worst workload activation scenario for subtask jobs of τ_i for Global EDF.

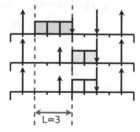
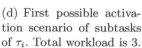
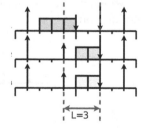

(d) First possible activation scenario of subtasks of τ_i. Total workload is 3.

(e) Second possible activation scenario of subtasks of τ_i. Total workload is 4.

(f) Third possible activation scenario of subtasks of τ_i. Total workload is 5.

Fig. 5. Workload analysis for external subtasks

Example

Back to the DAG task τ_i from Figure 5(a). According to the precedence constraints between its subtasks, the activation scenario of its subtask jobs is shown in Figures 5(d)-5(f). We consider an interference interval of length $L = 3$. Each Figure in 5(d)-5(f) shows a possible position of the interference interval w.r.t. to the interfering subtasks. For example, Figure 5(d) considers that subtask $\tau_{i,1}$ starts at the beginning of the interfering interval, and its total workload is 3. While Figure 5(e) considers that subtasks $\tau_{i,2}$ and $\tau_{i,3}$ start at the beginning of the interval and the total workload is 4. However, the maximum workload happens in Figure 5(f), in which the interference interval starts within subtask $\tau_{i,1}$ and it ends at the deadline of $\tau_{i,2}$ and $\tau_{i,3}$. In this case the total workload is 5.

Based on this example, we conclude that in order to calculate the maximum workload of external subtasks of the same DAG, we have to analyze all the possible positions of interference interval w.r.t. the activation of subtasks, and this is done at each time instant in the interfering interval.

Lemma 4. *The external interference $\widehat{Ie}_{k,h}^{i,j}$ of subtask $\tau_{i,j}$ on subtask $\tau_{k,h}$ in an interval, whose length is equal to the absolute deadline $D_{k,h}$ of $\tau_{k,h}$, is bounded by:*

$$\widehat{Ie}_{k,h}^{i,j} \leq N_{i,j}(D_{k,h})C_{i,j}+ \tag{12}$$
$$min(C_{i,j}, D_{k,h} + D_{i,j} - C_{i,j} - N_{i,j}(D_{k,h})T_{i,j})$$

where

$$N_{i,j}(D_{k,h}) = \lfloor \frac{D_{k,h} + D_{i,j} - C_{i,j}}{T_{i,j}} \rfloor$$

Proof. The maximum interference workload from the external subtask $\tau_{i,j}$ on subtask $\tau_{k,h}$ happens based on the execution scenario described in [9] and shown in Figure 4. The calculations of workload is based on number of interfering jobs which lie completely within the interfering window plus the last job in the interval which may contribute partially in the interference. More details about these equations can be found in [9].

A schedulability test for DAG tasks using any work conserving algorithm on m identical processors is provided as follows:

Theorem 1. *A DAG set τ is schedulable on m identical processors using any work conserving algorithm if:*

$$\forall \tau_{k,h} \in \tau_k \in \tau$$

$$\sum_{\tau_{k,i} \in sibling(k,h)} min(\widehat{Ii}_{k,h}^{k,i}, D_{k,h} - C_{k,h} - j'_{k,h})+$$

$$\sum_{\tau_{i,j} \, ; \, i \neq k} min(\widehat{Ie}_{k,h}^{i,j}, D_{k,h} - C_{k,h} - j'_{k,h})$$

$$\leq m(D_{k,h} - C_{k,h} - j'_{k,h})$$

Proof. Knowing that the interference of a subtask in a given interval can never exceed the workload of this subtask in the same interval, we can transform the interference schedulability bound on subtask $\tau_{k,h}$ described in Lemma 3 into a workload bound of schedulability of the same subtask. However, the internal and the external interference are based on their respective workload calculations shown in Equations 11 and 12,

The schedulability test described in the above theorem can be used to optimize the release jitter value of each subtask. Based on the test, the optimized release jitter can be calculated for each successor of the subtask. If the calculated release jitter is more than the actual release jitter (the maximum release jitter by default), then the calculated value is discarded and the actual release jitter will not be modified.

In order to analyze the performance of our schedulability test, we compare it with another test found in literature. Bonifaci et al. in [7] provided a GEDF schedulability test for DAG set on m identical processors. The test depends on the global parameters of the DAG tasks without considering the internal structure and the execution flow of the subtasks. Our schedulability test provided in Theorem 1 is provided for any work conserving algorithm. For the sake of simulation, we derived a special case of this test for GEDF scheduling algorithm and the results are shown in Figure 6.

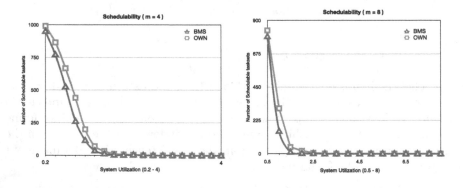

Fig. 6. Simulation results

We generated a large number of random DAG tasksets, and we applied both GEDF-schedulability tests on the sets of utilization that range from 0 to 8. As shown in Figure 6, our own scheduling test (denoted by *OWN*) performs better than the test from [7] (denoted by *BMS*). For each system utilization, our test schedules more DAG sets than the *BMS* test.

The simulation results provided in this section proves the importance of the internal structure of DAG tasks in the schedulability analysis.

6   Conclusion

In this paper, we were interested in the scheduling of parallel real-time DAG tasks on multiprocessor systems. Our motivation was to show that the scheduling of real-time DAG tasks is affected by the internal structure of the DAG and the execution flow of its subtasks. Hence, we applied the scheduling algorithms at subtask-level instead of DAG-level. This means that the scheduling decisions are based on local parameters of subtasks instead of the global parameters of DAGs.

We modified the subtasks by adding local parameters such as local offset, deadline and release jitter for each subtask. Then we provided interference and workload analyses for any work conserving scheduling algorithm.

As a future perspective, we aim at extending our work to analyze common scheduling algorithms such as EDF and DM, so as to provide precise schedulability test for each algorithm. Also, we aim at providing further analysis for subtask-level schedulers including performance metrics such as speedup factor and approximations ratio. These metrics can be used as an indication of the performance of our proposed scheduling method.

References

1. Davis, R.I., Burns, A.: A survey of hard real-time scheduling algorithms and schedulability analysis techniques for multiprocessor systems. ACM Computing Surveys (2011)
2. Lakshmanan, K., Kato, S., (Raj) Rajkumar, R.: Scheduling Parallel Real-Time Tasks on Multi-core Processors. In: Proceedings of RTSS (2010)
3. Saifullah, A., Agrawal, K., Lu, C., Gill, C.: Multi-core Real-Time Scheduling for Generalized Parallel Task Models. In: Proceedings of RTSS (2011)
4. Liu, C., Anderson, J.H.: Supporting Soft Real-Time Parallel Applications on Multicore Processors. In: Proceedings of RTCSA (2012)
5. Chetto, H., Silly, M., Bouchentouf, T.: Dynamic scheduling of real-time tasks under precedence constraints. In: Real-Time Systems (1990)
6. Li, A.J., Agrawal, K., Lu, C., Gill, C.: Analysis of Global EDF for Parallel Tasks. In: Proceedings of ECRTS (2013)
7. Bonifaci, V., Marchetti-spaccamela, A., Stiller, S., Wiese, A.: Feasibility Analysis in the Sporadic DAG Task Model. In: Proceedings of ECRTS (2013)
8. Qamhieh, M., Fauberteau, F., George, L., Midonnet, S.: Global EDF Scheduling of Directed Acyclic Graphs on Multiprocessor Systems. In: Proceedings of RTNS (2013)
9. Bertogna, M., Cirinei, M., Lipari, G.: Schedulability Analysis of Global Scheduling Algorithms on Multiprocessor Platforms. IEEE Transactions on Parallel and Distributed Systems (2009)

Integrated Schedulers for a Predictable Interrupt Management on Real-Time Kernels

Sergio Sáez and Alfons Crespo

Department of Computer Engineering
Universidad Politécnica de Valencia
{ssaez,alfons}@disca.upv.es

Abstract. To analyse the timeliness behaviour of a real-time system is one its key aspects. A big effort has been performed by the real-time community to develop accurate and more general schedulability analysis that can ensure the correct execution of the system. However, few works have analysed the side effects introduced by the scheduler and undesired execution of *Interrupt Service Routines*. Previous works addressed the interrupt interference by proposing an *Integrated Interrupt Model* that avoids unpredictable disturbance from external interrupts. Even so, the scheduling overhead due to the unnecessary activation of low priority tasks remains still unaddressed in this model. This work proposes a new *Virtual* implementation of an *Integrated Interrupt Event-Driven Scheduler* that copes with this pending issue. It also analyses the behaviour of the commonly used dual queue scheme under this kind of schedulers and proposes a more appropriated data structure to avoid unnecessary overheads.

1 Introduction

Real-time computing systems cope with its intrinsic complexity by decomposing the system software in a set of concurrent tasks with timing constraints. These timings constraints, that must be met for correct operation, are usually represented by a deadline and a task period. To guarantee such constraints, extensive research has been performed on schedulability analysis of real-time systems [1]. Schedulability tests are designed to take into account the system workload characteristics and the kind of scheduler used by the real-time operating system. Fixed-priority scheduler is one of the most popular and widely accepted real-time schedulers, and therefore it is present in almost all the commercial real-time operating systems [2]. However, a wide gap still exists between scheduling theory and its implementation in operating system kernels, since the system scheduler is usually assumed to be executed without any kind of overhead.

Few works have analysed the side effects introduced by the scheduler and the associated operating systems routines [3–5]. These works analyse the temporal behaviour of real-time schedulers classifying them into *event-driven*, that relies on an external hardware device that generates interrupts upon task arrivals, or *timer-driven*, that uses periodic interrupts from a programmable hardware timer

L. George and T. Vardanega (Eds.): Ada-Europe 2014, LNCS 8454, pp. 134–148, 2014.

to execute the scheduler at fixed intervals. Katcher *et al.* emphasize the importance of integrating timer interrupts into the scheduling scheme in order to avoid unnecessary interrupts, i.e., timer interrupt that will wake up a low priority task while a higher priority task is in execution. This *integrated interrupt model* has been further extended by Leyva-del-Foyo *et al.* in [6–8] to include all hardware interrupts that can be produced in a real-time kernel. These authors introduce an integrated model for task and interrupt management and propose different hardware and software implementation approaches. This integrated model is carefully analysed under each proposed implementation and the utilization bound reductions compared with the one obtained from a non-integrated model.

The integration of hardware interrupts and real-time tasks gives rise to a real-time task set composed by *Hardware Activated Tasks* and *Software Activated Tasks* respectively [8]. The release of Harware Activated Task is strictly controlled by an *Interrupt Hardware Abstraction Layer* in [7] or more loosely controlled using an optimistic approach in [8]. However, the Software Activated Tasks are normally released by means of a timer interrupt, and this fact is not addressed in these works. For example, on [7] is suggested that the timer interrupt still could be considered an Interrupt Service Routine, since it will never be handled by the application. This approach, although reduces the unnecessary overhead introduced by the Interrupt Hardware Abstraction Layer, could give rise to an unnecessary invocations of the system scheduler when the task that is woken up has a lower priority than the currently executing task. An integrated event-driven scheduler, as proposed by Katcher *et al.*, could cope with this scenario whenever the *Hardware Interrupt Controller* was able to manage multiple prioritized timers. However, this capability is usually not available in the hardware interrupt controller integrated in nowadays processors.

This work proposes to complete the integrated interrupt model with an integrated event-driven scheduler that modifies the hardware timer to interrupt only when a higher priority task has to be woken up. This kind of scheduler could avoid unnecessary task activations, reducing the disturbance introduced by the operating system kernel. The adequacy of traditional scheduling implementations based on a dual queue scheme, a ready-queue and a wait-queue, to implement this new kind of scheduler is also addressed. Finally, a new fixed-priority scheduler based on a Cartesian tree [9] is proposed to overcome the detected drawbacks of the traditional dual queue approach.

The rest of the paper is organized as follows: next section describes the system model and the notation used in the rest of the paper. Section 3 introduces the model of integrated interrupt management. Then section 4 presents how the scheduler can be integrated in this new model. Section 5 presents dual-queue scheduling schemes, its computational cost and main drawbacks when used in an integrated interrupt model. Section 6 presents a new scheduler that avoids previous drawbacks. Finally section 7 presents some additional considerations and then section 8 summarise some of the main results.

2   System Model and Notation

The notation used in this work is based on the one presented in [7] but with some small differences. It can be summarized as follows:

HAT *Hardware Activated Task.* A task that is released by an external interrupt.
SAT *Software Activated Task.* A task that is activated by a timer interrupt or by other task.[1]
τ_x Real-Time task with period T_x, worst-case execution time C_x and priority p_x.
r_x Next activation instant of task τ_x while it is in the wait queue.
$H(i)$ Set of tasks with a priority higher than task τ_i. $H_{\text{SAT}}(i)$ are the SATs that belongs to $H(i)$. A similar definition holds for $H_{HAT}(i)$.
   $H_{\text{SAT}}(i) \bigcap H_{HAT}(i) = \emptyset$.
$L(i)$ Set of tasks with a priority lower than or equal to task t_i. $L_{\text{SAT}}(i)$ and $L_{HAT}(i)$ are defined as in $H(i)$.
R **and** W Represents the tasks present in the *ready queue* or *wait queue* respectively. The number of tasks in these queues will be represented as N^R and N^W. Intersection with task sets $L(i)$ and $H(i)$ will be denoted by using superscripts, e.g., $H^R(i) = R \bigcap H(i)$.

The notation for system overheads is shown next:

δ^{isr} Total processing time for the enter and leave code of an *Interrupt Service Routine*, including basic communication with the *Hardware Interrupt Controller* (interrupt ack, end-of-interrupt, etc.).
δ^{hic} Communication cost with the *Hardware Interrupt Controller* to mask undesired external interrupts.
δ^{ctx} Time required to perform a task context switch, including CPU registers context, MMU context (if required), etc.
δ^{Sched} Processing time required to determine the next task to be executed. It can be differentiated in $\delta^{\text{Sched}-A}$, when it is computed during a task activation, or $\delta^{\text{Sched}-T}$, if it is computed when the active task is going to be suspended. It can also be suffixed as δ_T^{Sched} or δ_I^{Sched} to differentiate between *traditional* schedulers and *integrated interrupt* schedulers proposed in this work.

3   Integrated Interrupt Management Model

An extended explanation of the *Integrated Interrupt Model* is presented in this section along with the issues that still remains unaddressed. A complete explanation of this model can be found in [7, 8].

The Integrated Interrupt Model proposes to use a common priority space where real-time tasks and traditional Interrupt Service Routines (ISR) are mapped. This gives rise to a set of *Hardware Activated Tasks* (HAT) and *Software*

---

[1] However, this work only considers the software activated task released by a timer interrupt.

Activated Tasks (SAT) which timely execution can be analysed using well known methods [10, 1]. This model avoids to perform a probably unbounded number of ISR executions while high priority tasks are in execution, but also introduces additional system overheads.

3.1 Hardware Activated Tasks

The conversion of the existing ISRs into HATs allows the system to control when a given external interrupt is attended with respect to traditional real-time tasks, i.e. SATs, and the rest of HATs by means of a correct priority assignment. The disturbance associated to the execution of ISRs, that previously affect to all priority levels due to the independence of priority spaces, is moved to a given priority level in the common priority space where higher priority tasks will not be affected. The reduction of CPU utilization due to the interrupt disturbance for a given task τ_i is denoted in [7] as U_{iS}. That work also concludes that the time required to process the enter and leave code of the ISR, δ^{isr}, is replaced by a usually larger time required to perform the context switches of the implied HAT, δ^{ctx}. Whether the utilization reduction due to this new overhead is lower than the previous lost of utilization U_{iS} or not, allows the system designer to determine the adequacy of the integrated interrupt model for a given real-time system.

This integrated priority space for tasks and interrupts requires to change the interrupt priority level[2] of the *Hardware Interrupt Controller* (HIC) each time a new task enters into or exits from execution to avoid the undesired activation of HATs. If the HIC is not included inside the CPU encapsulation, then the communication with this external device through the input/output subsystem could carried out an important overhead that also has to be incorporated into the schedulability tests. Moreover, if the HIC does not support an interrupt priority level, a *Virtual Custom Programmable Interrupt Controller* can be incorporated to *Interrupt Hardware Abstraction Layer* to offer this functionality. As this Virtual Custom PIC emulates the availability of the interrupt priority level by means of *interrupt masking* on the real HIC, additional overheads are introduced to compute the adequate mask for each priority. These additional operations performed during task activation and deactivation are the ones that introduce a higher context switch time. A complete analysis of these overheads can be found in [7, 8].

3.2 Software Activated Tasks

Although the integrated model allows the system designer to control the activation of HATs by means of properly assigned priorities, the correct activation of SATs remains unaddressed. SATs are theoretically activated by software mechanisms such as semaphores, mutexes, barriers, execution time timers, timing events and so on. While the tasks activated by semaphores, mutexes, barriers

---

[2] This level specifies the minimum priority of an interrupt for the CPU to be notified.

and suspension objects are released by code executed directly or indirectly by other task, in the case of temporal events, it is the ISR of the timer interrupt the final responsible of producing the timed event. In such a way, a subset of the SATs, in particular the real-time periodic tasks, are indirectly activated by the occurrence of a hardware interrupt. After this SAT activation, the scheduler is executed in order to determine if the recently activated task has a higher priority than the one is currently under execution. If the activated task has a lower priority, then the current task is resumed. However, an unnecessary activation procedure has been performed that has introduced an unexpected overhead during a higher task execution. This overhead is similar to the one produced by hardware interrupts in a non-integrated model, but with the additional overhead of executing the system scheduler.

The interference due to unnecessary SAT activations, U_i^{SAT}, is the decrease of least upper utilization bound at priority level p_i and can be computed as follows:

$$U_i^{\mathrm{SAT}} = \sum_{\tau_k \in L_{\mathrm{SAT}}(i)} \frac{\delta^{\mathrm{isr}} + \delta_T^{\mathrm{Sched-A}}}{T_k} \tag{1}$$

where $\delta_T^{\mathrm{Sched-A}}$ can be typically decomposed in the following actions: to remove the time event from the wait queue, $\delta_{wq}^{\mathrm{Sched-A}}$, to insert the newly activated task τ_k into the ready queue, $\delta_{rq}^{\mathrm{Sched-A}}$, and to check the top of the ready queue to find out which task will be the next running task, $\delta_{next}^{\mathrm{Sched-A}}$.

$$\delta_T^{\mathrm{Sched-A}} = \delta_{wq}^{\mathrm{Sched-A}} + \delta_{rq}^{\mathrm{Sched-A}} + \delta_{next}^{\mathrm{Sched-A}} \tag{2}$$

While $\delta_{next}^{\mathrm{Sched-A}}$ can be considered constant when a new SAT has been activated, the other two overhead terms, $\delta_{wq}^{\mathrm{Sched-A}}$ and $\delta_{rq}^{\mathrm{Sched-A}}$, depends on the data structures used to maintain the ready and wait queues. These overheads are analysed in section 5.

This scheduling overhead can also be expressed as an additional blocking time, that higher priority tasks can suffer from lower priority tasks, and it should be taken into account during the Response Time Analysis [1] when traditional interrupt models are used. The next equation summarises this additional blocking time:

$$B^{\mathrm{SAT}}(i) = |L_{\mathrm{SAT}}(i)| \times (\delta^{\mathrm{isr}} + \delta_T^{\mathrm{Sched-A}}) \tag{3}$$

In order to avoid this effect, the integrated interrupt model has to grant that no timer interrupt that activates a lower priority task ($\tau_k \in L_{\mathrm{SAT}}(i)$) will be raised during the execution of a higher priority task τ_i. This can be achieved using an *Integrated Interrupt Event-Driven Scheduling* scheme as it is proposed by Katcher *et al.* in [3]. Next section briefly introduces this kind of schedulers and proposes a software-based implementation.

4 Integrated Interrupt Event-Driven Schedulers

In *Integrated Interrupt Event-Driven Scheduling* systems all the tasks are initiated by external interrupts which have priorities that fully match the software task priorities. Upon the activation of each task τ_i an interrupt is posted to the processor that only starts the corresponding ISR if the priority p_i is higher than the priority of the currently running task τ_r, i.e., $\tau_i \in H(r)$. If task τ_i does not belong to $H(r)$, then the activation interrupt of task τ_i remains pending. This behaviour requires a special hardware within the processor or a HIC that holds the active task's priority in a register and raises a real interrupt only when the pending interrupt with the highest priority has a priority greater than the current priority level. A similar *Custom Programmable Interrupt Controller* (CPIC) is described in [6] with some differences: As all the tasks are considered HATs, the CPIC has to provide enough hardware timers, with its associated priority level, to implement all periodic real-time tasks in the system.

As the functionalities to be provided by the HIC are not commonly available in current processors or PICs, an approach similar to the *Virtual CPIC* presented in [7] is proposed next.

4.1 Virtual Integrated Interrupt Event-Driven Schedulers

This work proposes the use of a *Virtual Integrated Interrupt Event-Driven Scheduler* (VIIED Scheduler). Under this kind of scheduler, while the current task τ_r is running, the HIC is programmed to raise only timer interrupts belonging to activation instants of higher priority tasks, $\{r_h : \tau_h \in H_{\mathrm{SAT}}(r)\}$. The activation instants that belong to lower priority tasks, $\{r_l : \tau_l \in L_{\mathrm{SAT}}(r)\}$, are ignored, including the case in which an activation instant r_l is closer than the closest r_h. This behaviour prevents the scheduler to wake up a task with a lower priority than the current one. Thus, if a VIIED scheduler is incorporated to the integrated interrupt mode presented in [7, 8], a fully integrated interrupt model can be achieved and the system can avoid disturbances shown in sections 3.1 and 3.2.

To achieve this behaviour, each time the scheduler is invoked to determine the next ready task with the highest priority, τ_r, it has to examine the wait queue to find out which of the suspended tasks, τ_p, with a priority higher than p_r, has the closest activation instant. We call this task, τ_p, the *next preemptor* of τ_r and it can be expressed as:

$$\tau_p \in H^W(r)/ \; \nexists \tau_q \in H^W(r) : r_q < r_p \tag{4}$$

Once τ_p is determined, the HIC has to be programmed to raise the next timer interrupt at time r_p. If $H^W(r)$ is empty then there is no task into the wait queue with a higher priority than the current one, and therefore, the timer interrupt does not need to be programmed. In such a case, the currently active task will run until its suspension, at which time the system scheduler is invoked again. This can only happen when the highest priority task is running.

Taking into account the new functionality that has to be implemented by the scheduler in this model, the new scheduling overheads $\delta_I^{\text{Sched}-A}$ and $\delta_I^{\text{Sched}-T}$ can be expressed as follows:

$$\delta_I^{\text{Sched}-A} = \delta_{wq}^{\text{Sched}-A} + \delta_{rq}^{\text{Sched}-A} + \delta_{next}^{\text{Sched}-A} + \delta_{np}^{\text{Sched}-A} \tag{5}$$

$$\delta_I^{\text{Sched}-T} = \delta_{rq}^{\text{Sched}-T} + \delta_{wq}^{\text{Sched}-T} + \delta_{next}^{\text{Sched}-T} + \delta_{np}^{\text{Sched}-T} \tag{6}$$

where δ_{np} is the time required to find the next preemptor on each case, and $\delta_{rq}^{\text{Sched}-T}$, $\delta_{wq}^{\text{Sched}-T}$ and $\delta_{next}^{\text{Sched}-T}$ are the execution times required to remove the active task from ready queue, to insert its next activation on the wait queue and to determine the next activate task among the ones found in the ready queue.

The efficiency of a VIIED scheduler will strongly depend on its ability to perform all the steps included in $\delta_I^{\text{Sched}-A}$ and $\delta_I^{\text{Sched}-T}$ in a fast and bounded manner. A lot of study has been carried out to analyse the behaviour and temporal costs of different kinds of priority queues, including under the real-time perspective [11]. Next section analyses common data structures used to implement the ready and wait queues on several real-time kernels. The main drawbacks that arise when they are used to implement a VIIED scheduler are also analysed.

5   Dual-Queue Scheduling Schemes

Today's real-time operating system kernels are usually based on a dual-queue scheduling scheme. This scheme uses one queue to store active tasks, called *ready queue*, and the other one to store timed events, called *wait queue*. Timed events stored in the wait queue usually has a reference to the suspended task that has to be woken up upon the arrival of such an event.

Several open source real-time kernels found in the bibliography have been analysed and the differences found among them in the scheduling scheme are mainly centred in the data structures used to implement these queues. While *PartiKle* [12] and *MarteOS* [13] use priority bitmaps plus an array of ordered linked lists to implement the ready queue and a heap to implement the wait queue, *Open Ravenscar Kernel* [14] and *Shark* [15] kernels implement both queues with ordered linked list. The only one that does not follow the dual-queue approach is RT-Linux [16] that uses a very simple scheme based on a single one unsorted queue.

5.1   Time Complexity of Queue Operations

The ready queue operations usually required by a scheduler to implement a fixed-priority scheduling policy are: `insert`, `delete` or `delete-min`, and `find-min`. Among the structures used to implement the ready queue, the priority bitmap clearly outperforms any other data structure since it has a constant temporal cost ($\Theta(1)$) with respect to the number of ready tasks[3] in all the required operations.

---

[3] The temporal cost is $O(P)$, where P is the number of priority levels, but this value is fixed in a given system.

The queue operation required to implement the wait queue in a conventional event-driven scheduler are the same than in the ready queue. As the normal key used for storing timed events are absolute activation instants, and they are not bounded, the priority bitmap cannot be used for wait queues. In these situations a typical data structure to be used is any binary tree that offers a good temporal behaviour on the required operations. As shown above, one of the preferred ones is the binary heap [17]. In this case, the temporal cost of `find-min` operation is $\Theta(1)$ and $\Theta(\log(n))$ for `insert` and `delete-min`. Other binary trees as AVL and Black-Red trees[17] can also be used, as they have similar temporal costs, although the constant that multiply any operation cost is usually higher than the one of binary heaps.

However, to implement a VIIED scheduler a new queue operation `find-pre-emptor` is required to be implemented in the wait queue, as it is shown in equation (4). This operation is not commonly available in used data structures, as it needs a second key to sort the wait queue nodes: the priority of the task to be activated. Since data structures used to implement wait queues only uses one key, the cost of finding the item that accomplishes the *next preemptor* condition has an asymptotic upper bound of $O(N^W)$, being N^W the number of timed events stored in the wait queue.

When a sorted linked list is used to implement the wait queue, the nodes can be traversed by increasing activation instant. Since the *next preemptor* condition holds for the closest timed event with an associated task priority higher than the current one, the `find-preemptor` operation can stop as soon as one node fulfils the *higher priority* condition. This gives rise to lower temporal bound of $\Omega(1)$ and an average-behaviour that depends on the distribution of timed events inserted in the wait queue. However, due to the temporal cost of the `insert` operation ($O(n)$), the linked lists are only useful for real-time system with small real-time task sets.

On the other hand, as the ordering of siblings in a binary heap is not specified by the heap property, no order about nodes can be assumed and no *in-order* traversal is possible. Then, the tight temporal cost of the operation `find-preemptor` is $\Theta(n)$. As some implementations of AVL trees can maintain an in-order linked list together with the binary tree, they could be a good substitution of binary heaps when used on VIIED schedulers with a large number of tasks.

From here on, the worst case execution time of a queue operation will be referred as Q^R_{oper} and Q^W_{oper} for the operation `oper` over the ready and wait queue respectively.

5.2   Dual-Queue Scheme Drawbacks

As shown in the previous section, the temporal behaviour of the queue operations used by a fixed-priority real-time scheduler can be tightly bounded by using the appropriated data structures. Despite of the inability of the currently used data structures to efficiently address the `find-preemptor` operation, the major drawback of the dual-queue scheduling scheme is the use of separate queues for ready and suspended tasks. This section describes the disadvantages derived from this dual-queue scheme.

Given a running task, τ_r, a VIIED scheduler prevents the activation of lower priority tasks by means of avoiding the unnecessary timer interrupts. However, when the *next preemptor* task τ_p is activated, the lower priority tasks which activation is pending still remain in the wait queue. Being τ_p the next preemptor of τ_r, this set of pending tasks $P_p(r)$ can defined as:

$$P_p(r) = \{\tau_k \in L^W(r)/r_k \leq r_p\} \tag{7}$$

Then the number of tasks, N_p, that have to be moved to the ready queue while activating τ_p is $N_p = |P_p(r) \cup \{\tau_p\}|$.

When evaluating the cost of removing these pending tasks, it has to be taken into account that some wait queue implementations are not able to perform a `find-min` operation without performing a set of `delete-min` operations to remove the previously activated tasks $P_p(r)$. This is the case of the commonly used *heap*. If the wait queue has this constraint, then the scheduling overhead $\delta_I^{\text{Sched}-A}$ is defined as:

$$\delta_I^{\text{Sched}-A} = N_p \times (Q_{\text{delete}-\min}^W + Q_{\text{insert}}^R) + Q_{\text{find}-\min}^R + Q_{\text{find}-\text{preemptor}}^W \tag{8}$$

Although the $Q_{\text{find}-\min}^R$ can be considered constant, as it is known that the highest priority task is going to be τ_p, the term $N_p \times (Q_{\text{delete}-\min}^W + Q_{\text{insert}}^R)$, referred as *pending task processing time*, could give rise to an important execution time overhead during the activation of τ_p.

On the other hand, when the running task finishes, the system has to determine the next running task and the next preemptor. This implies to update the ready queue and wait queue, before determining the next running and preemptor tasks. This scheduling overhead is shown next:

$$\delta_I^{\text{Sched}-T} = Q_{\text{delete}-\min}^R + Q_{\text{insert}}^W + Q_{\text{find}-\min}^R + Q_{\text{find}-\text{preemptor}}^W \tag{9}$$

Additionally, due to the internal design of the scheduler, these scheduling overheads, $\delta_I^{\text{Sched}-A}$ and $\delta_I^{\text{Sched}-T}$, are in fact *blocking times*, since the system scheduler is commonly designed as an uninterruptible routine. Therefore, no higher priority tasks can be activated while the scheduler structures are being updated.

Schedulers Implementation Comparison. In order to determine if this implementation of the integrated interrupt model is adequate for a given real-time system, the overhead introduced by a traditional interrupt model, δ_T, due to the tasks that have to be activated during the execution of τ_r has to be compared with the new δ_I.

When using a traditional scheduler, the maximum overhead at a priority level p_r, referred as $\delta_T(r)$, is:

$$\delta_T(r) = \delta^{\text{isr}} + 2 \times \delta^{\text{ctx}} + \delta_T^{\text{Sched}-A} + B^{\text{SAT}}(r) + \delta_T^{\text{Sched}-T} \tag{10}$$

On the other hand, from equations (8) and (9) the overhead at a priority level p_r when using a VIIED Scheduler, $\delta_I(r)$, can be summarised as:

$$\delta_I(r) = \delta^{\text{isr}} + 2 \times (\delta^{\text{ctx}} + \delta^{\text{hic}}) + \delta_I^{\text{Sched}-A} + \delta_I^{\text{Sched}-T} \tag{11}$$

Thus, the condition that has to be fulfilled by a VIIED scheduler to worth its use into an integrated interrupt model can expressed as:

$$\delta_I(r) \leq \delta_T(r), \forall \tau_r \tag{12}$$

although the condition could be applied only to the critical priority levels.

Taking into account that in the worst case scenario N_p is limited by the number of tasks with a priority lower than p_r, i.e., $N_p \leq |L_{\text{SAT}}(r)| + 1$, the inequality shown in (12) can be simplified as follows:

$$2 \times \delta^{\text{hic}} + 2 \times Q_{\text{find}-\text{preemptor}}^W \leq |L_{\text{SAT}}(r)| \times (\delta^{\text{isr}} + \delta^{\text{ctx}} + Q_{\text{find}-\text{min}}^R) \tag{13}$$

Therefore, as $Q_{\text{find}-\text{min}}^R$ has a constant execution time in an efficient ready queue implementation, the maximum temporal cost at a given priority level p_r for $Q_{\text{find}-\text{preemptor}}^R$ can be $O(|L_{\text{SAT}}(r)|)$. As currently used wait queue implementations do not use the priority to sort the timed events, the computational cost for finding the next preemptor is usually $O(N^W)$. In such cases, the system will need an additional data structure that are able to sort pending timed events in priority order to find the next preemptor with a tighter computational cost. A possible data structure to perform this task could be a priority-indexed array of sorted event queues, as it has $O(|L_{\text{SAT}}(r)|)$ for $Q_{\text{find}-\text{preemptor}}^W$.

Despite of the accomplishment of this inequality, the dependency of $\delta_I^{\text{Sched}-A}$ with the number of blocked task in $P_p(r)$ introduces an additional undesirable behaviour: the release jitter of task τ_p, defined as the interval between the expected activation r_p and the real activation $r_p + \delta^{\text{isr}} + \delta^{\text{ctx}} + \delta_I^{\text{Sched}-A}$, becomes significantly incremented.

These disadvantages are normally intrinsic to the dual-queue scheduling scheme. The next section presents a VIIED scheduling algorithm based on a single queue model that tries to avoid both problems: release jitter and pending tasks processing time.

6   A Scheduler Based on Cartesian Trees

This section describes a VIIED scheduler that uses only one data structure to store ready and suspended tasks. This data structure is based on Cartesian trees and it is intended to reduce the temporal cost of finding the next preemptor, $Q_{\text{find}-\text{preemptor}}$, to constant time. It was already presented in a previous work to implement a real-time scheduler [18].

Cartesian trees were introduced and named by Vuillemin [9]. The name is derived from the Cartesian coordinate system for the plane. A Cartesian tree for a set of points has the sorted order of the points by their x-coordinates, and it has the heap property according to the y-coordinates of the points. In this work the x-coordinates will be the task priorities and the y-coordinates their activation instants. In such a way, the Cartesian tree becomes a heap structure that stores the closest activation instant in the root node. However, as each node also have a priority, the final tree has an interesting property: the left child of each node is the next task to be activated with a priority lower or equal than its parent node and the next task to be activated with a priority higher than the parent node is the right child. So, the *next preemptor* of a given task is directly located in its right child node, and therefore, to find the next preemptor of any task can be performed in constant time. We denote this usage of the Cartesian trees: *Scheduling Cartesian Tree* or SC-Tree.

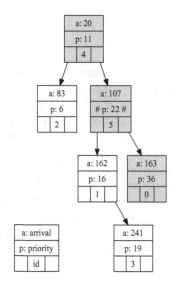

Fig. 1. A Scheduling Cartesian tree

Figure 1 shows an example of a SC-Tree with 6 tasks. Each task τ_i, is represented by three parameters: its identifier, i, its activation instant, r_i, and its priority, p_i. As it can be observed the activation instants of the nodes maintains no order but the heap property.

Let the node 4 represents the currently running task τ_4. All the suspended tasks with a higher priority, $H^W(4)$, can be found in the right sub-tree, and the lower priority ones, $L^W(4)$, in the left sub-tree. Moreover, the closest suspended task of $H^W(4)$, i.e., the next preemptor, can be found directly on the right child of node 4, i.e., the node 5. The right branch, depicted in grey in Figure 1, will be referenced as *preemptors branch*, and it contains the only tasks that can preempt the previous one in the branch during its execution. As it will be explained bellow, this preemptors branch has interesting properties.

Although this structure reduces $Q_{\text{find-preemptor}}$ to constant time, provided that a reference to the current task's node is available, this does no avoid the rest of drawbacks presented for the dual-queue scheduling schemes. So, the followed approach in this work is to use the SC-Tree not only as a heap of timed events with fast next preemptor operation, but also use the same SC-Tree as ready queue.

Let us follow the explanation with the depicted example of Figure 1. When task τ_5 becomes active at instant 107, no modifications will be performed on the SC-Tree, but just a change in the *currently running task* reference to point to node 5, that was the previous preemptor. At this time, the node 4 is the parent of currently running task τ_5. Task τ_4 is still active but it is not the highest priority task any more. Task τ_2 is also active, but it does not matter, since has a lower priority than τ_5 and τ_4. The next preemptor will be τ_0 with an activation instant $r_0 = 163$, which is the absolute time value used to program the next timer interrupt into the HIC. If the activation instant r_0 is reached before task τ_5 completes is execution, the task τ_5 will be preempted, and the scheduler would behave as in the later case, moving the currently running task reference to task τ_0. If task τ_5 finishes is execution before r_0 and ask for delaying its execution until its next period, the node 5 is modified with the new activation instant and pushed down until its new location in the SC-Tree. The new currently running task will be τ_4, i.e., the old parent of τ_5 that still remains active. The next preemptor would be τ_0 only if the new activation instant of τ_5 is not lower than r_0.

SC-Tree Computational Cost. As it has been explained, the structure of the SC-Tree only changes when a task finishes its execution. When a task becomes active there are no actions to perform but to change the currently running task reference to the previous preemptor (right child), so the time required to determine the next active task $Q_{\text{find-min}}^{SA}$ has a constant computational cost ($\Theta(1)$) and also to determine the next preemptor $Q_{\text{find-preemptor}}^{SA}$ once the currently running task reference has been updated. In such a way, the scheduling overhead due to task activation $\delta_I^{\text{Sched-A}}$ will be:

$$\delta_I^{\text{Sched-A}} = Q_{\text{find-min}}^{SA} + Q_{\text{find-preemptor}}^{SA} \tag{14}$$

which are both constant time. This behaviour allows the system to minimize the release jitter of a task under this VIIED scheduler.

On the other hand, when a preempting task finishes, the task that must be resumed is the task located at the parent node, so $Q_{\text{find-min}}^{ST}$ has also a constant execution time. Therefore, only the time to push down the next activation of the finished task is significant in the preemption process. This new operation **push-down** for a given finished task τ_f has a worst-case execution time $Q_{\text{push-down}}^{ST}$ that depends on the number of pending activations between *now* and r_f. In the worst case, the number of tasks will be N^W and, therefore, the cost will be $O(N^W)$.

SC-Tree Blocking Time. Another important advantage of the SC-Tree is that the `push-down` operation is only executed when the task finishes its execution. If some higher priority task is activated during the `push-down` operation, the operation can be preempted and resumed when the higher priority tasks finishes. Although the SC-Tree would remain in an inconsistent state until the operation was resumed, the interesting property is that the *preemptors branch* is never modified by a lower priority task, and therefore, the inconsistent SC-Tree still can be used to determine the next preemptor of the running task until pending `push-down` operations are concluded.

7   Additional Considerations

This section presents some additional considerations that have to be taken into account when a fully Integrated Interrupt Model is used in a real-time system.

In the traditional interrupt model, the scheduler cost of changing the priority of the running task, e.g. when it enters/leaves a protected object and the Immediate Priority Ceiling Protocol is used, is considered negligible or has a constant asymptotic cost.

When an Integrated Interrupt Model is used, to change the priority of the current task requires to update the system priority level. To avoid unnecessary interrupts when the system priority level changes, the HIC has to be reprogrammed and the next preemptor has to be computed when the task enters and leaves the protected object. The cost of these operations can be considered excessively high to be applied each time a task access to a protected object.

However, if the base priority is p_b and the real inherited priority, p_a, is not enforced by the VIIED Scheduler, any task τ_i with a priorities $p_i \in (p_b, p_a]$ will be activated but not executed. Additional blocking times have to be computed for these tasks similar to the one presented in equations (3) and (10).

$$B^{PO}(i) = \sum_{k \in L(i) - L(b)} \delta^{\mathrm{isr}} + Q^W_{\mathrm{delete-min}} + Q^R_{\mathrm{insert}} + Q^R_{\mathrm{find-min}} \qquad (15)$$

This blocking time is equivalent to the one for the traditional interrupt model but only for the task between priorities p_b and p_i. This overhead has to be compared with the overhead due to update the system priority level when the tasks enters and leaves the protected object that is presented next:

$$Q^{PO} = \delta^{\mathrm{hic}} + Q^R_{\mathrm{insert}} + Q^R_{\mathrm{delete-min}} + 2 \times Q^R_{\mathrm{find-min}} + 2 \times Q^W_{\mathrm{find-preemptor}} \qquad (16)$$

where Q^R_{insert} represents the overhead of inserting a pseudo-task at the new priority level p_a and $Q^R_{\mathrm{delete-min}}$ is the overhead to remove this pseudo-task at the end of the protected action. In the case of the SC-Tree, Q^R_{insert} is replaced by $Q_{\mathrm{push-down}}$.

To compute the cost of these operations for a given system scheduler allows the system designer to decide if it is worth following a fully integrated interrupt model or if it could be relaxed during the execution of protected actions.

8   Conclusions and Future Work

Previous works addressed the interrupt interference by proposing an *Integrated Interrupt Model* that avoids disturbance from external interrupts. However, the overhead of processing unnecessary activations of lower priority Software Activated Tasks has not been properly addressed in this model.

This work proposes a new *Virtual* implementation of an *Integrated Interrupt Event-Driven Scheduler* that avoids the hardware requirements of an Integrated Interrupt Event-Driven Scheduler. A new data structure based on Cartesian trees has been proposed to avoid the main drawbacks of implementing a Virtual Integrated Interrupt Event-Driven scheduler following a dual-queue scheduling approach. A comparison of the run-time behaviour of system schedulers used in an integrated model has been previously presented in [18].

The proposed SC-Tree scheduler has shown to be better suited for a fully integrated interrupt model, completely avoiding release jitter and scheduling blocking times that arise with conventional dual-queue schedulers.

Also a complete analysis of the implied overheads and blocking times when the integrated interrupt model includes Software Activated Tasks has been presented. This analysis allows the system designer to determine if the fully integrated interrupt management is suited for the real-time system under development.

Future work will try to extend the analysis to fully integrated interrupt management systems based on dynamic priorities and the suitability of the SC-Tree scheduler in such environments.

Acknowledgements. This work has been partially supported by the Spanish Government's projects COBAMI (DPI2011-28507-C02-02) and Hi-PartES (TIN2011-28567-C03-01-02-03) and the European Commission's MultiPARTES project (FP7-ICT-2011.3.4, Contract 287702).

References

1. Audsley, N., Burns, A., David, R., Tindell, K., Wellings, A.: Fixed priority preemptive scheduling: An historical perspective. Real-Time Systems 8(2/3), 173–189 (1995)
2. POSIX.13: IEEE Std. 1003.13-1998. Information Technology-Standardized Application Environment Profile-POSIX Realtime Application Support (AEP). The Institute of Electrical and Electronics Engineers (1998)
3. Katcher, D., Arakawa, H., Strosnider, J.: Engineering and analysis of fixed priority schedulers. IEEE Transactions on Software Engineering 19(9), 920–934 (1993)
4. Jeffay, K., Stone, D.L.: Accounting for interrupt handling costs in dynamic priority task systems. In: Proceedings of Real-Time Systems Symposium, pp. 212–221 (1993)
5. Burns, A., Tindell, K., Wellings, A.: Effective analysis for engineering real-time fixed priority schedulers. IEEE Transactions on Software Engineering 21(5), 475–480 (1995)

6. Leyva-Del-Foyo, L.E., Mejia-Alvarez, P.: Custom interrupt management for real-time and embedded system kernels. In: Proceedings of the Embedded Real-Time Systems Implementation (ERTSI 2004) Workshop 25th (December 2004)
7. Leyva-Del-Foyo, L.E., Mejia-Alvarez, P., de Niz, D.: Predictable interrupt management for real time kernels over conventional PC hardware. In: RTAS 2006: Proceedings of the 12th IEEE Real-Time and Embedded Technology and Applications Symposium, pp. 14–23. IEEE Computer Society, Washington, DC (2006)
8. Leyva-Del-Foyo, L.E., Mejia-Alvarez, P., de Niz, D.: Predictable interrupt scheduling with low overhead for real-time kernels. In: International Workshop on Real-Time Computing Systems and Applications, pp. 385–394 (2006)
9. Vuillemin, J.: A unifying look at data structures. Commun. ACM 23(4), 229–239 (1980)
10. Joseph, M., Pandya, P.: Finding response times in real-time systems. The Computer Journal 29(5), 390–395 (1986)
11. Mhatre, N.: A comparative performance analysis of real-time priority queues. Master's thesis, Florida State University (2001)
12. Peiro, S., Masmano, M., Ripoll, I., Crespo, A.: PaRTiKle OS, a replacement of the core of RTLinux. In: 9th Real-Time Linux Workshop (2007)
13. Aldea Rivas, M., González Harbour, M.: MaRTE OS: An ada kernel for real-time embedded applications. In: Strohmeier, A., Craeynest, D. (eds.) Ada-Europe 2001. LNCS, vol. 2043, pp. 305–316. Springer, Heidelberg (2001)
14. Puente, J., Zamorano, J., Ruiz, J.F., Fernandez, R., Garcia, R.: The design and implementation of the open ravenscar kernel. ACM SIGAda Ada Letters XXI(1), 85–90 (2001)
15. Gai, P., Abeni, L., Giorgi, M., Buttazzo, G.: A new kernel approach for modular real-time systems development. In: Proceedings of the 13th IEEE Euromicro Conference on Real-Time Systems (June 2001)
16. Barabanov, M.: A linux-based realtime operating system. Master's thesis (1997)
17. Knuth, D.E.: The art of computer programming, 2nd edn. Sorting and searching, vol. 3. Addison Wesley Longman Publishing Co., Inc., Redwood City (1998)
18. Sáez, S., Lorente, V., Terrasa, S., Crespo, A.: Efficient alternatives for implementing fixed-priority schedulers. In: Vardanega, T., Wellings, A.J. (eds.) Ada-Europe 2005. LNCS, vol. 3555, pp. 39–50. Springer, Heidelberg (2005)

PDP 4PS : Periodic-Delayed Protocol for Partitioned Systems*

Antoine Jaouën, Etienne Borde, Laurent Pautet, and Thomas Robert

Institut Telecom, TELECOM ParisTech, LTCI - UMR 5141
Paris, France
firstname.lastname@telecom-paristech.fr

Abstract. ARINC 653 systems have to comply with strong require-ments with respect to time determinism and resource consumption. How-ever, interacting processes may introduce significant overheads and in-duce pessimism in schedulability analysis. In this paper, we restrict the ARINC 653 execution and communication models so that a message is delivered as if it was sent at the sender deadline. We take advantage of dedicated inter-partition buffers to provide predictable and efficient implementations for kernel and application suppliers.

Keywords: real-time, partitioned systems, inter-partition communica-tion, deterministic communication protocol, scheduling, ARINC 653.

1 Introduction

Safety critical systems are systems whose failure can result in loss of life. In the avionic domain, several standards have been defined to guide the design of such systems. In particular, the avionic industry defined the ARINC 653 standard [1] for designing space and time partitioned real-time systems. These systems enable applications of different levels of criticality (under DO-178B [2] definition) to coexist independently on the same hardware. We call this property the isolation goal. Both the space and railway industries are now interested in this approach based on partitioned systems [3].

N→1 message passing communications (N producers to 1 consumer) are used for several purposes. A typical use concerns data fusion for system monitoring. Data fusion is the process of integrating multiple data, from multiple sources, into a consistent and accurate representation. Another use of N→1 communications occurs for fault tolerance techniques that rely on hardware/software redundancy and voting mechanisms such as Triple Modular Redundancy [4]. Mahadevan et al. in [5] described a critical avionic system involving N→1 communications used in the two circumstances previously described.

In this paper, we propose an approach to implement ARINC 653 N→1 com-munication channels with a deterministic message delivery order and a limited number of non-preemptive function calls. Our approach is designed to be used

---

* This work was partially funded by the FSF/IRT-X project.

L. George and T. Vardanega (Eds.): Ada-Europe 2014, LNCS 8454, pp. 149–165, 2014.

in only some parts of the system, leaving the possibility to use regular ARINC 653 communication channels in the remaining system.

In section 2, we describe the context of this work. Section 3 presents the issues raised when designing N→1 communications in ARINC 653. In section 4, we present our approach which results in two implementations described in sections 5 and 6. Section 7 summarizes our experimentation. Section 8 compares our approach with related works and section 9 concludes this paper.

2   Context and Motivations

N→1 message passing communications introduce schedulability analysis issues. First, as the message delivery order is not fixed, a non-deterministic number of concurrent accesses to shared resources occur. Second, preserving data consistency during these concurrent accesses requires to use lock mechanisms or non-preemptible sequences of instructions. At last, protected operations have an execution time that should not be neglected, especially when privileged execution domains are required. Designers have to over-approximate delays due to these shared resources. These issues deeply affect the schedulability analysis.

In [6], we define a deterministic N→1 communication mechanism implemented without lock mechanisms or non-preemptible sections. This paper aims at defining a N→1 deterministic and lightweight communication mechanism for ARINC 653 systems.

The ARINC 653 standard defines partitions (comparable to Real-Time POSIX processes). They are isolated in terms of space and time: space isolation means two partitions cannot share the same memory space; time isolation is materialized by a static allocation of time intervals for the execution of partitions. These time intervals (named Partition Windows or PW) are statically scheduled over the hyperperiod (named MAjor time Frame or MAF) of partitions, which are periodically executed [7]. Partitions contain processes, which can be compared to Real-Time POSIX threads. Processes in the same partition share memory and are executed under the scheduling policy of their partition. The user configures processes, partitions, ports, etc in XML-based files. A qualified tool generates from them parts of the kernel (i.e. scheduling tables).

In order to allow communication between processes, ARINC 653 defines intra and inter-partition mechanisms. We focus on inter-partition communications since intra-partition communications have already been addressed in [6]. An ARINC 653 channel is a communication link from one source partition to one or more destination partitions. Partitions have access to channels via ports and each port is either the source or destination of a channel. Two types of channels are defined in ARINC 653: queuing or sampling channels. We focus on the queuing mode since it raises issues on queue dimensioning and messages order. The messages are stored in source port, under FIFO order. ARINC 653 does not specify the instant or the mechanism for transferring messages between partitions.

A last concern in the safety-critical domain, and in particular in the avionic domain, is the certification process. The DO-178B certification standard requires evidences that the system source code is completely exercised by tests derived from requirements. All components of the system have to be certified and the certification depends on the criticality level of the component: the higher the criticality level is, the more difficult it is to certify. The ARINC 653 execution platform has to be certified at the higher criticality level and evolutions of such execution platforms require lots of time and efforts.

3   Problem Statement

This section presents and analyzes some of the main issues encountered in providing N→1 communications for real-time ARINC 653 applications.

In general, communication mechanisms entail scheduling dependencies between tasks. They originate from locks or system calls, violating the preemption hypothesis of most schedulers, both potentially delaying highest priority task execution. Since ARINC 653 aims at providing time isolation, such scheduling dependencies should be avoided as much as possible. In [6], N→1 communications have been studied for fixed priority preemptive scheduling. More precisely, an implementation strategy has been proposed to avoid both locks and non-preemptible code such as system calls. Preemptive scheduling of sending processes with variable execution leads to highly variable ordering of messages in N→1 message queues using FIFO queuing policies. ARINC 653 hierarchical scheduling of processes and partitions increases this phenomenon as preemptions are enforced at both process and partition levels.

Data transfers between partitions cannot be implemented directly within partitions as they cannot share memory. Data flows through a trusted component of the highest level of criticality, the ARINC 653 kernel. Data transfers between partitions rely on three steps: (i) store data to be transferred into the output port (triggered by a call to the ARINC 653 API for sending data), (ii) let the ARINC 653 kernel transfer data to the receiving partition (usually executed during PW switches), and (iii) retrieve data received on the input port (triggered by a call to the ARINC 653 API for receiving data). As a consequence of time and space partitioning, the implementations of steps (i) and (iii) include a non-preemptible sequence of instructions causing preemption delays. Indeed, partitioning memory relies on processors enabling memory access control (e.g. with MMU). Bypassing these controls requires privileged non-preemptible code execution. Moreover, the execution time of the memory copy is proportional to the amount of data to be transferred. Thus, these inter-partition transfers are sources of non-trivial delays on highest priority process execution, and impair schedulability analysis.

In its current version, ARINC 653 does not allow to link a channel composed of several source ports and one destination port. In other words, N→1 communications are natively not supported by ARINC 653-compliant kernels. Although the ARINC 653 standard does not give explicit reasons for this restriction, industrial partners provide us with the following explanations:

C1. A faulty process could produce more messages than expected and overflow the receiving buffer. Therefore, processes from other partitions would not be able to deliver their own messages and the faulty process would indirectly impact non-faulty processes from other partitions.

C2. The receiving process cannot identify the sending process of a given message and eventually the origin of an erroneous message. Extra information has to be carried out by messages for this purpose.

Besides, the ARINC 653 standard states that N→1 communication may be implemented on top of queuing or sampling ports. In other words, this design requires N unicast channels (1→1). Such an architecture addresses the issues stated above: (i) the space and time segregation is guaranteed by using N unicast channels, and (ii) since there is one port per partition, the sending partition can be easily identified in case it sent an incorrect message. However, this architectural solution does not address our initial issues :

1. the management of the message queue in the sending and receiving partitions is left to the responsibility of the developers. Its implementation can be very expensive and error-prone (see [5]). Moreover, the message delivery order may not be deterministic.
2. inter-partition communications heavily rely on not-interruptible sequences of instructions: one per emission or reception on a given port. Such an implementation generates important overheads at runtime and increases the pessimism of schedulability analysis.

In order to tackle these issues, we propose to adapt the Periodic-Delayed Protocol (PDP) model (originally presented in [6]) to take into account the specificities of partitioned architectures. In the next section, we introduce the main lines of the original PDP [6] which is the basis of our solutions to provide deterministic inter-partition communications.

4 PDP 4PS General Approach

As stated before, one of our objectives is to ensure a deterministic message delivery order. We characterize this determinism by the ability for a sending ARINC 653 process to transfer its messages in a predefined order and predict when they should be read by the receiver.

In [6], we described how to derive timing constraints on messages state (*i.e.* available, consumed, or outdated) from attributes of communicating processes. We propose to adapt this approach for ARINC 653 processes in order to cope with non-determinism of message transfers based on N→1 communications.

4.1 Execution and Communication Models

We first focus on processes to derive timing constraints of messages.

Execution Model: the system activity is carried out by a fixed set of processes characterized by T_i (name of process i), P_i (period of process T_i) and D_i (deadline of process T_i). The repetitive execution of a process on intervals delimited by an activation time and a deadline is called a job. As we assume synchronous activation of all processes at time 0, the execution of the kth job takes place within the time interval $[(k-1)*P_i,(k-1)*P_i+D_i[$ where $(\forall T_i : D_i \leq P_i)$. Therefore, the kth job of a process T_i is computed as a function of the time and not as a counter of T_i's activation. As ARINC 653 processes may have identical process ids on different partitions, we define global process ids to uniquely identify all the processes of the ARINC 653 system using PDP communication mechanisms. In the remaining, we designate as process ids these global and unique process identifiers.

Communication Model: communications correspond to message transfers from N sending processes to 1 receiving process. In order to follow ARINC 653 philosophy, sending processes push their messages through ports. Similarly, the receiver reads messages from its receiver port, as long as it has messages to retrieve. Sender and receiver ports can be located in distinct partitions. From the application programmer point of view, the *send* (respectively *receive*) function is called to send (resp. receive) one message to (resp. from) a port. Our purpose is to conceal from application programmers the implementation complexity (of these functions) required to ensure deterministic communication. We hide this complexity by providing an implementation method for these functions.

Our communication model is based on the following principles: in order to master queues dimension, (i) emission rate of messages has to be bound (as usually done during the design of real-time systems) and (ii) messages are only available for readers during a finite time interval. We assume that: (i) during each job exactly one message can (and has to) be sent on each sending port of a process and (ii) a message is only available after the deadline of the sender and during the following activation of the receiver. More formally, consider a message sent from a sender T_s to a receiver T_r. Assuming that T_s is released at time t_s, then its message is delivered to T_r at time $t_r = \left\lceil \dfrac{t_s + D_s}{P_r} \right\rceil * P_r$. The message is then available during the time interval $[t_r, t_r + D_r]$. A message can be read by a unique job of the receiver process. No assumptions are made about the period duration of senders. Thus, a sender can produce multiple messages during one activation of the receiver, if its period duration is lesser than the receiver's one.

An additional feature is to control the message delivery order. When messages are sent from different output ports, the order in which they are delivered to the receiving process is critical. We order messages according to the deadline of jobs of sender processes. When deadlines of sender jobs are simultaneous, we use a pre-defined order (*e.g.* based on processes id) noted $\prec$.

Such communications are said to be Periodic Delayed. In the remainder, ports, function names, or other related data structures are associated with PDP acronyms standing for Periodic Delayed Protocol to distinguish them from regular ARINC 653 artifacts. An implementation of such communications already exists in the case of non-partitioned systems (*i.e.* with shared memory). This solution is a building block of our approach and needs to be presented first.

4.2 PDP Communications for Non-partitioned Systems

Our contributions rely on the approach described in [6]. In [6], the authors proposed an implementation of the communication model described above in case processes can share memory. This implementation relies on a fixed size and shared circular buffer to store and access messages. This structure was designed to enable wait free insertion and extraction of messages from the buffer.

The number of slots in the buffer is denoted L. *send_PDP* (respectively *receive_PDP*) computes the slot index in (resp. from) which a message should be inserted (resp. extracted) and then perform the corresponding action. Slot indexes are computed with formulas attaching to each message a unique sequence number. These formulas allow computing indexes concurrently on each sender without synchronization between them. We define the following notations :

- PT_q is the set of processes sending messages towards a PDP port q. The single receiver would usually be denoted T_r.
- In order to deterministically sort messages with simultaneous deadlines, we define $\prec$ as a total order among senders.
- $SEJD(q, t)$ defines the cardinal of the set of messages that are supposed to be stored before t on q.
- $Followers(q, j, k)$ is the number of jobs, of processes belonging to PT_q, with same deadline as the kth job of T_j such that their process id is higher than T_j with respect to $\prec$.
- $PR(r, t)$ identify the next release time of receiving process T_r at time t.
- $MSN(q, j, k)$ (or Message Sequence Number) computes the sequence number of a message send by T_j from its kth job to the PDP port q.

$$SEJD(q, t) = \sum_{T_j \in PT_q} \left(\left\lfloor \frac{t - D_j}{P_j} \right\rfloor + 1 \right) \tag{1}$$

$$MSN(q, T_j, k) = SEJD(q, k * P_j + D_j) - Followers(q, T_j, k) \tag{2}$$

Sending a Message: A process T_j calls *send_PDP* once during its kth job. It computes $MSN(q, T_j, k) \bmod L$ and stores the message passed as parameter at this index in the buffer. As k is computed based on the period and the deadline of task T_i, an attempt to send multiple messages during a period is automatically detected (see [6] for more details). This approach was designed to store successive messages in contiguous position in the buffer.

Receiving Messages: The receiver can read messages with indexes from $SEJD(q, (k - 1) * P_r) + 1$ to $SEJD(q, k * P_r))$ during its kth activation. Modulo buffer size has to be applied to find the correct slot. When the slot is empty, the receiver automatically detects and identifies which sender failed to produce its message. The buffer size is a key feature of this mechanism as memory space is often the weakness of wait free queues. Let D_{max} the largest deadline of sending processes. Then, a sufficient number of slots in the buffer, denoted L, is:

$$L = \sum_{T_j \in PT_q} \left(\left\lfloor \frac{2 * P_r + D_{max}}{P_j} \right\rfloor + 1 \right) \tag{3}$$

To complete the presentation of this approach, note that it combines two advantages: first, messages are sorted in the order they should be delivered to the receiver, and senders store their messages concurrently without relying on locks. However, in partitioned systems, the memory space of partitions are disjoint. Thus, this solution cannot be used without adaptation.

4.3   Adaptation to Partitioned Systems

A simple implementation of PDP consists in writing and reading messages from a buffer stored in a memory space shared by sending and receiving processes. However, a message transfer requires three different steps when processes communicate without having access to a shared memory (i.e. processes from different partitions): (i) the sending process stores the message in a memory space of the partition referenced by the kernel, (ii) the kernel transfers (through a system call) the message from the sending partition to the receiving partition, and (iii) the receiving process consumes and uses the message. As a consequence, the implementation of PDP on a partitioned system must be adapted.

PDP relies on the principle that, for each job of a sender process, a dedicated slot can be identified in the buffer viewed by the receiver process. Since we can have P sending processes in N partitions sending messages towards one receiving process in one partition, messages are stored in each sending partition before being transferred to the receiving partition. The identification of the slot dedicated to each message must be done twice: once in the memory space of the sending partition, and once when the message is transferred to the queue viewed by the receiving process.

In order to implement PDP over a partitioned system, two alternatives are available from a software architectural point of view. Either data transfers from partitions to partitions are done through standard ARINC services (reducing maintenance effort), or data transfers are done through dedicated mechanisms provided by a specialized kernel (reducing non-interruptible calls).

Figures 1 and 2 illustrates the architecture of each solution (respectively with and without dedicated kernel services). The implementations of each solution are described in sections 5 and 6. In this section, we present the common principles of both solutions. Note also that data structures and functions of these implementations are part of the kernel or a system library and cannot be jeopardized unintentionally. This partially contributes to enforce the isolation goal.

Message Conditioning Before Transfer: this activity verifies the absence of message overproduction (a sending process sends more than one message during

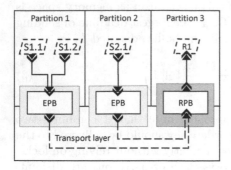

Fig. 1. K-PDP architecture

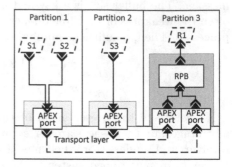

Fig. 2. A-PDP architecture

its period), and stores the message in the queue of the sending partition. In order to proceed to faults detection and message queue reconstruction on the receiver side, messages are annotated with (i) the identifier of the sending process, and (ii) the job counter of the sending process. This extra information is used to compute the message number as explained in equation (2).

Message Actual Transfer: messages being temporarily stored in sending partitions have to be transferred out from the memory of the sender partition and copied to the receiver memory. The actual transfer does not need to occur during the execution of the *send_PDP* function, but needs to occur before the next PW of the receiving partition.

Message Conditioning After Transfer: this step provides to the receiving process a message queue structure similar to the one presented at the beginning of this section. This means we have to proceed to the fusion of messages coming from different partitions, and to re-order these messages. This step also detects message omissions.

This approach complies with the IMA methodology. When designing IMA systems, the system integrator specifies to application suppliers the different production rates of messages exchanged by the partitions they are in charge of. When message rates are periodic, our approach can be applied whether the messages are produced by logical or physical tasks. For instance, in fault tolerance techniques relying on hardware/software redundancy and voting mechanisms such in [5], the production rates of sender components are fully specified and mapped onto periodic tasks. For non-periodic messages, the application suppliers have to use the regular inter-partition communication mechanisms.

This approach also preserves the constraints from section 3. For instance, let assume a sender produces two messages during the same period. As the job counter is computed based on the emission time, the period and the deadline, the **Message Conditioning Before Transfer** step will issue the same job counter and therefore store the messages in the same slot. For the second message, as its slot is not empty, a null message is stored to denote an incorrect message as well as an incorrect partition. The same mechanism applies during the **Message**

Actual Transfer step. During the **Message Conditioning After Transfer** step, the receiver will read messages produced during a given time interval. When one of these messages is a null message, this denotes the sender either failed to produce its message or produced multiple ones. In any case, the slot index corresponds to a specific partition which can be declared as erroneous.

The next section describes how these steps are actually implemented either on top of, or integrated to, the ARINC 653 kernel.

5   PDP 4PS for Kernel Supplier

In this section, we assume a role of ARINC 653 kernel supplier and we implement at kernel level a deterministic and wait-free solution for N→1 communication named K-PDP. The main ideas have already been described in the previous section. This section gives some implementation specificities made possible because of the kernel sources availability. Without loss of generality, let us assume we have only one N→1 channel to deal with.

5.1   Architecture

Figure 1 describes the architecture of a K-PDP channel and in particular the buffers used on the sending and receiving sides. We first focus on the sender side.

As N sending processes are spread over M partitions ($N \geq M$), let N_P designate the number of the processes co-located on the same partition P. Each of these sending partitions has an unique port linked to the port of the receiving partition. Therefore, N_p sending processes share the same port on partition P. We implement each partition port with a PDP buffer (named Emission PDP Buffer or EPB_p) allocated in the memory space of partition P. This buffer mainly provides these N_p sending processes with a wait free access to the port. During its job k, a sending process T_j stores in slot $MSN(EPB_p, T_j, k)$ mod $length(EPB_p)$ its message but also its process id and its job counter. This extra information on the sending process is used on the receiving side to globally order messages from several partitions. A sending partition also preserves $lastMSN$, the index of the last message transferred to the receiving partition.

We now focus on the receiving side. The receiving partition also maintains a PDP buffer (named Reception PDP Buffer or RPB) allocated in its memory space. This buffer allows the partition to order messages from all the sending processes of different partitions. For the sake of consistency, the RPB buffer also includes extra information as does any EPB buffer. This information is transferred for consistency reason but it also helps the receiving partition to identify a partition responsible for an erroneous message. Indeed, the receiving partition maintains a sequence table with the process id and its job counter of the messages to receive over an hyper-period. This table $MtoPID$ helps retrieving the process id from the index of the message in the RPB buffer. It is used to ignore messages coming from a partition that is deemed to be unreliable.

Note that the M EPB buffers and the RPB buffer are implemented as regular PDP buffers. Therefore, the MSN values used to store messages in these buffers are pre-computed either as a constant table or as a function [6].

5.2 Implementation

To explain the rational behind the architecture of a K-PDP channel, we now get back to the steps introduced in 4.3. In this context, the kernel supplier provides the new implementation of the send and receive functions. The different tables they depend on can be automatically generated by qualified development tools from the XML-based configuration file describing the ARINC 653 system.

Message Conditioning Before Transfer: As already stated, a sending partition P is equipped with a PDP buffer named EPB_p configured for N_p sending processes and one receiving partition. One of the goals of this step is to check that the current sending process T_j has not already produced a message in the buffer of port q during its current job k. This is easily done by checking that the slot $MSN(EPB_p, T_j, k)$ mod $length(EPB_P)$ is still empty. As described in the previous subsection, the EPB_p buffer includes the message produced by T_j but also an extra information such as its process id and its job counter. This extra information is crucial to enforce the actual transfer and to store the message at the right slot in the RPB buffer of the receiving partition.

Message Actual Transfer: the kernel performs this step when it starts executing a partition window (PW) of the receiving partition R. Let t_R^b be the activation time of such a PW. At t_R^b, we transfer messages produced by each sending partition P involved in the K-PDP channel. We first determine the messages produced by the N_p sending processes on partition P that have to be transferred from the EPB_p buffer to the RPB buffer. We transfer messages if and only if they might be consumed by the receiving process T_r during the current PW. To achieve this, we compute the release time of the last job of T_r occurring before t_R^e the completion time of the current PW. The last job of T_r occurs at time $\left\lceil \dfrac{t_R^e}{P_r} \right\rceil * P_r$. Therefore, we transfer from EPB_p to RPB the messages and their extra information from slot $lastMSN + 1$ to $SEJD(q, t_R^e)$. Note that before this transfer, the impacted slots can be first reinitialised to ease the detection of missing messages. Once the transfer achieved, $lastMSN$ is updated. Note that all these numbers are known statically and can be computed off-line to preserve performances.

In the event of a faulty sending partition which would produce more messages than expected, our methodology will prevent from RPB overflow. Indeed, the kernel determines which message to transfer from sending to receiving partition, without relying on some information contained in partition memory space. Thus, only expected number of message is transferred into the RPB.

Message Conditioning After Transfer: Once the messages to transfer from a sending partition P to the receiving partition R have been determined, the kernel dispatches them in the RPB buffer. As stated before, each message m comes with an extra information including the process id of T_j and job counter k of the sending process. The kernel assigns to m a slot $MSN(RPB, T_j, k)$ mod $length(RPB)$ in RPB. Before consuming a message m in RPB, the receiving process checks the validity of the process id and the job counter attached to m with those stored in the corresponding slot of the $MtoPID$ table. If they do not match, the message is actually missing and the receiving process can declare the process id from $MtoPID$ as faulty.

6   PDP 4PS for Application Supplier

In this section, we assume a role of ARINC 653 application supplier and we implement at APEX level a deterministic solution for N→1 communication. The main ideas have already been described in 4. The architecture of A-PDP channels is very close to the K-PDP channel's one. We focus on the implementation specificities due to the unavailability of the kernel sources.

6.1   Architecture

N_p designates the number of the processes co-located on a given partition P. As the ARINC 653 standard does not enable to have N→1 channels, we use M ARINC 653 unicast channels to implement one A-PDP channel, M being the number of partitions. Thus, each sending partition S has a unique ARINC 653 source port and the receiving partition has M destination ports, one per sending partitions. The size of ARINC 653 source and destination ports is set to the one of the EPB buffer that partition S would have in the K-PDP solution. This architecture is illustrated on figure 2. As we rely on ARINC 653 services, concurrent accesses to this source port from N_p co-located processes is delegated to the ARINC 653 send operation. Then, messages are sent via the source port with the sending process id and its job counter. As for the K-PDP channels, this extra information helps to enforce a global message delivery order on the receiving partition.

We now focus on the receiving side. The receiving partition has M ARINC 653 destination ports. its also maintains a PDP buffer (named Reception PDP Buffer or RPB) allocated in its memory space. This buffer allows the partition to order messages from N sending processes located on M partitions. The kernel flushed messages to at most M destination ports before activating a PW for the receiving partition. The receiving process dispatches the received messages in the RPB buffer using the process id and the job counter attached to messages. The receiving partition also maintains $MtoPID$, a sequence table with the process id and its job counter of the messages to receive over an hyper-period. This table allows to retrieve the process id with its index given a slot in the RPB buffer. The RPB buffer is implemented as regular PDP buffers. Therefore, the MSN values used to store messages in these buffers are pre-computed as they were in the K-PDP solution.

6.2 Implementation

To explain the rational behind the architecture of a A-PDP channel, we now get back to the steps introduced in 4.3. In this context, the application supplier provides an implementation of the send and receive functions in overlay of corresponding APEX functions. The different tables they depend on can be automatically generated by qualified development tools from the XML-based configuration file describing the ARINC 653 system.

Message Conditioning Before Transfer: As already stated, a sending partition P is equipped with a ARINC 653 source port. One of the goals of this step is to check that the current sending process T_j has not already produced a message on source port during its current job k. This is easily done by maintaining a counter associated at each sending process. This counter holds the number of sending function calls during each period of its associated process. As described in the previous subsection, a message produced by T_j is sent on the A-PDP channel with extra information used to store the message at the expected slot in the RPB buffer.

Message Actual Transfer: As message transfer between partitions relies on ARINC 653 channels, the actual message transfer between partition is performed by the ARINC 653 kernel. While the ARINC 653 standard specification does not specify the exact instant for transferring messages between partitions, it has to be done before any activation of the receiving partition.

   In the event of a faulty sending partition which would produce more messages than expected, our methodology will prevent from RPB overflow. Indeed, the A-PDP architecture being based on M ARINC 653 unicast channel, in this event the ARINC 653 channel linking the faulty partition to the receiving partition can be discarded without impact on the A-PDP channel.

Message Conditioning After Transfer: The receiving process executes an immediate ARINC 653 *receive_queueing_message* call on each of the M ARINC 653 channels and merges the received messages in its RPB buffer. This operation occurs when the receiving process invokes our specific receive operation at each period activation. As stated before, each message m comes with an extra information including the process id of T_j and job counter k of the sending process. The receiving process assigns to m a slot $MSN(RPB, T_j, k) \bmod length(RPB)$ in RPB. Before consuming a message m in RPB, the receiving process checks the validity of m and may detect a faulty process.

7 Experimentation

Experimenting with the K-PDP proposal requires to have access to the sources of an ARINC 653 kernel. For this purpose, we used POK (Partitioned Open Kernel [8]). POK is a generic kernel for partitioned systems and it comes with an ARINC 653 personality. Of course, POK is also used to evaluate the A-PDP proposal. In order to illustrate the PDP 4PS approach, we introduce a simple

Table 1. Process Id and Job Counter Associated to Message Number in Current MAF

Message Number	0	1	2	3	4	5	6	7	8	9	10	11	12	13
Process Id	S1	S2	S2	S3	S1	S2	S1	S2	S3	S1	S2	S1	S2	S3
Job Counter	0	0	1	0	1	2	2	3	1	3	4	4	5	2

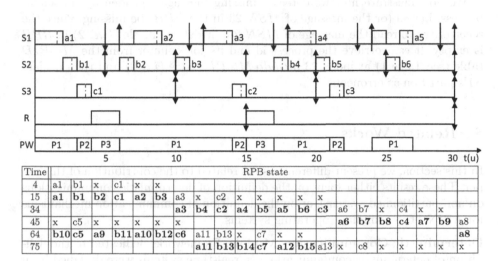

Time	RPB state																				
4	a1	b1	x	c1	x	x															
15	**a1**	**b1**	**b2**	**c1**	**a2**	**b3**	a3	x	c2	x	x	x	x	x							
34							**a3**	**b4**	**c2**	**a4**	**b5**	**a5**	**b6**	**c3**	a6	b7	x	c4	x	x	
45	x	c5	x	x	x	x	x								**a6**	**b7**	**b8**	**c4**	**a7**	**b9**	a8
64	**b10**	**c5**	**a9**	**b11**	**a10**	**b12**	**c6**	a11	b13	x	c7	x	x								a8
75							**a11**	**b13**	**b14**	**c7**	**a12**	**b15**	a13	x	c8	x	x	x	x	x	

Fig. 3. Receiver Buffer Content At Each Receiver Activation

example describing common configuration tables of K-PDP and A-PDP internal mechanisms and a short execution diagram. For the sake of clarity, we will focus only on the receiving side.

A system has three partitions : $P1$, $P2$ and $P3$. Process i is described as follow (T_i, P_i, D_i, C_i), C_i being the execution time of T_i. $P1$ has two sender processes $(S1, 6, 5, 2)$ and $(S2, 5, 5, 1)$ under Rate Monotonic Scheduling, $P2$ one sender process $(S3, 10, 10, 1)$ and $P3$ one receiver process $(R, 15, 15, 2)$. The RPB is 21 slot sized. The $MtoPID$ table is 14 slot sized (see Table 1).

The figure 3 presents the execution of the system introduced above over a MAF (at time 30). The PW line represents the Partition Windows allocated to each partition over a MAF. An up (resp. down) arrow represents an activation (resp. a deadline) of a process. A doted line designate the production of a message. The aX, bX, cX notation denotes the Xth message produced by respectively $S1$, $S2$ and $S3$.

Table from figure 3 describes the state of the RPB at each activation of process R. The symbols with a bold font represent available messages. These contiguous intervals are determined as described in subsection 4.2. The symbols with a normal font represent messages that will be available at the next receiver's period. Some of these messages have already been transfered, some messages marked as 'x' have not yet been transfered. This situation illustrates a A-PDP configuration. In a K-PDP configuration, only messages available in the PW of the receiver are transferred. The available message sequence is repeated every MAF. This allows to define a bounded size table *MtoPID* which gives the sender id and its job counter for a given message number in the current MAF (see Table 1). We retrieve the message number of a message, by applying its corresponding *MSN* modulo the size of the *MtoPID* table *MtoPID_size*.

We now illustrate how we detect a missing message and identify its sender process. Let $a9$ (or the message of *MSN* 23 in the *RPB*) be missing. Once the receiver try to read the message of *MSN* 23 , it detects its slot (*i.e.* 2) in *RPB* is empty. It can retrieve the process id and its job counter from the *MtoPID* table (see Table 1) at index 23 *modulo MtoPID_size* (*i.e.* 9) and then declare *S*1's partition as erroneous.

8   Related Works

In this section, we present different results related to the contribution of this paper. These results either focus on the definition of deterministic communications on non-partitionned systems, or on the definition of communication mechanisms for ARINC 653 compliant operating systems.

Deterministic Communication Models. Frameworks dedicated to the definition of deterministic communications in real-time systems were designed both for local communications (communications between tasks on the same processing unit) and remote communications (communications between tasks on different processing units). OASIS [9] automates the implementation of local communications based on a time-triggered semantics. Applications are designed with an extended version of the C language called ψC. Programmers express time intervals in which communications are triggered by a dedicated scheduler included in the kernel. In between such intervals, no data transmition is implemented. OASIS extracts from ψC sources the communication intervals such that message passing can be performed at predefined instants. This approach provides a deterministic communication model, which can be implemented without locks. However, OASIS differs from our approach since it requires a detailed description of the communication instants, based on ψC. In order to implement communications as specified in ψC, an automatic configuration of the kernel is required. Besides, since this configuration is done at a very precise granularity, it requires to adopt a specific execution environment. Beyond local communications, determinism is also of great interest when considering remote communications on a given network. For instance, time-triggered protocols [10] help to analyse and configure the usage of real-time networks. To illustrate this, the product ^{TTE}COM *Layer ARINC 653* is interfaced with *VxWorks 653* in order to handle time triggered remote communications in an avionic architecture. Note that deterministic remote communications (such as time-triggered communications) are complementary with the results we present in this paper: both approaches could be coupled to have determinism on local and remote communications. SynDEx [11] is a component-based framework relying on a synchronous data flow semantics. This model has been used to automate the deployment (by production of scheduling tables) of functions on processing units in order to guarantee the schedulability of tasks and communications. SyndDEx relies on a deterministic communication semantics, and addresses the configuration of both local and remote communications. However, the applicability of this framework to ARINC 653 applications has not been demonstrated yet. In [12], the authors study the usability of SIGNAL (a framework based synchronous data flows) in order to model and deploy applications on an ARINC 653-compliant kernel. This paper shows the advantage of this technology in terms of analysis of a design model, but does not detail how the ARINC 653 services are actually implemented. Thus, it is difficult to assess the precision of their schedulability analysis, or the impact of their approach on the certification efforts.

Low-Level Implementations of ARINC 653 Communications. When it comes to the low-level mechanisms used to implement ARINC 653 communications, different strategies have been proposed. We study such contributions in the remainder of this section. XtratuM [13] is a hypervisor designed for real-time embedded systems. XtratuM can run several applications in a robust partitioned environment, very similar to the ARINC 653 standard. Communications are conducted by the kernel, which copies messages from a dedicated memory space (in the kernel memory) bound to the sending partition to a dedicated memory space (in the kernel memory) bound to the receiving partition [13]. Send and receive operations execute a syscall in order to access their dedicated memory space. Thus, the kernel controls the data flow and performs message copy at specific instants, which increases the reliability of the system. As opposed to our solutions, XtratuM does not rely on a deterministic communication model. As opposed to our solution, this framework does not tackle the issues of scheduling dependencies and ordering of messages raised by classical implementations of ARINC 653. Implementing inter-partition communication with two buffers is a common practice. Rushby [14] proposed a more efficient communication mechanism via memory mapping between a sending and a receiving process, using the services of a memory management unit (MMU). The sending process has only writing permissions in the memory space, while the receiving process has only reading rights. This solution has several benefits in terms of execution time and memory footprint. However, a faulty sending process can write anywhere in the shared buffer and the receiving one must perform time consuming verifications under this assumption. Contrasting with our approach, this result does not propose a mechanism to detect the occurence of an erroneous communication. In [15], the authors focus on the impact of ARINC 653 kernel on the composability of timing properties associated to software components of a software architecture. Authors clearly identified ARINC 653 inter-partition communication as an issue for time composability. However, their results focus on improving the scheduling algorithm rather than on the definition of a deterministic communication model. Our results are thus complementary: design of ARINC 653 compliant kernels can take improve time composability by taking advantage of both solutions.

9 Conclusion

In this paper, we propose two implementations of N→1 communications for AR-INC 653 systems that provide a deterministic message delivery order and require no non-preemptive function calls. They ease the schedulability analysis and also respect the ARINC 653 standard requirements. The first implementation, K-PDP, is dedicated to platform suppliers as it requires an access to the kernel sources, when the second one, A-PDP, is more suitable for applications suppliers as it is based on the ARINC 653 services API. K-PDP has been implemented on top of POK, our free ARINC 653 kernel and A-PDP has only been evaluated with a manually generated implementation. We plan in future works to automate the A-PDP solution thanks to our AADL modeling environment and its modeling transformations for automatic code generation.

References

1. Airlines Electronic Engineering: Avionics Application Software Standard Interface. Technical report, Aeronautical Radio, INC (1997)
2. RTCA: DO-178B: Software Considerations in Airborne Systems and Equipment Certification (1982)
3. Alena, R., Ossenfort, J., Laws, K., Goforth, A., Figueroa, F.: Communications for integrated modular avionics. In: IEEE Aerospace Conference, pp. 1–18 (2007)
4. Lyons, R.E., Vanderkulk, W.: The use of triple-modular redundancy to improve computer reliability. IBM Journal 6(2), 200–209 (1962)
5. Mahadevan, N., Dubey, A., Karsai, G.: Application of Software Health Management Techniques. In: SEAMS, pp. 1–10 (2011)
6. Cadoret, F., Robert, T., Borde, E., Pautet, L., Singhoff, F.: Deterministic Implementation of Periodic-Delayed Communications and Experimentation in AADL. In: ISORC (2013)
7. Hang Lee, Y., Younis, M., Zhou, J.: Partition scheduling in apex runtime environment for embedded avionics software. In: RTCSA, pp. 103–109 (1998)
8. Delange, J., Pautet, L., Kordon, F.: Design, implementation and verification of mils systems. Softw., Pract. Exper. 42(7), 799–816 (2012)
9. Louise, S., Lemerre, M., Aussagues, C., David, V.: The OASIS Kernel: A Framework for High Dependability Real-Time Systems. In: HASE, pp. 95–103 (November 2011)
10. Kopetz, H., Grünsteidl, G.: Ttp-a protocol for fault-tolerant real-time systems. Computer 27(1), 14–23 (1994)
11. Grandpierre, T., Lavarenne, C., Sorel, Y.: Optimized rapid prototyping for real-time embedded heterogeneous multiprocessors. In: CODES, Rome, Italy (1999)
12. Gamatié, A., Gautier, T., Le Guernic, P.: Example of Synchronous Design of Embedded Real-Time Systems based on IMA. In: RTCSA, Gothenburg, Sweden (2004)
13. Crespo, A., Ripoll, I., Masmano, M.: Partitioned Embedded Architecture Based on Hypervisor: The XtratuM Approach. In: EDCC 2010, pp. 67–72 (2010)
14. Rushby, J.: Partitioning in avionics architectures: Requirements, mechanisms, and assurance. Technical Report (March 1999)

15. Baldovin, A., Mezzetti, E., Vardanega, T.: A time-composable operating system. In: WCET, pp. 69–80 (2012)
16. Delange, J., Lec, L.: POK, an ARINC653-compliant operating system released under the BSD license. In: 13th Real-Time Linux Workshop (2011)
17. Feiler, P.H., Gluch, D.P.: Model-Based Engineering with AADL: An Introduction to the SAE Architecture Analysis & Design Language, 1st edn. Addison-Wesley Professional (2012)
18. Cadoret, F., Borde, E., Gardoll, S., Pautet, L.: Design patterns for rule-based refinement of safety critical embedded systems models. In: ICECCS, pp. 67–76 (2012)

OBUs' Development and Maintenance of a Train Control System for Low Density Traffic Lines

Gerhard Hanis and Burkhard Stadlmann

University of Applied Sciences Upper Austria, Campus Wels – School of Engineering
and Environmental Sciences, Wels, Austria
{gerhard.hanis,burkhard.stadlmann}@fh-wels.at

Abstract. This paper sketches the evolution of a train control system (TCS) and its on-board unit (OBU) for low density traffic lines. The train control system represents a distributed real-time control system consisting of on-board computers on each train, a traffic control center as well as a data radio system. The safety critical software components have been implemented in Ada95 and the system is constantly adopted for different industrial and research projects. The latest modifications dealt with the exchange of the communication mechanisms over the data radio system, the exchange of the data radio system itself and sensor replacements. These modifications have been performed within the realm of the EU funded research project SATLOC and tested in field.

Keywords: train control system. GPS based train control system. real-time systems. communication-based train control.

1 Basic Idea of the Train Control System

The train control system relies on the same operational principles as radio-based operational train control (in German: Zugleitbetrieb mit Sprechfunk), but receives computer-aided support with the addition of a data radio system for communication between trains and the traffic control center. The traffic controller performs the same routines as before, but now via the aid of a computer instead of paper and pencil. Train drivers obtain their movement authority via the driver machine interface (DMI) instead of listening to and acknowledging over voice radio and logging it manually into a journey report. The systems goal is to omit track side installations and therefore the trains shall determine themselves were they are along the line, report this information to a centralized control and supervision system. The traffic control center monitors the trains and informs them up to where they are allowed to move. Since this kind of system heavily relies on the communication between the system elements it can be classified as a Communication Based Train Control (CBTC) system [6]. The system development started in 1999 and a first version is described in [1]. In the meantime the system has been developed further and is currently deployed on 5 low density lines in Austria [2].

L. George and T. Vardanega (Eds.): Ada-Europe 2014, LNCS 8454, pp. 166–176, 2014.
© Springer International Publishing Switzerland 2014

2   System Architecture

The TCS is a distributed real-time system with a proprietary data-radio system as the shared network layer and centralized control for dispatching. The communication between the traffic control center and the trains relies on a line-specific bi-directional data radio system, thus no expensive further line-side equipment is required. The system utilizes a digital line atlas which contains line specific information like geography and topology. It can be interpreted as simple track database and it is stored on each on-board computer as well as at the traffic control center. Originally all safety relevant parts of it like the management and emission of conflict free movement authorities, collision avoidance and driver supervision have been implemented in Ada95. In order to simplify system development as well as to get the advantages of strong typing and due to recommendations in EN50128 Ada has been chosen as the main programming language. Initially the TCS has been approved for SIL0 [3] though the design process was already implemented to achieve a higher level like SIL2. The approval for SIL0 was done as it represents an addition to the previously used voice system and due to economic restrictions.

2.1   Traffic Control Center

The traffic control center (TCC) consists of two separate software modules. The safety kernel has been developed in Ada95 and is responsible for conflict-free generation of movement authorities (MA), maintaining the communication to the trains via the data radio system and the transmission of locally generated Radio Technical Commission for Maritime Services (RTCM) correction data to the trains. The RTCM correction data contains information which is used by the trains to improve their self-localization via satellite based systems. The other part has been coded with Java and provides an interface to the traffic controller which shows a complete real-time view of the line. The schematic view shows the line on one hand and a scaled electronic time table including both the planned and actual train runnings on the other hand.

Fig. 1. Traffic Control Center

2.2   On-Board Unit

The on-board unit (OBU) consists of an on-board computer (OBC), driver machine interfaces (DMI) for cab-signaling, navigation sensors, a data radio modem and is connected to the emergency brake system as well as other train relevant digital I/Os. The on-board computer is responsible for determining the train's location along the line, which is mainly based on Global Navigation Satellite System (GNSS) position data and other sensors. The result of the sensor fusion is matched against a digital line atlas to retrieve a position in a line-based coordinate format. Due to omitted track side signals, the train driver is informed via cab-signaling of the most important information, like current location, system state and received MA. Consequently, the computer supervises the correct execution of the MA by the train driver. Moreover, it also monitors the movement of the train and will automatically activate the emergency brake if the driver tries to pass beyond the limitations of the given movement authority. Depending on the configuration and state of implementation the speed of the train is supervised too.

3   Ada-Software Architecture

The safety related software of OBC and TCC do have a limited shared code basis e.g. digital line atlas, telegram structures and generic packages in common. Due to the nature of the system the remaining bigger portion of the code is separated, but does follow the herein described principles.

3.1   Task Structure

The software of the TCC as well as the OBC consists of several loosely coupled tasks of which each serves one distinctive purpose. The overall structure is:

- One task is responsible for starting the system in a defined order. This task initially loads the configuration files as well as the digital line atlas. Afterwards it starts further tasks and supervises them by monitoring heartbeats. Therefore this task is referred to as "Task_Supervisor".
- The other tasks have to offer the rendezvous method "Start".
- The inter-task communication is realized via an asynchronous messaging mechanism.
- The tasks send cyclic heartbeats to "Task_Supervisor".
- If heartbeats of a task are missing for a certain period of time the system either restarts automatically or prompts the user to restart it.
- Cyclic tasks with appropriate predefined priorities and cycle times are used.

3.2   Inter-task Communication

The inter-task communication is implemented as a message handling system with an appropriate amount of buffers using generic protected message buffers [1]. Therefore each task has its own buffer from which it receives incoming messages. A message is a record which consists of two values: an ID as enumeration type and Data as Unbounded_String.

In order to create and retrieve proper messages so-called task message packages have been introduced. These packages define the message ID as enumeration type and the content of the Unbounded_String depends on the message ID. To ensure proper data exchange explicit routines for creation and parsing the Unbounded_String have been implemented for each message ID. In order to provide consistency these packages have been named after the task which receives the messages. There have been two arguments for using the dynamic structure Unbounded_String: (1) The safety of the TCS is based on the combination of technical support by the computer as well as from a system point of view the operational procedures themselves and (2) the concerned railway guideline [3] only recommends avoiding dynamic structures or objects for SIL3 or higher.

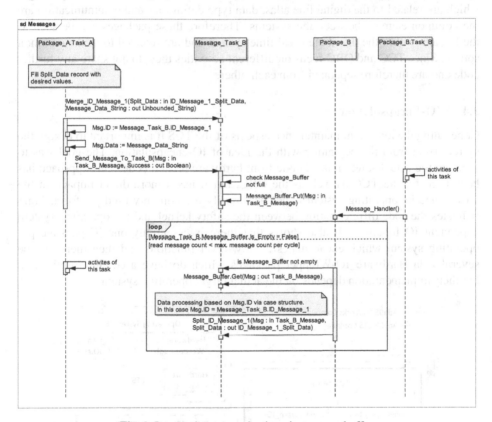

Fig. 2. Inter-task communication via message buffer

The task package implements a message handler procedure which is only visible within it and this routine shall only be called by the task and not in any other way indirectly by procedures or functions. For message processing the task calls this handler every cycle and therefore checks whether messages are available and will process them accordingly to their ID. Since the design rule is to use a case structure for handling the enumeration type and to not use the keyword "others", the Ada compiler ensures all values of the enumeration are included and handled. Fig.2 illustrates the implemented architecture and the required steps in order to transmit a message with data from Task_A to Task_B.

The advantage of this approach is to have one straightforward, longterm base structure for data exchange whereas the obvious downsides are the required amount of processing resources for data conversions as well as the additional code to perform them.

3.3   Code Structure

From the development perspective certain code elements are shared between the software of the TCC and the OBC. The concerned code elements are generic packages for reusability like buffers and finite-state machines. On the other hand packages which are related to the digital line atlas, data type definitions and communication are the common element between the systems. Therefore these packages can be seen as the linkage within the distributed real-time system and are referred to as the common source. Since TCC and OBC focus on different activities they do not share any further code and are therefore separated from each other.

3.4   IO-Encapsulation

Concerning the long term maintenance aspects of the TCS it is important to design the system right from the beginning with the idea of IO-encapsulation. The goal was to separate the actual safety related code from hardware related code. This approach has been used for the TCC as well as the OBC, but it has a more direct impact on the OBC since its operating system is not necessarily a commonly used platform. Fig.3 indicates the code differentiation between the safety kernel and the operating system dependent IO functions. It also shows that there is essentially one IO-package per operating system which encapsulates all low-level functions and then there can be several Ada Hardware_IO-Wrapper packages which do have a common definition, but their implementation depends on the actual target operating system.

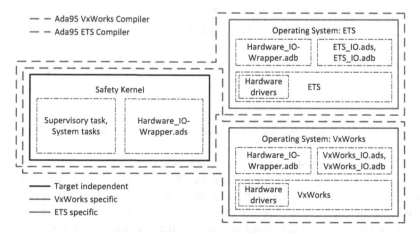

Fig. 3. Operating system and hardware dependent IO-encapsulation

4   System Evolution

After the successful deployment in 2005 at the Gmunden line of Stern&Hafferl and its final approval in 2006 [4] the system got modernized. Due to new features specified by the user and new legal requirements and an end of operating system maintenance of the OBC platform it was decided to move on to a modern target. Therefore the OBCs' operating system has been exchanged from the Windows based ETS to VxWorks which also forced a change of the used Ada95 compiler. In consequence a VxWorks system image with all relevant custom hardware drivers had to be developed. This step was followed by a simple exchange of the OS dependent IO-functions as shown in Fig.3.

4.1   Stern and Hafferl

The Train Control System in Upper Austria [1] [4] has been enhanced with numerous additional features based on the experience of the daily operation in combination with user generated new features. Examples are the automatic location controlled lubrification of the track to reduce squeezing of the wheels or the control of the moveable step for easy access of the passengers and the supervision of the switch positions.

4.2   RZL-Pinzgau

For the deployment at Pinzgaubahn [2] several system elements had to be exchanged or added in order to improve safety to SIL2 which have been implemented within an additional research project. The main system extensions were support of "track selectivity", improved supervision and control as well as a mechanism for enhanced integrity and authenticity checks of exchanged telegrams between OBC and TCC. Previously the OBC was not capable of determining on which parallel track it was driving. In order to add this functionality so-called balises, which represent passive RFID tags, have been mounted onto track sleepers. In consequence balises and its balise-reader have to be supported, which forced a major extension in the system architecture. This affected the TCC, the OBC as well as the data exchange over the digital radio system. The shared parts of the system, the data telegrams and the digital line atlas have been extended accordingly.

Adding the new navigation sensor, the balise reader, to the system has been done with the following steps:

- Adding Task_Balise_Reader as child task to the already implemented Task_Location_Determination.
- Adding a "Balise-Buffer" in order to communicate detected balises to the parent task.
- Extending the train location state by last crossed balise.
- Monitoring the activity of Task_Balise_Reader is realized within Task_Location_Determination.

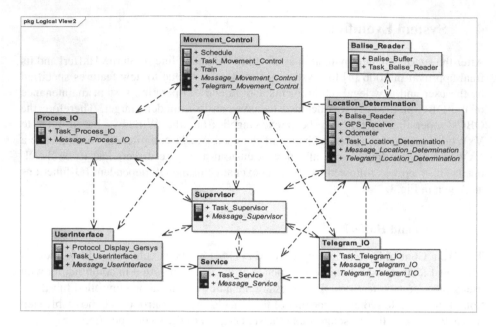

Fig. 4. Package and task structure of RZL-Pinzgau

Fig.4 gives an overview of the OBCs' software architecture and it mainly consists of 8 packages and its child packages where each one contains one task. Task_Balise_Reader has not been further integrated into the system, since it represents a subpart of the location determination task. The supervision of it is realized via monitoring the communication with Task_Location_Determination. Since the balise reader reports detected balises and after an idle timeout sends a heartbeat, the parent task is able to monitor if the hardware as well as the child task is still active. If a problem or timeout occurs Task_Location_Determination reports the event via the already implemented mechanisms. In consequence it was not necessary to perform modifications to Task_Supervisor. By now this implementation is tested in field for over two years and has proven to not cause issues on the systems performance.

Within Europe there are several different railway control systems, which hinder cross country rail traffic. In order to overcome this situation and provide an interoperable train control system across Europe, the EU initiated the development of the European Train Control System (ETCS). ETCS provides different levels of functionality and currently it is mandatory to be equipped on new high speed lines within Europe. The train side equipment consists of a vital computer, DMI, balise reader, odometry module, Juridical Recording Unit and a Euroradio module [8]. Euroradio is the standardized ETCS system for communication between trains and the Radio Block Centers (RBCs) which is based on GSM-R [8]. GSM-R itself is a railway specific standard of GSM including e.g. definitions for service quality levels focused on high speed lines. Furthermore within Euroradio a method for message authenticity and integrity checks, generation of random session keys as well as the telegram structures is specified.

Due to the required features to the data radio communication of the RZL-Pinzgau certain elements of Euroradio have been implemented. Since the basic TCS [1] did not feature message authenticity checks it has been decided to integrate Euroradio's method: CBC-MAC and triple DES. The required modifications to the base TCS [1] mainly dealt with the communication related common code and therefore they have been implemented in Ada95. The other features of Euroradio have not been integrated into the system, because on the one hand field proven proprietary hardware has been used and on the other hand ETCS compatibility was not required.

4.3   SATLOC

SATLOC is an EU funded research project which tackles the question of how a cost efficient train control system for low density traffic lines can be realized. The system utilizes GNSS-based train localization, cab-signalling as well as an adopted version of ETCS Euroradio data radio communication as well as a modified ETCS RBC. The project's long-term goal of SATLOC is to promote the usage of GNSS as safe method for train navigation in the railway domain focused on low density traffic lines.

Since the required operational procedures are similar between the Pinzgau – RZL and the ETCS principles an adopted OBU version of the Pinzgau – RZL system will be used. However the main difference between ETCS and Pinzgau – RZL is that the former is dedicated to high speed lines across Europe while the latter focuses on lines with low speed and low traffic density.

On-Board Unit

The previously used hardware for the OBC and DMI remains the same, whereas data radio modem, balise reader and GNSS-receiver are exchanged. These components had to be replaced in order to support the required features and functionalities of this research project. The exchange of the GNSS-receiver was simple, since the hardware interface is the same and the data protocol is in both cases NMEA 0183. In contrast to this, the balise reader interface as well as the data protocol changed completely. Once again this hardware exchange proofed to be of limited work, since it was only neces-sary to exchange the concerned package Balise_Reader against a version which sup-ports the new hardware while communication with Task_Location_Determination remains as before. Furthermore, since the original system was designed to be used only by German speaking personal and the fact that SATLOC is a European project, it was required to support multilanguage output on the DMI. In order to achieve this feature a generic package has been implemented which offers support for multiple languages. These languages are loaded from configurable predefined static tables which belong to the configuration of the OBC. During runtime it is possible to switch the displayed language via the DMI.

Traffic Control Center

The TCC consists of a visualization unit, a communication unit and the software of Invensys SIL4 ETCS RBC, which has mainly been developed in Ada.

Data Radio

Since the data radio system is the shared media between OBU and TCC it was necessary to agree on a standardized solution under consideration of the economic constraints of low density traffic lines. In the case of SATLOC the major system modification was related to the data radio communication between TCC and OBU.

Within the scope of this research project, the OBU has to be able to communicate with an ETCS RBC. Since the project focuses on low density lines which budgets are rather strict, it was not applicable to use standard Euroradio for communication. If standard Euroradio would have been used, it would have been necessary to deploy and maintain the cost intensive circuit-switched GSM-R network, which is mandatory for Euroradio, as well as the concerned equipment. Since this would have exceeded the given economic boundaries, and SATLOC itself is a research project, it was chosen to utilize the broadband network of local mobile carriers and therefore to implement a version of ETCS over packet-switched technologies like GPRS and UMTS. From the TCC point of view it was only necessary to add a Wrapper-Layer to encapsulate the used TCP/IP mechanisms from the standard ETCS RBC. From the OBCs' perspective it meant introducing a conversion module from the RZL-Pinzgau communication system to an adopted Euroradio system.

As the topic of Euroradio over GPRS is currently investigated by a UNISIG working group [5], the SATLOC implementation is based on the proposed ideas but does not necessarily comply with them in all aspects. In order to be on the OBC mainly in line with Euroradio the layers Application, Safety and Transport including a Wrapper-Layer have been introduced. These Layers have been integrated as tasks, since they perform independent actions of each other. The combination of Transport and Wrapper-Layer is responsible for handling the TCP/IP socket; the Safety Layer performs the session key management as well as the message authenticity and integrity check. In order to fully integrate the adopted Euroradio into the OBC software the application layer has to perform the conversion from RZL to Euroradio application messages. Since the message structures and their actual content are not totally compatible to each other, a message conversion layer has been incorporated into the internal implementation of the ETCS application layer. Concerning the base OBC software it meant integrating these new tasks and re-routing certain application messages via an "ETCS Translator" to the new ETCS Application Layer, see Fig.5.

The current implementation contains only a subset of a full ETCS [7], but within the scope of SATLOC it is sufficient to handle all relevant operational procedures like: authorizing train movement, monitoring train movements, issuing emergency stops from the TCC.

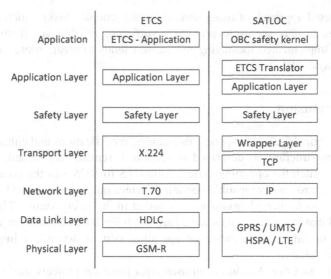

Fig. 5. ETCS vs. SATLOC layer architecture

Field Tests

During the second half of 2013 field tests have been carried out and they showed that the OBC was able to communicate with the adopted ETCS RBC. Therefore the driver could obtain a Movement Authortiy from the RBC while the traffic controller at the TCC was able to monitor the trains' movement along the line. Hence the implemented subset of Euroradio, ETCS over TCP/IP, and the exchange of the balise reader hardware seems to be working properly. During the test period communication failures in the sense of outtake of mobile broadband did not occur, hence this indicates good mobile broadband coverage along the test track. The implemented multilanguage feature proved to be very helpful for the multinational test crew, since it was possible to change the displayed language from German to English and Romanian. In 2014 further tests will be carried out to clarify and demonstrate system capabilities.

5   Experiences

System development started in 1999 and the first official deployment was in 2005 at Stern&Hafferl [4]. Ever since the TCS has been developed further in order to support new features like track selectivity, improved train monitoring and supervision, switch control and switch supervision.

Meanwhile the OBC hardware and operating system have been completely exchanged. Considering the headcount of the R&D team this challenge proved to be of limited scope due to the architecture of the system with implemented IO-encapsulation and other features as well as the features of Ada. The main work focused on creating a functional VxWorks image for the selected hardware, which includes the self-written hardware drivers.

The selected approach of using several loosely coupled tasks which communicate via message buffers seems to provide a sufficient reliable yet flexible approach, though the implemented messaging mechanism tends to create more module dependencies than desired.

6   Conclusion

While the original TCS [1] experiences changes, modifications and enhancements, the basic system structure, as described in section 3, remains untouched. When it was required to switch the operating system from ETS to VxWorks the core task was the creation of a hardware compatible operating system image including IO-encapsulation in Ada, thus no further adoptions were required in the safety kernel. Therefore it can be assumed that in this case the selected approach for IO-encapsulation via distinctive definitions in Ada and hardware or operating system dependent implementations proved to be suitable.

Due to the fact that Ada has been used right from the projects start in 1999 to develop all safety relevant functions, it provided a solid framework for a first system deployment in 2005 as SIL0 system. With further features and enhancements it was possible to deploy a low cost SIL2 train control system at Pinzgaubahn in 2012 [2].

References

1. Stadlmann, B.: Ada-Development for a Basic Train Control System for Regional Branch Lines. Ada User Journal 22(1) (March 2001)
2. Stadlmann, B., Kaiser, F., Maierhofer, S.: Rechnergestütztes Zugleitsystem für die Pinzgauer Lokalbahn. In: SIGNAL+DRAHT 5/2012, pp. 28–33. Eurailpress (May 2012)
3. EN 50128: Railway applications – Communications, signaling and process systems – Software for railway control and protection systems
4. Stadlmann, B.: Basic Train Control System for Regional Branch Lines - Field Test Report. In: Eleventh International Conference on Computer System Design and Operation in the Railway and Other Transit Systems, pp. 253–262. WIT Press (2008)
5. UNISIG: Protocol Stack main Alternative 1 ETCS over GPRS (v3). UNISIG (2012)
6. Pascoe, R., Eichorn, T.: What is communication-based train control? IEEE Vehicular Technology Magazine 4, 16–21 (2009)
7. UNISIG. System Requirements Specification. Subset-026-1 v2.3.0. UNISIG (February 24, 2006)
8. Stanley, P.: Institution of Railway Signal Engineers: ETCS for Engineers. Eurailpress, Hamburg (2011)

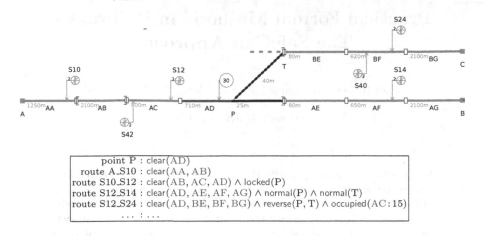

point P	: clear(AD)
route A_S10	: clear(AA, AB)
route S10_S12	: clear(AB, AC, AD) ∧ locked(P)
route S12_S14	: clear(AD, AE, AF, AG) ∧ normal(P) ∧ normal(T)
route S12_S24	: clear(AD, BE, BF, BG) ∧ reverse(P, T) ∧ occupied(AC : 15)
...	: ...

Fig. 1. A simple junction and an excerpt from its control table

The first three are the fundamental safety properties that may be reasoned about at a specification level abstracting away from minute details of physical track topology and the setting in which the track is laid. The remaining two require consideration of concrete track geometry, topography, train exploitation characteristics and prospective service requirements.

A schema must be free from collisions. A collision happens when two trains occupy the same part of a track. Reasoning about collisions must take into an account concrete topology, requires an explicit train notion, the definition of laws of train movement and assumptions about train driver (either human or automatic) behaviour. Note that if train drivers choose to ignore whatever means of indication of track occupation states are available to them (e.g., track side signals) there is nothing preventing two trains from colliding. Hence, the absence of collisions is ensured by demonstrating the compatibility of specific topology, signalling and certain driving rules.

The basic safety mechanism is that of route locking and holding. A train is given permission to enter an area of a railway once there is a continuous and safe path through this area assigned exclusively to this train. Such a path is normally called a *route* and is delineated by *signals* — either physical track-side signals with lamps or conceptual signals displayed to a driver via a computer screen. Two-aspect signals (red/green or stop/proceed) are positioned at the maximum braking distance from each other and this defines the smallest train separation. 3- and 4- and higher aspect signalling allows trains to come closer by advising drivers on the safe speed and the extent of free track available in front.

In Fig. 1, one route example is route S10_S12 between signals S10 and S12. This route consists of two train detection circuits: AB and AC. A train detection circuit is a part of a railway (a sub-graph in an abstract topology) with some equipment capable of reporting the presence or absence of a train in this part. An additional circuit AD is also in the dependency of this route playing the role of an *overlap*. An overlap is an extra part of track reserved together with a route to

Practical Formal Methods in Railways - The SafeCap Approach

Alexei Iliasov, Ilya Lopatkin, and Alexander Romanovsky

Newcastle University, UK

Abstract. This paper presents the SafeCap Platform approach to the verification of railway safety properties. We discuss how the hierarchy of formal theories is used to capture the railway domain and interface with verification tools; we explain the contribution of each individual theory to the overall task of safety verification and capacity assessment. Finally, we briefly relate our experience of using two independent verification chains to validate concrete track layouts and control tables against the SafeCap safety theories.

1 Introduction

Ensuring and demonstrating railway system dependability is crucial for the way our society operates. Formal methods have been successfully used in developing various railway control systems. The best-known examples include the use of the B Method [1] for designing various metro and suburban lines, and airport shuttles all over the world [5, 8]. The formal methods here are used to trace the requirements to system models and to ensure and demonstrate the system safety. Our work builds on this work.

The SafeCap Platform [19] is an integrated modelling environment aimed at a railway signalling engineer. Its focus is the microscopic analysis of a railway node (station, marshalling yard, complex junction) with the purpose of investigation, with the maximum level of detail, the performance of a node under various service patterns, train types and stability margins. Central to achieving this goal is an efficient and scalable approach to the verification of operational safety. Indeed, any change in track layout, train detection circuit boundary and control rule potentially renders a node unsafe. It is our goal to address the highly challenging verification problem in such a way that it does not unnecessarily distract an engineer from the primary goal of optimization. This means a push-button approach where no expertise in verification technology is required and a feedback is presented promptly and in a friendly manner.

We continue with the discussion of principal problems and objectives of railway signalling verification. Within the hierarchy defined by Fokkink and Hollingshead [22], we focus exclusively on the middle interlocking layer leaving out details of lower layer of physical equipment functioning and upper layer of railway logics and exploitation largely out of the view. We identify five kinds of railway safety verification concerns.

L. George and T. Vardanega (Eds.): Ada-Europe 2014, LNCS 8454, pp. 177–192, 2014.

protect a train running slightly past a red signal (when, for instance, rail adhesion is lower than normal and a driver misjudges the stopping distance); alternatively, it is an area to automatically engage train brakes should a driver fail to notice a red signal (this is generally known as an automated train protection (ATP) system).

When a route is locked, all the movable equipment such as *points* or level crossings must be set and detected in a position that would let a train safely travel on its desired route. They must remain locked in such a state until the train passage is positively confirmed.

A schema must be free from derailments. A derailment may happen when a train moves over a point that is not set in any specific direction and thus may move under a train. To avoid this, a point must be positively confirmed to be *locked* before a train may travel over it. In a control table one writes a condition defining when a point reconfiguration may happen. For the example in Fig. 1 such a rule requires that circuit AD is clear.

Another reason for derailment is driving a train through a curve at an unsafe speed. As a train goes over a curve, the combination of gravitational, centripetal and centrifugal forces exerts a rolling force on train carriages and a substantial lateral force on rails. This effect can be mitigated by track canting although no single canting is a perfect fit for all train types. Hence, enforcing a safe speed limit before a train enters a curved track area is an essential safety consideration. There are several ways of doing this. One is a static speed limit. This can be a sign board warning a driver (circle with number 30 over circuit AD in Fig. 1) or an electronic signal sent to an on-board computer. A speed restriction may be also enforced by signalling: a signal does not switch into a permissive aspect until a train is detected to occupy some preceding detection circuit for a duration time. A combination of such time duration and track length gives an upper train speed limit. Example in Fig. 1 uses this technique for route S12_S24: the control table mandates that a train travelling over the route occupies AC for at least 15 seconds.

Flank protection Consider the example in Fig. 1 and assume some train (2) approaching to and stopping at signal S40 (going right to left) while some other train (1) travels over route S12_S14; also, assume that there is no overlap track for route S40_S42. Should train 2 fail to stop at the signal it might roll into the path or hit the side of train 1. Another common scenario is having no signalling in operation at siding BE, BF, BG. A train approaching from a siding would be operated on sight or using less restrictive shunting signalling. If the siding goes up a slope there is an additional danger of carriages rolling freely onto the main line A_B. Avoidance of such situations is generally known as *flank protection*. Defining route overlaps (e.g., requiring AD to be clear and point P set in reverse) would generally provide a sufficient safety margin albeit at a cost of lower performance and extra signalling equipment. An alternative is to set points in such a way that any interfering traffic would be diverted away or even derailed using *trap points*. In our example, we protect main line route S12_S14 by setting *flanking point* T to normal (straight) direction to divert any interfering traffic coming from the siding.

Physical layout properties. A range of properties pertinent to safety requires analysis of land topography over which track is build. As one example, it must be ensured that physical signals have certain minimum sighting distance giving a sufficient time for a driver to react. Sometimes tracks are so close together that carriages of a train going through a curve may come into a contact with carriages of a train located on a parallel track. A signalling engineer must identify and protect such areas (known as *fouling points*) via signalling rules. Further examples include gradients at stopping points (e.g., signals) that may be unsafe for heavy trains, parts of track susceptible to landslips, derbies on the track due to nearby trees and overpasses, and so on. An important consideration is the spacing between signals and speed restriction signs: it must be possible for all trains to brake within the given limits to meet signal or speed limit restriction. Signal positioning and speed restriction would be wastefully conservative if one does not consider specific properties of traffic, in particular train acceleration and braking performance.

Quality of service. It is never sufficient to consider the safety aspect of a railway in isolation from its performance. Indeed, setting all signals permanently to red (stop) state trivially satisfies all the safety concerns discussed above. As a less extreme example, there could be a signalling mistake preventing or hindering train progress but not violating safety properties. Typically, when signalling a station or a junction, an engineer would have access to a provisional time table. A time table defines traffic class and station calling and dwelling times. It must be ensured that signalling is able to accommodate such traffic with some extra margin for unaccounted or delayed traffic. Simulation of train runs is the common way to check quality of service requirements.

2   Safety Verification

In this section we discuss requirements to verification of railway signalling, in particular verification of control tables, and characterise major approaches used in the industry and proposed by academia. We start with the summary of *aspects* of verification - the prominent traits we believe to be relevant to industrial adoption. Our focus is largely on the application of formal verification to railway signalling.

2.1   Aspects of Verification

Rigour. A good verification technique is both exhaustive and thorough; this should be a natural consequence of innate properties of an applied technique rather than achieved through measures of extra diligence or man power. Clearly, a truly rigorous techniques must be based on an objective, formal handling of safety-related artefacts expressed in a mathematical notation. The results achieved with a rigorous technique must be readily reproducible from the record of verification activity: a property highly desirable for the certification of signalling solutions.

Productivity. It is not enough to simply offer a rigorous techniques; there must be means available and accessible to an engineer to apply the technique with some definite prospect of success within a given lapse of time. It means that a technique must provide automation for most of the routine activities and allow an engineer to assess the problem at differing levels of detail. A good presentation of railway artefacts and verification concerns is also an important issue.

Expertise. Signalling engineers are expected to be experts in railway signalling but are rarely also experts in formal verification. Conversely, formal method experts are rarely proficient in the signalling domain. Hence, a technique levying an unlikely blend of expertise - i.e., the knowledge of both formal modelling and railways - would be costly to apply in practice. Lowering of expertise requirements is always welcome as it correlates with the reduction of user involvement and increase in productivity.

Scalability. Safety verification is a pressing issue for truly large and complex stations and junctions. Small-scale signalling may be confidently executed by an experienced engineer without need for any advanced modelling and verification techniques. A large layout, however, is beyond mental capacity of a human being and has to be processed in a piece-wise manner greatly increasing the chance of both oversights and overly conservative decisions. Therefore, to be truly useful, a verification technique must be able to scale to the level of a large station or an area spanning several stations.

Expressiveness. In Section 1 we have presented the main classes of verification conditions. A perfect verification techniques would address all of them in a satisfactory manner. For this, the notation employed to express verification conditions must be rich and flexible enough to capture verification goals without undermining legibility and, by extension, productivity. Automation tools must also be capable of dealing with the complete notation, not just a subset of it.

Feedback. Although it is valuable to know whether a control table and layout are safe, it is even more valuable to obtain an explanation of why a given combination of a control table and layout are not safe and what steps should be taken to make it safe. Thus, the value of a verification technique is also determined by the form and kind of feedback a verification activity presents to an engineer. A feedback in the terms of logical constructs obtained through a mechanical translation of a railway model into a formal modelling notation is useless in a real life scenario. A simple yes or no is not good enough either as it leaves an engineer in the dark about the likely source of a problem. An ideal feedback would narrowly identify a responsible part and step an engineer through events and actions leading to a concrete manifestation of safety violation.

2.2   Techniques

In this section we discuss main approaches to signalling verification. In practice, several techniques may be combined although this has unclear implications on the overall rigour.

Manual review. Just as compilation of control tables is often a manual process, verification may also be accomplished via a carefully set up but otherwise manual review procedure. In most cases, to facilitate legibility, control tables are written in a highly structured tabular form following a common standard, i.e., UK Railway Group Standard GK/RT 0202 [17] although historic and regional peculiarities are not uncommon. One possible arrangement is having one company to design signalling and a competing company to verify it. The reasoning is that this way both parties are incentivized to do their best.

Manual review is a slow process with very high requirements to reviewers' expertise. It does not deliver any objective proof of safety. At the same time, it does not suffer from any limitations of a formal verification process.

Simulation. Railway industry widely employs railway simulation tools. These range from coarse-grained simulation of a national railway network to a detailed simulation of various aspects of mechanical performance of specific engines and carriages in a combination with specific rail and balast types. Verification concerns span from analysis of digital communication protocols connecting trains and regional control to stressing of tunnels and bridges by passing trains. Simulation is widely applied for time table optimisation and interactive 3D simulation is sometimes used for driver training. RailSys [16] and OpenTrack [15] are two of the more well-known simulation suites applied in time table optimisation and general analysis of signalling performance.

The main attraction of simulation is that it does not require deep understanding of railway functioning. Simulation tools present many aspects of railway performance in an intuitive, visual manner helping to quickly obtain the big picture of overall layout and signalling performance. There is, however, no guarantee of safety as simulation can only ever consider a tiny proportion of all scenarios.

Model checking. The safety challenge of railways and the fact that collision and derailment properties may be dealt with within the setting of discrete, inertia-less train movement makes railway safety verification especially appealing for formal method practitioners. The principal idea of railway model checking is quite simple: a model of train movement laws is combined with the definitions of track topology and signalling rules. A model checking tool attempts to go through all or many execution scenarios to confirm that unsafe scenarios are ruled out. The list of modelling notations used in this setting is practically endless. Notable examples include Coloured Petri nets [7], process algebra CSP [11], a continuation work based on the model-based notation ASM [12], an algebraic language Maude [9] and the B Method together with ProB model checking tool [14].

Almost all model checking approaches allow automatic instantiation of template models making application of model checking relatively straightforward for engineers. Many tools are able to report a sequence of steps leading to a safety violation. While model checkers are able to analyse many more scenarios than a simulator this comes at a price of reduced expressiveness (i.e., inability to reason about track geometry) and proof certificate is generally not ultimate: there could be a false negative (i.e., the absence of an error report in case an error is present but not discovered) when a model is too large to analyse exhaustively.

Table 1. Characterisation of major verification techniques and the SafeCap approach

	Review	Simulation	Theorem proving	Model checking	SafeCap
Rigour	−−	−−	++	+	+
Productivity	−−	~	−−	+	++
Expertise	−−	++	−−	+	+
Scalability	+	−	++	−−	+
Expressiveness	++	++	~	−	−
Feedback	+	++	−	+	~

Theorem proving. Model checking imposes limitations on the model size and performs best with a relatively limited logical language. Theorem proving overcomes these limitations and offers potentially unlimited opportunities for verifying safety with the utmost level of rigour. Theorem proving is not necessarily an all-manual process: there is a large and successful community developing automated theorem provers [20]. At the moment, automated prove support is best in the domain of first order logic and set theory; an attempt at reasoning about continuous train dynamics is likely to require an intervention by a highly skilled verification expert - the kind of people mostly found in academia. From our experience, even reasoning about track geometry is surprisingly difficult as this is a problem outside of the typical application domain of verification tools. One success story with theorem proving is the ongoing application of B method in the railway domain [8]. J.-R. Abrial has published methodological guidelines on an economical use of basic logic and set theory to reason about railway safety in a discrete setting [4].

Theorem proving, even with excellent tool support, requires a high level of expertise in formal verification and mathematical modelling. The semantic gap between logic and railway concepts is formidable. This leads to generally low productivity (but we should notice efforts like the BART tool for automatic refinement of B models [13]), difficulties in interpreting tool feedback, and posing verification statements in a manner convincing to a non-expert reviewer.

Summary. Table 1 summarizes our assessment of verification techniques. Each aspect is given a score ranging from −− (very poor) to ~ (satisfactory) to ++ (excellent). The last column characterises the SafeCap verification approach discussed in the following sections. The approach, as the table illustrates, offers tangible advantages over both model checking and theorem proving: it scales better than model checking, offers good productivity and does not require a high level of expertise.

3   Safety Verification in SafeCap

The purpose of the SafeCap Platform is to enable railway engineers to analyse complex junctions by experimenting with signalling rules, signalling principles,

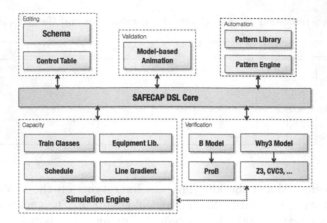

Fig. 2. SafeCap Platform architecture

track topology, safety limits (e.g., speed limits for points and crossings) while receiving an on-line feedback from automated verification and analysis tools.

We have build the Platform around Eclipse — a mature and extensible IDE framework. We used Eclipse Modelling framework (EMF) to realise our Domain Specific Language (DSL) [10]. One important consideration was the ability to benefit from the extensive EMF ecosystem which offers a tool-kit for model manipulation and the construction of graphical and textual editing tools. Apart from the editing tools, the main components of the Platform are transformation patterns, model-based animation, simulation and verification (Fig. 2).

The SafeCap platform aims to provide a versatile tool-kit for analysing railway node safety and capacity. The approach we have taken is based on a combination of theorem proving and constraint solving.

We have applied the Event-B modelling notation and its refinement methodology to develop a theory of safe railway. This theory explicitly describes train movements, signal operation and points control. It does not, however, deal with any specific topology or control table. The proof of safety (we consider absence of collisions and derailments, and protection of flanks) is done for some class of topologies and control tables. The proof of Event-B model, although challenging, is done once and for all.

An important by-product is the set of axiomatic conditions characterising the class of *safe topologies* and *safe control tables*. To establish that a given track topology and control table are safe we only need to check that they do not contradict the mentioned axiomatic conditions. We do not need to redo the proofs of Event-B model. Safety verification is accomplished by putting together the definition of a concrete topology, control table and the axiomatic conditions derived by the Event-B model. If a *constraint solver* does not find a contradiction in logical statements encoded by this composition then the concrete topology and control table are deemed safe. Returning to the Event-B domain, the absence of contradiction established by a constraint solver means that our generic Event-B

```
machine M
  sees Context
  variables v
  invariant I(c, s, v)
  initialisation R(c, s, v')
  events
    E₁ = any vl where g(c, s, vl, v) then S(c, s, vl, v, v') end
    ...
end
```

Fig. 3. Event-B machine structure

model of train behaviour is refined by a model instantiated with the given track topology and control table.

Schema topology and control table theories come in the form of a list of first order logic predicates; they do not define any state transitions or dynamic behaviour but rather well-formedness requirements to objects describing track topology and control table.

For constraint solving, we make use of two sets of formal notations and tools: B together with ProB [14], and Why3 [6]. In the short term, we aim to benefit from their complimentary strengths; in a longer term, the dual verification path provides a logical redundancy that makes a low-level encoding or tool bug unlikely to be left undiscovered.

3.1 Event-B

We apply the Event-B [2] formal modelling notation to specify and verify railway signalling. Event-B belongs to a family of state-based modelling languages that represent a design as a combination of state (a vector of variables) and state transformations (computations updating variables).

An Event-B development starts with the creation of a very abstract specification. A cornerstone of the Event-B method is the stepwise development that facilitates a gradual design of a system implementation through a number of correctness-preserving *refinement* steps. The general form of an Event-B model (or *machine*) is shown in Fig. 3. Such a model encapsulates a local state (program variables) and provides operations on the state. The actions (called *events*) are characterised by a list of local variables (parameters) *vl*, a state predicate *g* called *event guard*, and a next-state relation *S* called *substitution* or event *action*.

Event parameters and guards may be omitted leading to syntactic short-cuts starting with keywords **when** and **begin**.

Event guard g defines the condition when an event is *enabled*. Relation S is given as a generalised substitution statement [1] and is either deterministic ($x := 2$) or non-deterministic update of model variables. The latter kind comes in two notations: selection of a value from a set, written as $x :\in \{2, 3\}$; and a relational constraint on the next state v', e.g., $x :| x' \in \{2, 3\}$.

The **invariant** clause contains the properties of the system, expressed as state predicates, that must be preserved during system execution. These define the *safe states* of a system. In order for a model to be consistent, invariant preservation is formally demonstrated. Data types, constants and relevant axioms are defined in a separate component called *context*.

Model correctness is demonstrated by generating and discharging *proof obligations* - theorems in the first order logic. There are proof obligations for model consistency and for a refinement link - the forward simulation relation - between the pair of *abstract* and *concrete* models.

3.2   Discrete Driving Model

The discrete driving model is an Event-B model capturing train, signal and point behaviour. It proves that the described behaviour is contained within a certain safety envelope by formulating and proving, through a number of refinement steps, *safety invariants* corresponding to the first three verification objectives of Section 1. This model gives a formal definition of principal phenomena observed in railway operation: train movement, route reservation, point locking, route cancellation and so on.

To construct the proof we have used Event-B [3] and the Rodin Platform [18]. Train driving rules are encoded by Event-B events - atomic state transitions - so that the overall model defines a state transition system. The safety properties are stated as a system invariant: a subset of possible states where the dangerous situations may not occur. The proof is done inductively by examining the effect of each event on a given safety property and discharging relevant proof obligation (first-order logic theorems).

The model in Fig. 4 illustrates the notation and modelling style of Event-B. This particular model is the very first (abstract) model in the development chain.

The overall model is made of seven refinement steps with 470 verification conditions of which 301 were discharged automatically by Rodin theorem provers. Its development span over several months and several early versions were abandoned either due to misrepresentation of some railway concepts or unacceptable verification costs.

```
machine route0
  sees ctx_line
  variables
    t_line   // Train/line association
    t_r_hd   // Train head position on a line
    t_r_tl   // Train tail position on a line
  invariant
```
$t\_line \in TRAIN \nrightarrow LINE$
// A train is mapped to the id of a route occupied by the head of a train
$t\_r\_hd \in TRAIN \nrightarrow \mathbb{N}_1$
// correspondingly, $t\_r\_tl(t)$ is the id of the route occupied by the tail of train t
$t\_r\_tl \in TRAIN \nrightarrow \mathbb{N}_1$
$\mathrm{dom}(t\_line) = \mathrm{dom}(t\_r\_hd)$
$\mathrm{dom}(t\_line) = \mathrm{dom}(t\_r\_tl)$
// A train occupies a continuous route interval of route from tail till head
$\forall t \cdot t \in dom(t\_line) \Rightarrow t\_r\_tl(t) \mathrel{..} t\_r\_hd(t) \neq \varnothing$
The routes a train occupies are the routes defined by the train line
$\forall t \cdot t \in dom(t\_line) \Rightarrow t\_r\_tl(t) \mathrel{..} t\_r\_hd(t) \subseteq dom(Line(t\_line(t)))$
// Initially, there are no trains in the system
```
initialisation
```
$t\_line, t\_r\_hd, t\_r\_tl := \varnothing, \varnothing, \varnothing$
```
events
    // A train may appear in the system with this operation
  appear =
  any t, l where
```
$t \in TRAIN \setminus dom(t\_line)$ // a train must be not already in the system
$l \in LINE$
```
  then
```
$t\_line(t) := l$set the train line to l
$t\_r\_hd(t), t\_r\_tl(t) := 1, 1$ // set head and tails routes
```
  end
    // Moves the head of a train from one route to another
  move_route_hd =
  any t where
```
$t \in dom(t\_line)$
$t\_r\_hd(t) < LineLen(t\_line(t))$ // train head must not be on the last line route
```
  then
```
$t\_r\_hd(t) := t\_r\_hd(t) + 1$ // move the head one step forward
```
  end
    // Moves the tail of a train between routes
  move_route_tl =
  any t where
```
$t \in dom(t\_line)$
$t\_r\_tl(t) < t\_r\_hd(t)$ // a tail must be strictly behind the head of the train
```
  then
```
$t\_r\_tl(t) := t\_r\_tl(t) + 1$ // move the tail one step forward
```
  end
    ...
```

Fig. 4. An Event-B model of abstract, route-level train movement (an excerpt)

```
/* (1)   */  {} <<: NODE  &
/* (2.a)  */  {} <<: TRACK  &
/* (2.b)  */   TRACK <: NODE * NODE  &
/* (2.c)  */   elm(TRACK) = NODE  & /* all nodes are connected by tracks */
...
/* (10) */ AMBIT : LA --> (POW(NODE) * POW(TRACK)) &
/* (11) */ ! (a, q, p) . (a : ran(AMBIT) & a = ( q |-> p ) => p <: q * q & {} <<: p) &
/* (12) */ ! (a, q, p) . (a : ran(AMBIT) & a = ( q |-> p) => p~ <: p) &
/* (13) */ ! (a, q, p) . (a : ran(AMBIT) & a = ( q |-> p) =>
                   ! (n) . (n : q => closure(p)[{n}] = q) ) &
/* (14) */ union({p | # (a, q) . ( a : ran(AMBIT) & q <: NODE &
                   p <: TRACK & a = ( q |-> p))}) = TRACK &
/* (15) */ ! (a, b, r, s, t, q) . (a : ran(AMBIT) & b : ran(AMBIT) & a /= b &
                   a = (r |-> s) & b = (t |-> q) => s /\ q = {}) &
...
```

Fig. 5. Schema well-formedness rules (an excerpt)

Apart from its role in the validation of first two layers, the discrete operational rules of the third layer are used to visually animate train movements over a given schema. There are two main applications for such an animation: replaying the results of model checking of discrete driving rules in order to pin-point the source of an error in a topology or a control table; and helping an engineer to understand how trains may travel through a schema with a given set of control rules.

3.3   Schema Topology Theory

The schema topology theory is responsible for verifying logical conditions expressed over track layout (i.e., track connections, point placement) and logical topology (i.e., routes and lines as paths through a schema). Few examples of verification conditions include the connectivity property (no isolated pieces of track), continuity of routes and lines, absence of cycles, correct traversal of points and valid placement of train detection circuit boundaries.

As a whole, these conditions express what we understand to be a valid track topology. We have tested them against a number of large-scale real-life layouts and we able to discover some problem in already informally validated track topologies. In addition, semi-automated alteration and generation of track layouts (e.g., via the improvement patterns we are developing in the tool) necessitates a careful and strict inspection of these basic properties. An automated verification process ensures high productivity and enables an engineer to explore a large range of designs within a short time.

Figure 5 gives a sample of verification conditions written in the Classical B notation [1] and ready to be processed by model checking tool ProB [14]. Not shown is the encoding of DSL elements (track graph, control tables) as sets, relations and functions of a B model. For a real-life example, such a model may be 6-14 thousand lines long. The same conditions and constructs are also generated in the Why3 theory notation. It is not a direct translation of the B model and we intentionally use a different representation of relations and functions to introduce a form of modelling diversity. At the moment, for the topology theory, ProB and Why3 verifications chains deliver broadly similar performance.

```
...
/* @label (CT.1): A permissive signal may be lit only when all route ambits are clear */
! (l, r). (l |-> r : CTO_DOM => ! (n). (n : 1 .. RASPECT(l, r)-1 =>
                    routeambits(r) <: CT_CLEAR(l, r, n) )) &
/* @label (CT.2): A route with an overlap may have permissive signal only
  when its overlap is reserved and confirmed as clear  */
! (l, r). (l |-> r : ROVERLAP & r : dom(LINE(l)) => ! (n). (n : 1 .. RASPECT(l, r)-1 =>
                    TA[fst(ROUTE(LINE(l)(r)))] <: CT_CLEAR(l, r, n))) &
/* @label (CT.3.a): No point is set both normal and reverse */
! (l, r). (l |-> r : CTO_DOM => CT_NORMAL(l, r) /\ CT_REVERSE(l, r) = {} ) &
...
```

Fig. 6. Control table conditions (an excerpt)

3.4   Control Table Theory

On the platform of the topology verification we define the conditions of operational safety. These are derived, via a formal proof, from a set of discrete (inertia-less) train movement rules and expressed as a set of constraints over signalling rules.

In SafeCap, we depart from the convention of associating control rules with track-side signals. Instead, we consider a more general situation where different signalling rules are applied depending upon the ultimate train destination or train type and attach control logic to a pair of line and route. This permits, for instance, to model, on the same track, an express train using two aspect signalling and a freight train travelling over the same routes but in a three or four aspect mode. Such an arrangement may be used to achieve an optimal balance between headway and average speed in a heterogeneous traffic mix. Given the fact that in UK track-side signals are going to be made obsolete by 2030 [21] this represents a fairly modest scenario of using virtual signals to improve capacity.

The control table theory demonstrate such properties as the absence of potential collision (as may happen, for instance, when a proceed aspect is given while a protected part of track is still occupied) and derailment (due to incorrect point setting or point movement under a train). Other properties relate to the danger or circular dependencies between signals, dependencies between multi-aspect signals and operation of auto-signals, conformance with an ATP system, and verification of point and signal based flank protection. Certain properties, notably approach speed control via the timed occupation of a track section, are not verified at this stage as the formalisation at this layer does not capture train inertia. Speed limit conformance and other time-related properties are formulated at the final, most detailed layer.

A list of sample control table theory conditions is given in Fig. 6. For the shown rules, the outer quantification selects a pair of a line and a route that define a list of control rules (one per aspect). This model includes the topology model[1]. Constraint solving is the primary verification strategy: we try to detect a contradiction between concrete data structures defining topology and control tables and the verification conditions. Again, the model is given in both B and

---

[1] At the level, it is assumed that the topology theory has been verified and the topology constraints are turned into axioms.

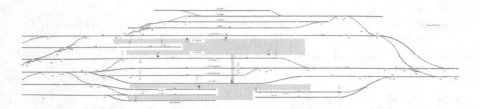

Fig. 7. The station area of Carlisle example (a SafeCap editor screenshot)

Why3 notations although this time the Why3 verification route is not successful for larger examples. In addition, for any mid to large scale schema we currently have to exclude the verification of flank protection properties as these require complicated computations over track topology. We are working on a program that would output a proof term for each instance of flank protection property so that a theorem prover or a constraint solver would only have to check the elementary steps of a prepared proof.

4   Experimental Results

We have tested our approach on a range of synthetic and real-life examples. Whenever possible, we have tried to accurately reproduce layout topology and control tables from paper-based documents provided by UK's Network Rail. A summary of verification experiments is given in Table 2. Control table verification scales very well; the solving of topology suffers mainly from the conditions establishing absence of cycles in the definitions of lines and routes. If these properties are known to hold (i.e., topology is taken from an existing layout) these properties may be suppressed.

One of the larger examples we have tackled is the Carlisle Citadel station with the North, South, and Caldew junctions. The modelled fragment is 2.6km long and comprises 70 train detection circuits, 63 points, 79 routes and 161 valid paths. The translation from a scanned PDF drawing and printed control tables took 45 man-hours. The verification of the topology theory constraints using ProB took just over 6 minutes on a PC with i7 3730 CPU and utilized

Table 2. Verification run times for several sample layouts

Benchmark	Points/Lines/ Routes	Conditions, topology	Conditions, control table	Run time, topology	Run time, control table
Station 1	8/12/14	117	230	4s	2s
Junction 1	23/4/21	280	602	24s	8s
Station 2	6/23/21	104	678	18s	6s
Carlisle, west	24/112/30	350	888	1m 17s	12s
Carlisle	63/161/79	892	1270	6m 4s	19s

just under 2GB of RAM. The Why3 [6] verification of the same theory takes approximately 70 minutes. The control table theory is verified under 20 seconds by ProB and not verified completely, with the current translation of conditions, using Why3. It worth noting that the control table verification time is by far more important as topology, once verified, changes rarely if at all.

The SafeCap Platform is freely available from [19] together with the verification models discussed in this paper.

5 Conclusions

In the paper we have surveyed the architecture of the verification infrastructure of the SafeCap Platform. Our approach has proven to be successful and we are working with our industrial partners to further improve the fidelity of the models and the robustness of the verification chain.

One of the advantages of applying formal modelling in the railway domain is the ability to transfer the modelling expertise accumulated analysing existing signalling laws to the verification of novel, unexplored ideas. The level of confidence a formal approach is especially valuable in overcoming a healthy scepticism over a novelty in a field known for its conservatism. We plan to extend our approach to cover moving block, virtual signals and automated train operation in a uniform and coherent manner. We hope this will allow us to reason about hybrid solutions combing elements of fixed and moving block principles, human driving and fully automated operation. As one example, we would like to model how several similar trains travelling through a junction may be temporarily signalled using the train convoy principle where train separation control may realised on a more relaxed assumption leading to smaller headway and less capacity consumption.

Acknowledgements. The work of SafeCap has been conducted as part of the U.K. EPSRC/RSSB SafeCap and SafeCap-Impact projects. This work was partially supported by the EPSRC/UK TrAmS-2 Platform Grant.

References

1. Abrial, J.-R.: The B-Book. Cambridge University Press (1996)
2. Abrial, J.-R.: Modelling in Event-B. Cambridge University Press (2010)
3. Abrial, J.-R., Mussat, L.: Introducing Dynamic Constraints in B. In: Bert, D. (ed.) B 1998. LNCS, vol. 1393, pp. 83–128. Springer, Heidelberg (1998)
4. Abrial, J.-R.: Train systems. In: Butler, M., Jones, C.B., Romanovsky, A., Troubitsyna, E. (eds.) Fault-Tolerant Systems. LNCS, vol. 4157, pp. 1–36. Springer, Heidelberg (2006)
5. Behm, P., Benoit, P., Faivre, A., Meynadier, J.-M.: Météor: A Successful Application of B in a Large Project. In: Wing, J.M., Woodcock, J., Davies, J. (eds.) FM 1999. LNCS, vol. 1708, pp. 369–387. Springer, Heidelberg (1999)
6. Bobot, F., Filliâtre, J.-C., Marché, C., Paskevich, A.: Why3: Shepherd your herd of provers. In: Boogie 2011: First International Workshop on Intermediate Verification Languages, pp. 53–64 (August 2011)

7. Janczura, C.W.: Modelling and Analysis of Railway Network Control Logic using Coloured Petri Nets. PhD thesis, School of Mathematics and Institute for Telecommunications Research, University of South Australia (1998)
8. Essamé, D., Dollé, D.: B in Large-Scale Projects: The Canarsie Line CBTC Experience. In: Julliand, J., Kouchnarenko, O. (eds.) B 2007. LNCS, vol. 4355, pp. 252–254. Springer, Heidelberg (2006)
9. Hagalisletto, A.M., Bjørk, J., Yu, I.C., Enger, P.: Constructing and Refining Large-Scale Railway Models Represented by Petri Nets. IEEE Transactions on Systems, Man, and Cybernetics, Part C, 444–460 (2007)
10. Iliasov, A., Romanovsky, A.: SafeCap domain language for reasoning about safety and capacity. In: Pacific-Rim Dependable Computing Conference (PRDC 2012), Niigata, Japan. IEEE CS (November 2012)
11. Winter, K.: Model Checking Railway Interlocking Systems. In: Proceeding of the 25th Australian Computer Science Conference, ACSC 2002 (2002)
12. Winter, K., Robinson, N.: Modelling Large Railway Interlockings and Model Checking Small Ones. In: Proceeding of the Australian Cumputer Science Conference, ACSC 2003 (2003)
13. Burdy, L.: Automatic Refinement. In: Proceedings of BUGM at FM 1999 (1999)
14. Leuschel, M., Butler, M.: ProB: A Model Checker for B. In: Araki, K., Gnesi, S., Mandrioli, D. (eds.) FME 2003. LNCS, vol. 2805, pp. 855–874. Springer, Heidelberg (2003)
15. OpenTrack simulator. Website, http://www.opentrack.ch/
16. RailSys simulation platform. Website, http://www.rmcon.de
17. Railway Group Standards. Signalling Design: Control Tables, http://www.rgsonline.co.uk/
18. Rigorous Open Development Environment for Complex Systems (RODIN). IST FP6 STREP project, http://rodin.cs.ncl.ac.uk/
19. SafeCap Project. SafeCap Platfrom website (2013), http://safecap.sf.net
20. TPTP. Thousands of Problems for Theorem Provers, http://www.tptp.org/
21. TSLG. The Rail Technical Strategy, RTS (2012), http://www.futurerailway.org/RTS/Pages/Intro.aspx
22. Fokkink, W.J., Hollingshead, P.R.: Verification of Interlockings: from Control Tables to Ladder Logic Diagrams. In: Proceedings of 3rd Workshop on Formal Methods for Industrial Critical Systems, FMICS 1998 (1998)

Author Index